Trust in International C

International Security Institutions, Domestic Politics and American Multilateralism

Trust in International Cooperation challenges conventional wisdoms concerning the part which trust plays in international cooperation and the origins of American multilateralism. Brian C. Rathbun questions rational institutionalist arguments, demonstrating that trust precedes rather than follows the creation of international organizations. Drawing on social psychology, he shows that individuals placed in the same structural circumstances show markedly different propensities to cooperate based on their beliefs about the trustworthiness of others. Linking this finding to political psychology, Rathbun explains why liberals generally pursue a more multilateral foreign policy than conservatives, evident in the Democratic Party's greater support for a genuinely multilateral League of Nations, United Nations and North Atlantic Treaty Organization. Rathbun argues that the post-World War Two bipartisan consensus on multilateralism is a myth, and that differences between the parties are growing continually starker.

BRIAN C. RATHBUN is an Associate Professor in the School of International Relations at the University of Southern California. He is the author of *Partisan Interventions: European Party Politics and Peace Enforcement in the Balkans* (2004), as well as articles in *International Organization*, *International Studies Quarterly*, the *Journal of Conflict Resolution*, *Security Studies* and the *European Journal of International Relations*, among others.

Cambridge Studies in International Relations: 121

Trust in International Cooperation

Cambridge Studies in International Relations is a joint initiative of Cambridge
University Press and the British International Studies Association (BISA). The
series will include a wide range of material, from undergraduate textbooks and
surveys to research-based monographs and collaborative volumes. The aim of
the series is to publish the best new scholarship in International Studies from
Europe, North America and the rest of the world.

Cambridge Studies in International Relations

Trust in International Cooperation

International Security Institutions,
Domestic Politics and
American Multilateralism

BRIAN C. RATHBUN

CAMBRIDGE
UNIVERSITY PRESS

CAMBRIDGE UNIVERSITY PRESS
Cambridge, New York, Melbourne, Madrid, Cape Town,
Singapore, São Paulo, Delhi, Tokyo, Mexico City

Cambridge University Press
The Edinburgh Building, Cambridge CB2 8RU, UK

Published in the United States of America by Cambridge University Press, New York

www.cambridge.org
Information on this title: www.cambridge.org/9781107603769

First published 2012

Printed in the United Kingdom at the University Press, Cambridge

A catalogue record for this publication is available from the British Library

Library of Congress Cataloguing in Publication data
Rathbun, Brian C., 1973–
Trust in international cooperation : international security institutions, domestic politics
and American multilateralism / Brian C. Rathbun.
    p.   cm. – (Cambridge studies in international relations ; 121)
Includes bibliographical references and index.
ISBN 978-1-107-01471-8 (hardback) – ISBN 978-1-107-60376-9 (paperback)
1. International cooperation.   2. International organization.   I. Title.   II. Series.
JZ1318.R375   2011
327.1'7 – dc23   2011033548

ISBN 978-1-107-01471-8 Hardback
ISBN 978-1-107-60376-9 Paperback

To Nina, Luc and Max – my circle of trust

Contents

Preface

This is not a modest book. In its pages, I contend that the way that most in the field go about explaining international cooperation and the creation of international organizations, as the rational and functional response to objective security environments marked by uncertainty, is almost always too narrow, often obvious, and sometimes exactly wrong. Drawing on insights from social psychology, I contend that trust, rather than distrust, drives the institutionalization of cooperation and the construction of multilateral institutions. And the type of trust that matters, the "generalized" variety, is dispositional, an attribute of decision-makers that varies even in the same structural situation. This book is decidedly "old school," seeking to provide better answers to old questions in the field – What explains international cooperation? Why do states create international organizations? – with new tools. In the course of writing this book, I have become convinced that some of the most foundational issues in international relations cannot be adequately addressed without attention to psychology. Like many, given our field's dispositions (and prejudices), I originally resisted its insights as reductionist and lacking external validity. I am now a convert. I hope to change readers' minds as well, including those already drawn to psychology but who self-ghettoize themselves in the field of foreign policy analysis with the mistaken belief that international relations is somehow a bridge too far.

Writing a preface for a new book is tremendously gratifying, particularly as books are always the culmination of a long process and each has its own story. This book about American multilateralism actually has its roots in Europe. It began with an observation I made while an undergraduate study abroad student in Vienna observing the tortured ratification process of the Maastricht Treaty in Western Europe in 1992. Sitting in Vienna cafés reading the now-defunct *European* newspaper, I noticed that conservative parties in particular seemed to resist encroachments on national sovereignty, but I didn't know why.

In 1994, I spent the summer in Berlin as a research assistant at the Wissenschaftszentrum Berlin für Sozialforschung, a position arranged for me by my undergraduate mentor, Joseph Grieco, who at the time was engaged in a prominent academic debate with Robert Keohane about the possibilities for significant international cooperation and the role of international organizations in world politics. My boss found for me a room to rent in his daughter's unfurnished apartment. With no friends, very poor German skills, and no television, I took to checking out issues of journals from the WZB's library such as *International Security* and *International Organization* to read at night. I remember reading Mearsheimer's "Back to the Future" at intermission in the German State Opera in what was once East Berlin. Thinking that I might want to attend graduate school in political science, I also set out to master Keohane's *After Hegemony*, a used copy of which I had bought at the college bookstore the previous semester. I remember agreeing more with Keohane than Grieco, although I dared not tell Joe as he had been so kind to me. In hindsight this was probably little more than a sense that international organizations (IOs) mattered, derived from my very interest in them. I was of course far, far away from developing my own unique voice on international relations. But it piqued my interest in international cooperation and reciprocity.

My very first paper in graduate school at Berkeley was on the integrationist instincts of leftist parties in the European Union, although it was full of anomalies and problems that I hoped to address when I turned back to it a few years ago, after graduate school. It seemed to me that the explanation for the formation of supranational institutions such as the EU that rationalists working in the Keohane tradition had developed – that they were a simple functional response to collaboration problems – simply did not work. International organizations did seem to serve some function; they were not just created for their own sake. But the process was simply too contested, too politically controversial, too emotionally charged to be explained with such coolness and calculation. The rationalist approach lacked a sense of real politics, but I could not put my finger on an alternative.

It was about this time that chance intervened. While an assistant professor at McGill, in pursuit of a free pizza, I stumbled upon a talk by Eric Uslaner on the "varieties of trust." I recognized in his description of "strategic trust" the logic of repeated games and cooperation that Keohane had given voice to in international relations. From this

I figured out that the implicit concept driving *After Hegemony* was trust. IOs solved problems of distrust by institutionalizing cooperation. This begged the question, however – how could those who did not trust one another collaborate in building an organization? But Uslaner also spoke of "generalized trust," an instinct to cooperate somewhat independent of circumstance that might explain the motivations of those political actors more predisposed towards international cooperation. This insight led me to invert the rationalist conventional wisdom – trust rather than distrust drives the formation of international organizations.

Another moment of clarity arrived when I was presenting a preliminary version of the argument to colleagues at Indiana University. A more rationalist-oriented colleague stopped me in the middle of the presentation to ask, "What game are they playing?" It only occurred to me after the talk that different political actors in the same situation saw their strategic environment differently and that they were playing different games based on their own subjective framing. Some trusted and were playing an assurance game; others did not and were in a prisoner's dilemma. Luckily I was hardly the first to have had this realization, and following this thread led me to a veritable treasure trove of work in social psychology on the effect of "social orientation" on cooperation almost completely ignored in international relations. And social orientation reduced to variation in levels of generalized trust. Had this been one or two articles only somewhat tangentially related to our subject of concern, it might be forgivable. But this was almost a half century of research on the very same questions with which we were grappling telling us that the economistic work the field has become so enamored of simply did not work in the real world. It is microeconomics and formal modeling that really has the problem with external validity.

Work on this book has spanned three universities, and along the way, a lot of colleagues and friends have helped me work through the argument. In no particular order, I thank Robert Keohane, Eric Uslaner, Andy Kydd, Jonathan Mercer, Craig Parsons, Rick Herrmann, John Odell, Alex Wendt, Charli Carpenter, Ned Lebow, Shiping Tang, Nicolas Onuf, Hendrik Spruyt, Brendan Green, Jacques Hymans, Colin Dueck, Peter Trubowitz, Joseph Jupille, David Andrews, Benjamin Fordham, Aaron Hoffman, Joshua Busby, Wade Jacoby, Regina Smyth, Mark Manger, and Juliet Johnson and audiences at Purdue University, Indiana University, American University, Scripps College and the University of Southern California for comments on this project at various stages of development. Debbie Larson, David Houghton and Nicolas Jabko revealed themselves to me as reviewers after the manuscript had been accepted, and I hope this final version shows the impact of their trenchant critiques. Research support was provided by the Advancing Scholarship in the Humanities and the Social Sciences initiative of the University of Southern California. Christina Faegri was an invaluable research assistant. Work done by Kevin Duska, my first undergraduate assistant at McGill, is finally seeing the light of day. John Haslam was an attentive and gracious editor from start to finish. Nicolas Wheeler, who co-edits this series along with Christian Reus-Smit, was a champion from the beginning. I appreciate his confidence. The School of International Relations at USC has served as a wonderful home to write the manuscript. I am so pleased to have come full circle, back to California.

My sons form bookends to this project. My first, Luc, was born just before I began. My second, Max, came into this world just after I finished the draft that went to Cambridge University Press. As always, my wife Nina Srinivasan Rathbun was my sounding board, shoulder to cry on, copy-editor, and critic. I dedicate this book to them.

1 | *Circles of trust: reciprocity, community and multilateralism*

In 2001, even before the terrible events of 9/11, a term once reserved for arcane discussions among academics began to seep into the public discourse – unilateralism. This was the characterization of a number of high-profile actions taken by the new Republican administration such as the "unsigning" of the International Criminal Court statute and a lack of serious engagement on the issue of climate change. Following the terrorist attacks in New York and Washington, the Bush administration decided to fight the war in Afghanistan largely alone, refusing an offer of NATO help. Then, of course, came Iraq. The American government, unable to garner the international community's endorsement of its aim of permanently disarming Saddam Hussein's regime by force, proceeded without the sanction of the United Nations. The government's unilateralism, it has been consistently maintained, marked a departure from the post-WWII tradition of American multilateral engagement and has attracted widespread disappointment and scorn on the part of American allies.

Even as the Bush administration was castigated for being unilateral, however, scholars and pundits alike failed to interrogate the term and its logical opposite – multilateralism. What are unilateralism and multilateralism and what are their sources? A convenient answer is that unilateralism is the desire to go it alone, one that simply emerges when a state's interests are out of line with those of other countries. Why, after all, would the United States seek to constrain itself multilaterally in the United Nations when other countries were not as threatened by the possibility of weapons of mass destruction falling into terrorists' hands?

Yet it seems there was something deeper at work in the Bush administration's preference for unilateralism, something ideological in nature, what psychological scholars would call a dispositional explanation. Unilateralism is not just the case-by-case resort of those whose interests do not match with others in particular instances. It is a general

1

inclination not to cooperate with others and not to restrain oneself in institutions. It is, in keeping with the term itself, an 'ism' in its own right.

That unilateralism is dispositional and ideological rather than structurally determined is given credence by the fact that unilateralism does not mark the views of the entire political spectrum in the United States. The preference for unilateral as opposed to multilateral action has become increasingly partisan in recent years, reflecting growing ideological divergence between the Republicans and the Democrats not only on foreign policy but also on domestic political questions. The result has, some maintain, been a shattering of the bipartisan consensus on projecting American power through the framework of international institutions that has marked American foreign policy since WWII.

Yet still we are left with the questions, Why is it that some are more inclined to cooperate than others in the same circumstances? What are the precursors of unilateralism and multilateralism? Why did the Bush administration depart from it? Why are political parties divided on the subject? To answer these questions I return to the origins of American multilateralism, its efforts to establish international security organizations in the wake of two wars – WWI and WWII – and in the early moments of another, different kind of conflict – the Cold War. In doing so, I find some surprising answers that overturn both theoretical and historical conventional wisdom concerning the factors promoting cooperation and institution building in international relations in general and the sources of American multilateralism in particular.

I argue that multilateralism is the expression of trust. In the context of strategic interdependence, trust is belief that cooperation will be reciprocated. Unilateralists resist collective solutions to common problems because they believe that others are not trustworthy. Multilateralism places one's interests in the hands of others in an effort to reach greater gains through cooperation. It requires trust. Those who do not trust will prefer unilateralism.

Trust has attracted considerable attention recently in the international relations literature, particularly on the part of rational institutionalists. Rationalism relies on a particular notion of trust, the "strategic" variety (Uslaner 2002). In this conceptualization, trust emerges when individuals have information that leads them to believe that specific others have a self-interest in reciprocating cooperation rather than violating their commitments (Hardin 2006). International organizations can help provide this information, reduce uncertainty and alter the situation so that potential cooperators' interests "encapsulate" one another. Distrust comes first, then the institution, and then trust (Keohane 1984). States act rationally to design institutions in such a way that they can secure their goals by calculating the likely alignments of interests among other parties and choosing the organizational form that suits them best. Scholars in the "rational design" school have sought to demonstrate that the greater the problems of distrust, the more authoritative and hierarchical the institutions fashioned to solve them (Koremenos, Lipson, and Snidal 2001; 2004).

The type of trust I am describing is different. It is "generalized" in nature, based on a broad belief that others are largely trustworthy (Uslaner 2002). Generalized trusters are more optimistic that others will live up to their agreements and that they do not wish them harm. Given the scope of such a belief, generalized trust must be moralistic, based not on an assessment of others' interests but on their character and honesty. It is ideological in nature, rooted in a broader worldview about the nature of social relations.

For almost half a century, social psychologists have demonstrated (and international relations scholars have largely ignored) the importance of generalized trust for cooperation. It helps states initiate cooperation in the absence of adequate or telling information about the trustworthiness of others. Generalized trust begins a *reciprocity circle* of trust, cooperation and enhanced trust. And it helps sustain cooperation when the exchange of benefits is not consistent or frequent over time. When generalized trust is present, the reciprocity circle can be more open-ended. This variety of trust also allows states to cooperate with new partners. It broadens the *community circle*, extending trust to others. With generalized trust, this circle is left open. Without it, states are forced into isolation or cooperation only with those about whom they have specific information or relationships, potentially forgoing larger gains with others.

Generalized trust also leaves an impact on the design of international organizations. To reach more collectively optimal outcomes, organizations often require that states cede some of their sovereignty, at least formally, through commitments made in international agreements. What Ruggie (1992) calls "qualitative" multilateralism allows states to harness the collective weight of a number of states to reach outcomes they could not unilaterally by establishing general rules of conduct that do not depend on the particular case. For instance, states agree that an attack on one is an attack on all, or that they will submit all their disputes to third-party mediation. This is a reciprocal exchange in which states tie their hands on some unknown issue in the future on the condition that others do the same.

Qualitative multilateralism, however, comes with the risk of opportunism because it places one's fate in the hands of others. States might not hold up their end of the reciprocal bargain and might abandon others by not submitting their disputes or not coming to the aid of a state in need. A binding security guarantee risks entrapment and free riding on defense spending. Conflict resolution mechanisms in which states allow international organizations to settle their disputes threaten exploitation and interference by others. Multilateralism is a double-edged sword. And this danger increases as the number of states participating grows, what Ruggie calls "quantitative" multilateralism. Whereas smaller organizations might more easily run on the basis of overlapping interests or specific reciprocity, qualitatively multilateral institutions with many members require diffuse reciprocity to function. This is particularly true of security organizations.

Because they rely exclusively on the strategic variety of trust, rationalists believe that states will find it hard to cooperate in these highly uncertain situations. But generalized trust can help states resolve these dilemmas in favor of cooperation. By lessening concerns about opportunism, generalized trust allows states to place their fate in the hands of others and create institutions with more binding commitments among more members. It generates the belief in diffuse reciprocity necessary for qualitative and quantitative multilateralism to operate. Rationalists systematically understate the possibilities for cooperation.

In short, where generalized trust is present, it serves as a form of what I call, by crossing the terms popularized by Hedley Bull (1977) and Robert Putnam (1993), *anarchical social capital* to create a basic system of rules and order in international relations. Because it rests on a judgment about the inherent trustworthiness of others, generalized trust allows for the transfer of trust beyond specific instances in which interests are thought to align. This type of trust is in a sense trust in international cooperation itself, a theme captured in the title of this book. It is a general belief that collaborating with others will yield joint benefits. Individuals or states do not cooperate for cooperation's sake. Trust in and of itself does not explain cooperation. But it facilitates collaboration if there is the possibility of mutual gain based on some complementary interests. In this book, the motivations are security and peace.

Looking at cooperation and institutional creation from this angle leads us to invert, or least significantly qualify, the rational institutionalist conclusions regarding international organizations that emerged with Robert Keohane's *After Hegemony* (1984). According to this view, the formation of international organizations is driven by distrust among states. Rationalist arguments have a certain intuitive appeal yet they lead to some counterintuitive results. For instance, following rationalist logic, we might conclude that distrust is higher amongst the members of the European Union, the most authoritative set of supranational institutions in the world, than among other countries in the world when the exact opposite seems to be true. Rationalist arguments beg the question of how states are able to come together to build institutions to solve problems of distrust without some reservoir of good faith in the first place. A focus on generalized as opposed to strategic trust leads to a directly opposite conclusion that helps answer this question. Trust rather than distrust leads states to create international institutions. It is a cause, not the effect, of international organizations.

Just as Keohane did, I import fresh insights from another discipline to upend certain conventional wisdoms regarding international cooperation and organizations. Strategic trust is situational in nature, a product of the particular constellation of interests in play at any particular time. Generalized trust, in contrast, is dispositional in nature, a trait of particular individuals but not necessarily of others. This points the way towards a uniquely *psychological* theory of international cooperation and international organization. The literature on "social orientation" in social psychology demonstrates that individuals in the same structural circumstances show remarkably different propensities to cooperate based on their different expectations of how others will behave (Kuhlman and Marshello 1975; Kuhlman and Wimberley 1976). "Cooperators" are generalized trusters who believe that cooperation, even in prisoner's dilemma situations, will be reciprocated. "Competitors," in contrast, lack generalized trust and consistently defect, even in assurance games. Rationalism, with its focus on the situational factors affecting cooperation, cannot explain the effect of social orientation.

Such findings wreak havoc with the premises of rational design theorists who claim that international institutions are efficient and functional responses to the particular objective strategic dilemma states face. Multilateralism might be less useful in helping states cope with prisoner's dilemma situations, but decision-makers will act on the basis of their subjective understanding of their country's position, something which varies even in the same structural conditions. Therefore, multilateralism is not just an institutional structure that all will embrace when it serves the national interest; it is an individual trait of some but not others. Psychology puts the "ism" in multilateralism and unilateralism. Generalized trusters are cooperators with a multilateral disposition more likely to frame a strategic situation in assurance terms. Non-trusters are competitors with a unilateral disposition who frame the same situation in prisoner's dilemma terms.

Placed in the same circumstances, generalized trusters are more likely to cooperate and more likely to construct institutions of a particular kind – those with more binding commitments, more members and less flexibility. Non-trusters want to retain more of their unilateral prerogatives such as vetoes, opt-out clauses and withdrawal provisions. They will limit the terms of their agreements and include fewer members.

Variation in inclinations to cooperate in the same structural circumstances points us towards an evaluation of domestic politics. Social orientation research suggests that divisions over multilateralism and unilateralism will become a contentious domestic political issue to the extent that generalized trust varies within countries. A cleavage between trusters and non-trusters might have its origins in any number of factors. However, the newly emerging consensus in political psychology is that the left is more trusting than the right. The notion that the left has a more benign view of human nature and sees the world as a less threatening place than the right is a longstanding observation, one for which there is increasing evidence both in social psychology and studies of elite and mass public opinion. Generalized trust and its absence find expression in both the domestic and the foreign policy positions of the left and right. They structure political attitudes. This leads us to expect significant partisan differences between left and right in countries on the issue of international cooperation and the design of international organizations as parties are the primary vehicle for ideological contestation.

I apply this argument about multilateralism to the cases that first come to mind when we think of the term – the American role in the construction of the League of Nations, the United Nations and the North Atlantic Treaty Organization (NATO). The standard account is that after 1945, the United States embarked upon a new international-ist strategy of engagement that broke with its previous grand strategy of political–military isolation, a course most evident in its policies con-cerning the creation of international organizations. Whereas the US declined to enter the League of Nations, it joined the United Nations and a few short years later signed and ratified the North Atlantic Treaty. Structuralists argue that the changing nature of military tech-nology, the US's unprecedented power, and the growing threat of the Soviet Union combined to put politicians of all stripes on a more inter-nationalist and multilateralist path after WWII (Lake 1999; Leffler 1979). Given its hegemonic position, the United States was willing to provide public goods despite free-riding opportunism by its part-ners (Keohane 1984). Ikenberry (2001) claims that American multi-lateralists were preoccupied mainly with making sure that US hege-mony was acceptable to others by binding itself down in multilateral institutions.

I take issue with this conventional wisdom as well. Keohane's initial problématique was how the American-sponsored multilateral institu-tional order might nevertheless persist "after hegemony" as the United States began to decline in the 1970s and 1980s. However, at the time of the creation of the League and the United Nations, the United States was not yet hegemonic. Even when it was, as in the smaller Western bloc of states which formed NATO, the United States was decidedly ambivalent about long-term institutionalized cooperation. For their part, America's partners were not at all concerned about American exploitation. Multilateralism was a mechanism for them not to hold the United States "down" but rather to keep them "in," as Lord Ismay's famous aphorism about NATO has long told us. The real puzzle is therefore why the United States was willing to make this commitment at all, not how it was able to solicit international support for it. This was cooperation after victory but *before* hegemony.

The key to the postwar American commitment to multilateralism both after WWI and WWII was trust of others, not how to make others trust the United States. Binding security institutions might have had the effect of constraining American power over time, but it was not the original motivation. The United States was not willing to allow unlimited free riding as a hegemon might. Even in the case of the North Atlantic Treaty, where the United States did possess overwhelming power among its partners, American multilateralists were not inclined to provide security without the expectation of European reciprocity.

Rationalists claim that the power of structure in propelling post-WWII multilateralism was evident in the overwhelming bipartisan support in the Senate for these agreements, which contrasted with the polarizing partisan politics and division during the debate on the League of Nations Covenant (Busby and Monten 2008; Kupchan and Trubowitz 2007). However, in the aftermath of WWII, American political elites again vigorously debated the wisdom of significant cooperation with other nations in the framework of international security institutions, first in the form of the United Nations and later in the North Atlantic Treaty. Even in the early post-WWII era, shown empirically to be the most bipartisan period in American foreign policy in the twentieth century, there was no ideological consensus. Structural circumstances did not dictate a unique solution to America's security problems after WWII any more than after WWI. There was no decisive break or new bipartisan consensus.

Both parties were composed, both after WWI and after WWII, almost entirely of internationalists, but there were two competing internationalisms at work. Democrats and Republicans differed over the relative merits of multilateralism and unilateralism, that is, whether security was best served by combining resources with others or going it alone. Even where there was a more compelling security logic, as was true in the NATO case, the United States still faced a choice between a cooperative and a unilateral solution to the threat. Democrats were again more ideologically inclined towards multilateral solutions to collective problems than Republicans in the same structural situation because of their different social orientations, their different levels of generalized trust. Cooperators expected reciprocity, whereas competitors anticipated free-riding, entrapment, exploitation and abandonment. This led them to support different visions for the design of these organizations.

The post-WWII period was different than the post-WWI period not in the absence of ideological differences, but in that the Democratic administration, learning from the mistakes of Woodrow Wilson, solicited Republican input behind the scenes during the negotiation of these two treaties so as to bridge differences before they were publicly debated in the ratification process. Any solution to the dilemma of post-war engagement had to reflect a compromise between the mainstream tendencies in both parties given the need for two-thirds Senate support for any treaty. Ideological divisions were pronounced, but unlike after WWI they were hidden from public view and resolved in private. The subsequent overwhelming consensus in the Senate and the lack of any significant political opposition has facilitated the development of a certain myth of "bipartisan consensus," giving a false impression of ideological convergence when what actually emerged was a carefully constructed compromise in which both sides received something in the deal.

This tells us much about the domestic politics of multilateralism in the United States today. There has always been contestation in the United States over whether and how to cooperate with others. Much of this was muffled during the Cold War. After NATO was created, hardening divisions between West and East papered over domestic ideological differences over the precise design of the alliance. And the United Nations was constructed so as not to significantly threaten American sovereignty in the first place. Therefore generic support for multilateralism did not elicit different responses from liberals and conservatives, as it asked little of the United States. After the Cold War ended, however, these tendencies, present from the beginning, reasserted themselves. And they worsened still after 9/11. Ideological differences between the parties have certainly become much more polarized in recent years. But they were always present.

In sum, generalized trust was an essential ingredient in America's tortuous movement from isolation to engagement over the course of the twentieth century and therefore for the creation of the post-WWII multilateral order. Generalized trust provided a source of social capital for cooperators, predominantly in the Democratic Party, without which the American multilateral security order might never have come into existence or at least would have looked very different. Given American power and its historical reluctance to engage internationally, the United States had great bargaining leverage in the creation and design of the League of Nations, the United Nations, and the North Atlantic Treaty. The form these organizations took was largely the result of American planning. However, the final shape of these institutions resulted from a domestic political compromise of cooperators and competitors, something that explains key features of the three organizations.

In the remainder of this chapter, I lay out an encompassing definition of trust and describe its relationship with related concepts such as reciprocity and cooperation. Defining two dimensions of trust provides the groundwork for drawing out the different varieties of trust. Strategic trust is first. I note its implicit use in rationalist institutionalist theories and explain how the conclusions they reach as regards the causal relationship between trust and IOs derive from this particular choice of trust. This generates a number of different puzzles and anomalies for rationalism. In Chapter 2, I introduce generalized trust, comparing it to the strategic variant and demonstrating how it resolves many of the difficulties the latter has in explaining multilateral cooperation. Generalized trust is a dispositional trait, one evident in the literature on social orientation reviewed next. From this point, after a brief consideration of constructivist approaches to trust and cooperation, it is possible to generate a number of distinct hypotheses for each approach. Finally I take up issues of case selection and measurement.

The dimensions of trust: reciprocity and community

Trust is the belief that one will not be harmed when his or her fate is placed in the hands of others. It entails a combination of uncertainty and vulnerability (Hardin 2006: 29; Hoffman 2006: 17; Kramer, Brewer and Hanna 1996: 25; Larson 1997: 19; Sztompka 1999). Trust always leaves the truster exposed to potential opportunism. Trusters put themselves in a vulnerable position because they do not expect harm to come of it. Yet if trust is involved, they do not know for sure.

In the context of cooperation, trust is the belief that others will cooperate when one cooperates, that they will not exploit one's vulnerability but rather respond in kind. Kydd (2005) has put it in game theoretic terms. Trust is the belief that another has assurance game rather than prisoner's dilemma game preferences, that he or she prefers mutual cooperation to exploiting and suckering others (Kydd 2005: 6–7). Whether to trust involves an assessment of the likelihood that another has cooperative intentions (Kydd 2005: 4–6). Trust is not altruism but rather the expectation of reciprocity (Ostrom and Walker

2003). Trust is particularly crucial in situations of "mixed-motives," or "collaboration games" in which there is an incentive to cooperate but also to defect if others cooperate (Keohane 1984; Olson 1971; Stein 1982).

Trust is critical for cooperation when there is no simultaneous exchange of benefits. The vulnerability involved in trust stems from its sequential nature (Hardin 2006: 18). As Luhman writes, "trust is paid . . . as an advance on success" (1979: 25). That exchange might take place over a short time frame "in a strictly delimited sequence," what is known as "specific" reciprocity (Keohane 1986). Where the level of trust is higher, individuals might engage in "diffuse" reciprocity, in which exchange occurs over a longer period of time, not following every individual transaction. Successful experience with specific reciprocity might build deeper trust and allow more diffuse reciprocity in the future. But where there is no trust, exchange must be simultaneous, eliminating any vulnerability and uncertainty.

Trust is not the only factor promoting cooperation, of course. *Ceteris paribus*, as the cost of defection increases for any player, cooperation becomes more difficult irrespective of trust (Jervis 1978). Even in situations marked by considerable faith in others, individuals might not risk cooperation if the costs of being double-crossed are extremely high.[1] Even leading theorists of trust miss that distinction.[2] Any effort

---

[1] Relatedly, if some player A values the same payoff for mutual cooperation more than another player B, and yet the two have similar assessments of the probability of opportunistic behavior on the part of some player C that would frustrate reaching that goal, player A will be more likely to take a chance on cooperation. This is known as risk propensity, which is not the same as trust. It refers to how willing individuals are to accept risk, not the overall evaluation of the level of risk. By virtue of player A's higher evaluation of the payoffs for cooperation, he or she is more willing to take a chance on cooperation at higher levels of the risk of opportunism. There is a risk of defection in any trust situation because trust is only an issue in situations of uncertainty. Less trusting individuals believe that cooperation is more risky than more trusting individuals. However, the concept of risk aversion applies to a lower evaluation of the payoffs for mutual cooperation. Trust is risky in that there is a potential downside with defection, but trust is not the same as risk propensity (Bueno de Mesquita 1988; Hoffman 2006: 21–2, 25; Kim and Bueno de Mesquita 1995; Luhmann 1979; Sztompka 1999: 28–31).

[2] Hardin writes that "seemingly honorable" people "turn out to be rascals in high stakes endgames." If being a rascal implies defection, as it appears, this still tells us nothing about trust or trustworthiness, as what is driving the breach of trust are the stakes (2006: 22).

to establish the effect of trust must distinguish its impact from the stakes.[3]

This encompassing definition of trust is agnostic on the basis on which trust is conferred and the extent to which trust extends. *How* do political actors know *who* to trust? We can conceive of these problems in terms of two circles of trust, the reciprocity and the community circles. The question of "how" we trust refers to the basis on which political actors make their decisions about the trustworthiness of their potential partners. On what grounds do potential cooperators make their decisions about whether prospective partners will honor their commitments? Different varieties of trust are based on different ideas about the foundations and extent of trust.

The literature on social capital often speaks of a "virtuous circle" in which trust is extended and honored, which then reinforces beliefs about the trustworthiness of others and induces more cooperation (Putnam 1993). Partners travel *around* what I call the *reciprocity circle*. Where reciprocity is diffuse, we can think of the circle as being more open-ended. It does not require an almost immediate exchange in order to continue. Reciprocity is left to a later day. Where trust is relatively more lacking, the circle is more closed. The cycle keeps its momentum only if cooperation is quickly matched. Variation in how individuals determine trustworthiness helps determine the openness of the reciprocity circle.

The question of "who" we trust refers to the scope or extent of trust. Who is admitted *into* the circle of trust? I refer to this as the *community circle*, which we can again conceive of in terms of open and closed circles. The community circle of trust might extend widely if many are regarded are trustworthy, or it might remain closed only to a few. If the community circle remains open, others can be added; if it is closed, they will find it hard to gain access.

Rationalism, strategic trust, and international cooperation

The literature on cooperation in international relations has been pioneered by the rationalist, earlier known as the neoliberal

---

[3] Trust is not the same as confidence either. Confidence implies a belief that the other is capable of meeting his or her end of the bargain, that he or she has the ability and the competence to do so (Barber 1983: Chapter 2; Hoffman 2002; Yamagishi and Yamagishi 1994: 131). Trust, at least as I will use the term, involves an assessment about others' intentions, not their capabilities.

institutionalist, approach. Scholars in this tradition focus largely on "mixed-motive" situations in which short-term incentives to defect undermine potentially more fruitful long-term cooperation among states, generally because of uncertainty about intentions (Keohane 1984; Olson 1971; Stein 1982). Rationalists call this "market failure." Although it is seldom if ever mentioned in this early literature, the problem posed by uncertain intentions is at its heart a question of trust. Not knowing whether others will meet their end of the bargain, states have a hard time cooperating for fear of being suckered.

Rationalist international relations theory rests on a particular notion of trust, what Uslaner (2002) calls the "strategic" variety. In this understanding of the concept, actors trust on the basis of beliefs about others' interests. Actors trust others when they believe that others' interests "encapsulate" their own (Hardin 2006). Trust is a belief that potential partners have a self-interest in cooperation, generally an incentive in building or sustaining a long-term, mutually beneficial relationship. Tyler calls this approach "calculativeness," and it does envision a cold, sober evaluation of the advantages and disadvantages of trust (2001: 287). Whether to trust, argues Hardin, is a "matter of prudential assessment, not moral choice" (2006: 22).

Actors make such judgments on the basis of information. Hardin writes that the two central elements of the rationalist account of trust are, first, the incentives of the trusted to honor the trust and, second, knowledge to justify the truster's trust (Hardin 2006: 44; Yamagishi and Yamagishi 1994: 139). Potential trusters can gain such information through direct experience or by examining potential trustees' previous histories of interaction with others, that is, their reputation (Keohane 1984; Mercer 1996). Of course there is also strategic distrust, the belief that another is untrustworthy based on his or her actions or reputation. International relations scholars have recently begun utilizing this conception of trust explicitly (Kydd 2005).

What is striking about strategic trust is the degree to which trust is limited and situational. Actors trust specific others in particular contexts in which they have enough relevant information about interests. Trust is confined to particular situations but not generalized beyond. As Uslaner writes, the etymology of strategic trust is "A trusts B to do X" (2002: 21). The implication is that even if there is an ongoing relationship of mutual self-interest in one area, those involved draw no general lesson about the partner that carries into other domains. The relationship might produce incentives for potential partners to honor their commitments in other fields but only through the mechanism of a linkage with previously existing areas of cooperation (Haas 1980; Keohane 1984). Actors do not make judgments about others' inherent trustworthiness, instead explaining and predicting behavior by reference to situational circumstances. Others might have an incentive to cooperate in one area and to defect in another.

In terms of the circle metaphor identified above, in strategic trust, the reciprocity circle is driven by information and interest and the community circle is limited to those with whom there are dense and "thick" interactions and for whom there is significant experience to draw on. Both circles are relatively closed. While we can separate the reciprocity and community circles conceptually for the purpose of a typology, they are connected logically. If trust is only based on an assessment of another's interests, the circle of trust is limited in scope. The "how" of trust dictates limitations on the "who."

As strategic trust has nothing to do with the attributes of the individuals cooperating, rationalist work on cooperation has focused almost exclusively on changing the structure of the situation to generate more cooperation. Most notably, Robert Axelrod demonstrated in a series of computer experiments that cooperating in a prisoner's dilemma becomes sustainable and rational when the game is repeated (1984: 31–2). Played only once, there is a dominant strategy to defect, even though the outcome is suboptimal for both players. However, when the game is repeated, the "shadow of the future" is lengthened, and individuals have an interest in sustained cooperation. In Hardin's terms, in a repeated game the player's interests "encapsulate" one another and strategic trust emerges.

Institutions and organizations can also help. By institutionalizing cooperation, international organizations facilitate cooperation otherwise inhibited by uncertain intentions by lengthening time horizons and creating a reputational stake in keeping promises (Keohane 1984; Oye 1985). They provide incentives for trustworthiness. Non-compliance would threaten beneficial cooperation in the future, in other issue areas, and with other partners. Institutions can also solve the problem of uncertain intentions directly by providing information about state behavior and detecting cheating (Abbott and Snidal 1998; Fortna 2003; Keohane 1982; K. Weber 2000).

The rationalist literature on cooperation, because it relies on strategic trust, specifies a particular cause-and-effect relationship between international organizations and trust. Distrust drives the creation of international organizations, which are the producers of strategic trust and cooperation. International organizations come before trust. They change incentives and provide information, altering the structure of the situation to solve the uncertainty problem that breeds distrust.

In recent years, the "rational design" school of international organization has gone beyond issue linkages and time horizons to apply the functionalist logic of rational institutionalism to develop more specific hypotheses about how states construct institutions (Koremenos et al. 2001; 2004). The core assumption is that states behave in a strategic and instrumental way to draw up institutions in such a manner as to solve the particular collective problem they face. Strategic distrust drives the process of institutional design just as it does institutional creation and is embedded in the design of international organizations.

For instance, following Stein (1982), Martin (1992) hypothesizes that international organizations created to cope with what Stein (1982) calls "collaboration" games will require more authority and power to generate cooperation than those that deal with "coordination" games. Whereas in the latter, there is no incentive to defect once an agreement has been reached, collaboration games involve mixed motives and contain incentives to defect on agreements that implicate trust. The claim that states create powerful and authoritative institutions in order to circumvent defection, sometimes called "hierarchy," is a common one in the rationalist literature (Abbott and Snidal 1998; Lake 1999; Moravcsik 1998; 2000; Pollack 1997; G. H. Snyder 1984; K. Weber 2000).[4] States can delegate control of policy implementation to international institutions. The latter can serve as executor of decisions in those situations in which violations are difficult to detect by national parties and when states do not trust one another or even themselves to implement or keep to an agreement in the future (Garrett 1992; Moravcsik 1998; 2000; Pollack 1997; K. Weber 2000). States

---

[4] Koremenos, Lipson and Snidal (2001) claim that in situations with larger incentives to cheat, institutions require "centralization" to enforce cooperation. Lake (1999) calls this "hierarchy," although he envisions the process occurring solely among sovereign states with a dominant power. Abbott and Snidal (2000) make the similar claim that states in these circumstances will settle on "hard law" with more precise obligations and more delegation, both of which limit sovereign decision making.

also have another option short of hierarchy. By pooling sovereignty, for instance in some sort of institutional council based on majority voting, states can outmaneuver and reach collective outcomes against the wishes of those they do not trust.[5] However, in these cases, states retain the ability to defect as they do not actually lose control over the implementation of policy.

These rationalist arguments are somewhat different than those offered by the first generation of rational institutionalists. Whereas lengthening time horizons and creating a concern for reputation involve creating incentives for trustworthy behavior, hierarchy involves removing control over policy from states so that defection is not an option and trust is not an issue. Strong institutions are the primary mechanism to allow "cooperation without trust" (Cook, Hardin and Levi 2005; Kramer, Brewer and Hanna 2004: 383; Ostrom 2003: 19; Sztompka 1999: 87). However, the logic is the same. Problems of distrust drive the creation of institutions. And the greater the distrust, the more powerful the organization.

Rationalist arguments about cooperation and hierarchy rest on the condition that states are able to calculate their interests and estimate the likely course that other members might take. Assuming that all states are under the same obligations, states are balancing the potential threat of transferring their own sovereignty against the gain of others doing the same. If states choose to delegate or pool sovereignty they are placing their fate in others' hands, but primarily to outmaneuver and reach collective outcomes against the wishes of other members they do not trust. Therefore, when uncertainty reaches such a degree that states are unable to make such strategic calculations, that of "uncertainty about the state of the world," rationalists argue that states behave differently. In these instances, states design institutions that establish individual control, such as a veto (Kahler 1992; Koremenos et al. 2001), "soft law" (Abbott and Snidal 2000) or escape clauses

---

[5] For instance, in the European Union, states delegate the implementation and management of key issue areas to the European Commission and European Central Bank because they do not trust other members to execute faithfully their agreements. Or they make decisions in a council of national state representatives but on the basis of non-unanimous voting. In the case of the Single European Act, scholars argue that members agreed to qualified majority voting to ensure the subsequent implementation of the Single Market in the face of mistrust of Spanish and Portuguese protectionist tendencies (Garrett 1992).

so they can withdraw if it turns out an agreement or participating in an organization is not in their interest. Flexibility allows states to wriggle out of obligations, reinstating sovereignty (Koremenos 2005; Rosendorff and Milner 2001). In short, they resort to unilateralism or its institutional equivalent.

At first glance this argument seems to directly contradict the previous claim about "locking in." In one instance uncertainty leads to sovereignty transfer, in the other to sovereignty retention. But they are linked by a common assumption that strategic distrust drives the design of international organizations. States do not place their fate in the hands of others by relinquishing sovereignty unless they can calculate the likely effects.

The limitations of rational institutionalism

Rationalist explanations of international cooperation and the design of international organizations suffer from a number of limitations. First, they have difficulty accounting for the initiation of cooperation. Once begun, ongoing relationships of mutual benefit and exchange might be self-enforcing. Strategic trust can sustain cooperation. But the strategic conception of trust is based on information derived from experience in cooperation and an incentive to preserve the relationship after it has begun. The process must begin with one side trusting enough to risk opportunism for the potential gains of cooperation. In other words, no one can be brought into the community circle unless there is already a reciprocity circle.

Rationalists might argue that cooperation is easier to initiate in reassurance games than prisoner's dilemmas, but the very essence of a reassurance game is that players are uncertain about the preferences of others, fearing they might be playing a prisoner's dilemma. In game theoretic language, both sides prefer mutual cooperation to all other outcomes, but they are not certain that others do not prefer defection. It is only through cooperation that the actual game matrix is revealed. Once one player makes a cooperative move, the mutually beneficial outcome is virtually assured, but the question of who will begin the process remains. Someone must take the "initial gamble" to initiate the reciprocity circle (Uslaner 2002: 14–15). Trust is necessary to begin the process of cooperation, but strategic trust cannot perform this function. Axelrod, one of the great rationalist theorists of reciprocity in international relations, notes the puzzle posed by the initiation and resorts to kinship ties (identity and altruism), which are then passed on through reproduction as dispositional traits (Axelrod and Hamilton 1981). But those mechanisms are not rationalist.

Rationalists might also rely on the notion of a "privileged group," an individual or group of individuals who value the gains created from cooperation so much that they are willing to make the first move irrespective of what others do. This is how Keohane (1984) and others explained the creation of much of the postwar institutional order, thereby sidestepping the question of how strategic trust instigates cooperation (Snidal 1985). However, in this case, trust is not present at all, as privileged groups provide certain goods despite the fact that others are defecting. This is not an instance of reciprocity or trust of any kind.

Perhaps a state has information about another's interests and trustworthiness based on its prior actions in other contexts, rationalists might say. There is always a history of interaction. However, rationalists still have difficulty explaining cooperation in larger contexts, in which the alignments of interests cannot be known given the sheer number of states or the sheer scope of an organization's ambit. Indeed rationalism tells us that states will generally limit the size of institutions when uncertainty about preferences and cheating are key concerns, as mentioned above. Large-N "quantitative" multilateralism is difficult to account for, unless these organizations are allowed to do very little (Ruggie 1992). Downs, Rocke and Barsoom (1998) argue that if they are to perform any significant functions, multilateral organizations must start with a small number of members, adding additional states over time piecemeal. Rationalists cannot explain larger community circles of trust.

Rationalists also have difficulty explaining how more open-ended reciprocity circles are sustained. They cannot account for diffuse reciprocity *over time*. Strategic trust rests on, indeed requires, specific rather than diffuse reciprocity. Individuals trust so long as another's cooperative behavior indicates to them that they have a vested interest in maintaining a cooperative relationship. Where the benefits of exchange are not relatively consistent, strategic trust disappears as it is the very repetition of cooperation that convinces states of the trustworthiness of others. It provides the information about the interests of others' cooperative intentions. And if there is no frequent exchange of benefits, there is no long-term relationship that provides the incentive to cooperate and the reason to trust.[6]

Rationalism and multilateralism

All three of these rationalist shortcomings – explaining the initiation of cooperation, significant cooperation in large settings, and diffuse reciprocity over time – share a common denominator. Rationalism cannot account for cooperation in situations of pronounced uncertainty in which states are not able to make strategic calculations, whether because of either the lack of information about preferences in a new setting of potential cooperation, or the complexity of decision making in an environment with many actors, or the inability to make specific exchanges of benefits given a lack of knowledge about when or whether promises might come due. States avoid cooperation in these instances. This is because they rely on a somewhat closed and shallow variety of trust.

As a consequence, rationalists have a hard time explaining the creation of multilateral security organizations. At least theoretically, international organizations should be most effective at reaching outcomes that benefit their membership when they ask states to make legally binding commitments that limit their future discretion. Ruggie calls this "qualitative multilateralism," "an institutional form which coordinates relations among three or more states on the basis of 'generalized' principles of conduct – that is, principles which specify appropriate conduct for a class of actions, without regard to the particularistic interests of the parties or the strategic exigencies that may exist in any specific occurrence" (1992: 51).

Multilateralism limits sovereignty in the sense of state discretion over foreign policy rather than actual control of policy, something which is only limited by hierarchy. States concede to such a limitation so as to mobilize the collective weight of a group of states and allow

---

[6] Rationalists can account for diffuse reciprocity over space. Multilateral trade regimes are an example. States do not benefit from the opening of their markets to every individual member of the regime, but even if they lose in particular bilateral contexts, they benefit from the broader multilateral arrangement. It is not that states expect to benefit only over the long term, but rather that they do not expect reciprocity across every bilateral relationship. As there is no time element to cooperation among many members across space, no trust of any kind is implicated.

outcomes that would not otherwise be possible. Absent such a loss of state discretion, the situation remains as it had been before the creation of an organization. Complete freedom of choice, without any real costs due to obligations from international agreements, is unilateralism. If states are allowed total discretion in some agreement over how to behave in each instance, there is very little difference between the situation before and after the commitment.

In the security arena, multilateralism involves two features. First, multilateral security institutions typically include some sort of security guarantee, a pledge to take a particular action in case one of the members is attacked. Second, they might also contain an obligation to resolve disputes peacefully and provide mechanisms for doing so. Both are efforts to reap the gains of cooperation by combining resources for the collective good. Security guarantees attempt to deter aggression and ensure that states fighting wars will have additional help and are more likely to win. Multilateral conflict resolution mechanisms aim at nipping conflicts in the bud before they escalate and draw in others. Reaping the gains of cooperation generally means making binding commitments. Security guarantees have a better deterrent effect if they are automatic in nature, unequivocally committing a state in advance to the defense of others. Conflict resolution is most likely to yield collective benefits if parties to a dispute commit to always submit their disputes to arbitration or mediation, have no say in the ultimate decision, and there are penalties for non-compliance or non-submission of disputes. Both security guarantees and conflict resolution pledges can be thought of as reciprocal exchanges. One state agrees to come to the aid of others and to allow others to mediate its disputes, in exchange for others doing the same.

However, states will commit to qualitative multilateralism only if they believe that states will not abandon their obligations by either refusing to abide by procedures for dispute resolution or not coming to the aid of others in case of attack. They cannot base this expectation on strategic trust. As Ruggie (1992) notes, qualitative multilateralism requires an expectation of diffuse rather than specific reciprocity. A commitment to come to the aid of others in case of attack is different from a commitment to liberalization in trade in that the former deals with contingencies that might never arise and cannot be directly exchanged. States in a multilateral alliance cannot engage in a specific exchange of actual benefits, only promises, as the exchange involves aggression that might never happen. Norway did not exchange aid from France in their efforts to fight an invasion from the Soviet Union in return for their aid when France was invaded by Germany. They couldn't. These types of contingencies could not be foreseen, and they would be extremely rare if they occurred at all. A multilateral security guarantee involves an open-ended commitment. In the absence of the possibility of specific reciprocity, encapsulated interest does not emerge and strategic trust cannot sustain cooperation.

Rationalists would argue that these promises might be credible if states share an interest in deterring a common threat. In these cases, trust is not necessary because interests are identical. France might fight for Norway not because of the expectation of reciprocity later, but because France has an interest in helping Norway now.[7] This is of course true and is the core of many alliances. But as multilateral security pacts grow in size, such identity of interest is harder to sustain, making diffuse reciprocity necessary. In other words, larger community circles make it more difficult to maintain open reciprocity circles.

In addition to abandonment, multilateralism comes with the potential price of other forms of opportunism, as this institutional form places a state's fate in the hands of others to some degree. The risks of a security guarantee are articulated nicely by Snyder (1984) and subsequently refined by Lake (1999). First, if security guarantees are automatic in nature, states can become ensnared in conflicts that do not serve their interests, triggered by the outbreak of hostilities on the part of any member. Security commitments might lead to moral hazard, leading states to take overly provocative acts with the expectation that others will bail them out if conflict breaks out. This is the problem of "entrapment."

Conflict resolution procedures come with their own pitfalls. They allow potential exploitation and interference. The ability of a state to have a say in others' affairs comes at the price of others having a say in one's own. States could use these institutional mechanisms to interfere in areas of vital interest to others, even if this is not in keeping with the spirit of the organization or agreement. For instance, IO members might use their power to resolve disputes not on the basis

---

[7] Note that identity of interest is different than encapsulated interest. In the former, cooperation, the explicit coordination of behavior, is not even necessary whereas in the latter it is.

of the merits of the various cases but rather purely on self-interested grounds.

Rationalists would expect states to commit to qualitatively multi-lateral institutions only if they can design other aspects of the institution in such a way as to reduce the problems of trust, uncertainty and opportunism inherent to this particular institutional design. First, rationalists point out that states can limit their exposure to untrustworthy behavior by insisting on control – unilateralism or its institutional equivalent. They can water down their security guarantees, making them contingent on particular conditions or not specifying the nature of action to be taken. The less automatic they are, the more state actions are not determined by the behavior of others. Conflict resolution can be diluted by making submission and adjudication contingent on the agreement of parties to the dispute, or by not providing for any penalty for non-compliance. Most obviously, states can insist on a veto for all matters affecting their sovereignty, whether it be taking action to enforce a security guarantee or consenting to conflict resolution or accepting its results. All of these steps reduce qualitative multilateralism by removing the general nature of commitments and making them more discretionary.

Second, states can limit the number of members in an organization, reducing quantitative multilateralism. They can improve the functioning of the reciprocity circle by closing the community circle. The problems of entrapment, free-riding, exploitation and abandonment increase as more members are added to an organization. Therefore rationalists expect states to be able to commit more easily to security guarantees amongst smaller groups of states as it is more likely that interests encapsulate one another. Specific reciprocity can drive cooperation, and monitoring of behavior is easier. It also makes the prediction of future alignments easier, allowing states to predict whether their interest is served by authoritative conflict resolution procedures. Small groups of states might form a "privileged group" (Abbott and Snidal 1998; Downs et al. 1998; Kahler 1992; Koremenos 2005). In other words, state preferences for qualitative and quantitative multilateralism are inversely related.

Third, states can make their arrangements more flexible, through the inclusion of withdrawal mechanisms that allow states to drop out of cooperation if their interests are not served. Another example of flexibility is the term of an agreement. For instance, security treaties vary in length. They might last only a few years, or be indefinite (Koremenos 2001; 2005; Koremenos et al. 2001; 2004; Rosendorff and Milner 2001).

Finally, states can impose some form of supranational hierarchy. This solution allows for limitations on all types of opportunism by taking control out of the hands of those who might act opportunistically. For instance, the creation of a multinational chain of military command makes abandonment in time of war more difficult (Abbott and Snidal 2000; Garrett 1992; Hawkins et al. 2006; Koremenos et al. 2004; Moravcsik 1998; 2000; Pollack 1997). Since states use such mechanisms to solve problems of strategic distrust, they prefer more authoritative arrangements only if they allow them to outvote or constrain their likely opponents. If they do not or cannot make such projections because the environment is too uncertain, as might occur as institutions increase in membership or scope, they will prefer unilateralism or its institutional equivalent to prevent exploitation.

All of these solutions to the problem of opportunism in multilateralism involve reducing uncertainty. Many, however, work against the reason for creating multilateral institutions in the first place. For instance, weakening a security guarantee through looser language or a veto limits the likelihood of entrapment but also limits the guarantee's deterrent effect. Adding a veto prevents interference and exploitation but also means that others can obstruct the business of an institution. Limiting the number of members means excluding those who might make a contribution to an organization in the hour of peril and who might increase the deterrent effect of the organization. Arrangements with long terms and no provisions for withdrawal are more credible and provide more assurance to members. And hierarchy is generally very costly. However, as the next chapter shows, there is another way. But it requires a different conception of trust.

2 | *Anarchical social capital: a social psychological theory of trust, international cooperation and institutional design*

Rationalists have difficulty accounting for multilateral cooperation because of their reliance on strategic trust. However, rationalism does not exhaust the varieties of trust, either theoretically or empirically. Social psychologists have centered their attention instead on *generalized trust*, a relatively optimistic view about the trustworthiness of others. Generalized trust is not tailored to individual circumstances or partners but serves as a general rule that guides behavior and choices about cooperation. The etymology of generalized trust is "A trusts" or "A is trusting." Generalized trust allows for a more open community and reciprocity circle.

Generalized trust is not based on a naïve belief that all others are trustworthy. Rather it is a default tendency to trust, *ceteris paribus*, unless there is specific information indicating that this is not wise (Mercer 2005: 95; Yamagishi 2001: 124). Brewer calls it "depersonalized trust" (1981: 356). As such, generalized trust is *not* inconsistent with distrust of specific others who have proved themselves to be unreliable and dishonest partners. As Uslaner writes, "It is hardly contradictory for someone who places great faith *in people* to check out the qualifications and honesty of *specific persons*" (2002: 24).[1] Nor is it a panacea. Even generalized trust might not promote cooperation if the costs of a breach of trust are dramatic. Vulnerability is not distrust.

Generalized trust cannot be based on information collected on all prospective interaction partners as this would be impossible to collect. As Sztompka writes, "Trustfulness may incline people to grant trust, and suspiciousness to withhold trust, quite independently of any estimate of trustworthiness. The origins of trustfulness or suspiciousness are not epistemological. They have nothing to do with knowledge

---

[1] Hardin dismisses generalized trust because he interprets it incorrectly as implying that we must trust everyone as much as our mother (2001: 11).

24

about the partners of future engagements"(1999: 70). Mercer writes that it involves "certainty beyond observable evidence" (2005: 95). Hardin, somewhat pejoratively, calls it a "non-cognitive" approach (2001: 5). Better stated, it is "non-calculative" in the utilitarian sense. It is most certainly cognitive in that it is based on a set of beliefs about others. In the context of cooperation, generalized trust is a belief that others are generally likely to reciprocate cooperation, a feeling that others have reassurance, rather than prisoner's dilemma preferences.

Because trust of the generalized variety cannot be based on specific information about others, it must be a kind of "moralistic" trust. It rests on a general belief in the benevolent character of others (Cook and Cooper 2003: 215; Uslaner 2002: 4). Rotter defines this variety of trust as the "generalized expectancy held by an individual that the word, promise, oral or written statement of another individual or group can be relied on" (Cook and Cooper 2003: 213; Messick and Kramer 2001: 91; Rotter 1980: 1). Trust of this sort is a "moral impulse" (Sztompka 1999: 97–8). Messick and Kramer are describing moralistic trust when they define trust as making decisions as if others will abide by ordinary ethical rules, most important of which are truth-telling and not harming others (2001: 91).

Moralistic trust is a "social conception of trust" in which trusters believe that intentions and behavior reflect traits of the trustee, rather than the situation (Tyler and Degoey 1996: 332).[2] Moralistic trust is based on "an implicit theory of personality," a belief that others have consistent personalities and traits that do not vary by situation (Mercer 2005: 95; Sztompka 1999: 75). When we trust moralistically, we are making judgments about the character of partners and their inherent trustworthiness (Larson 1997: 22; Yamagishi and Yamagishi 1994: 132). The reciprocity circle begins with an attribution about others' character, rather than their interests.

This element of generalized trust captures the conventional, commonsense notion of trust as having a moral element. Trust is generally associated with an expectation of integrity and upright behavior on the part of the trustee. Uslaner writes that when someone trusts, he or she presumes that others are "honorable" (2002: 15). One might argue that if we need to gather information and constantly verify

---

[2] Hoffman calls it "fiduciary trust" (2002: 20–2).

cooperative behavior, we are not really trusting. In the context of strategic interaction, moralistic trust is the belief that others will feel morally bound to reciprocate cooperation.

Moral attributions allow individuals to draw broader conclusions about the trustworthiness of others without the need constantly to collect information in every new situation. By ascribing a moral character to another or to others in general, trust is transferable to other potential areas of mutual benefit in a way that is not possible in rationalist conceptions of trust and cooperation. Therefore, generalized trust, as a kind of moralistic trust, serves as a "social lubricant" allowing for higher levels of cooperation without the need for costly enforcement and the collection of information (Cook and Cooper 2003: 209; Putnam 1993; Sztompka 1999: 62; Tyler 2001: 285). Generalized trust is a form of "social capital" (Putnam 1993; Tyler 2001: 285). Although the nature of social capital and its precise definition are contentious issues, I use the term merely to describe a resource of individuals, groups or societies that serves to promote more optimal levels of cooperation that leave all better off.

Social psychology, generalized trust and international cooperation

As a form of social capital, generalized trust promotes cooperation even in structural situations deemed inhospitable by rationalism. It helps address the shortcomings identified above. Generalized trust is particularly useful in situations of what Luhmann (1979) calls "social uncertainty," extreme uncertainty about the intentions of others akin to what Koremenos, Lipson and Snidal (2004) call "uncertainty about the state of the world." Individuals often do not have enough information to make a choice between cooperation and non-cooperation based on strategic trust or distrust alone.

First, generalized trust can get the ball rolling, allowing actors to initiate cooperation. Trust in the inherent morality of others helps begin the reciprocity circle by bringing even those one does not know into the community circle. Hayashi et al. (1999) call this the "sense of control," Kramer et al. "elicitative" trust (1996: 374). The former conducted a one-shot experiment with prisoner's dilemma payoffs, only they staged the moves so that players did not move simultaneously but rather sequentially. Rational choice expects the first player to engage in backwards induction. Recognizing that the second player will defect against cooperation and defection, he/she will protect himself/herself by not cooperating to begin with. However, the study found that when the first mover's choice is to be conveyed to the other player, first movers often cooperate because they believe they can induce others to reciprocate (Kramer, Brewer and Hanna 1996: 374; Larson 1997; Pilisuk and Skolnick 1968).

The kind of trust operating in this instance must be based on a belief that others feel morally compelled to reciprocate cooperation since there is no other sanction given the one-shot nature of the game (Kramer, Brewer and Hanna 1996: 374; Larson 1997; Pilisuk and Skolnick 1968). And this belief must be based on a general under-standing of how others in general will behave, as there is no history of interaction or prior experience with the other player. Similarly, gener-alized trust might begin the process of cooperation among states.

The sense of control might be aided by the ability to communi-cate and make commitments. Dawes, McTavish and Shaklee's (1977) famous study of behavior in a commons dilemma experiment showed that the ability of groups to communicate about a game before play-ing generated significantly more cooperative behavior. The possibility of making a pledge to cooperate improved mutual cooperative out-comes still further, even though the promise amounted to "cheap talk" because the structure of the game was identical to a one-shot prisoner's dilemma.[3]

Hardin, like others, dismisses the relevance of these studies, questioning the intelligence of players and their grasp of the logic of the game they were playing (2006: 52). Kydd rejects the notion that trust is playing a role for first movers in these instances, as this would make trust "irrational" (2005: 10). Working within the confines and premises of strategic trust, this is true. However, if subjects in experiments have reason to believe that moral norms are operative and their decision to trust will be met in kind, it is rational to cooperate.

---

[3] The aggregate defection level of groups, i.e. the percentage of non-cooperative choices among players, was 73 percent in groups that could not communicate at all and 65 percent in situations in which they could only engage in small talk unrelated to the game. However, the defection level plummeted to 26 percent in groups in which subjects could discuss the game and fell further still to 16 percent when they could make a pledge to cooperate. This again seems to point to the importance of elicitative trust and a norm of reciprocity.

Empirically, such a trusting act is actually strongly associated with reciprocity. In the Hayashi et al. (1999) study, second movers choose to meet cooperation with cooperation to a large extent, even though there is no prospect for continued gain given the one-shot nature of the game. Therefore it is often irrational for the first player not to trust in these situations On the basis of findings in a similar one-shot experiment showing substantial trust and reciprocity, the behavioral economists Berg, Dickhaut and McCabe (1995) come to the conclusion that reciprocity is a basic element of human behavior, an "economic primitive."

A belief that others are generally and inherently trustworthy provides the confidence needed to cooperate even when the gains from cooperation are inconsistent over a long period of time. It helps sustain, as well as begin, cooperation. Where generalized trust is lacking, states will insist on specific reciprocity, as they will be less certain that others will honor their agreements (Keohane 1986).[4] In the relationship between specific reciprocity and strategic trust on the one hand and diffuse reciprocity and moralistic trust on the other, cause and effect are reversed. Whereas strategic trust follows from specific reciprocity, the practice of diffuse reciprocity over time follows from moralistic trust. As Keohane notes, diffuse reciprocity rests on a "sense of obligation," of "duties" and on a "confidence in the good faith of others" (1986: 20–21, 25). Although he is not explicit, he is talking about moralistic trust. Where moralistic trust is lacking, actors must engage in simultaneous exchange or specific reciprocity. This is the "appropriate principle of behavior when norms of obligation are weak" (Keohane 1986: 24).

Generalized trust thereby facilitates the diffuse reciprocity often necessary for long-term cooperation. It can maintain the reciprocity circle even when it is relatively open. For instance, members of the North Atlantic Treaty Organization have to feel assured, even in the absence of specific reciprocity, that others will come to their aid. Only moralistic trust gives that assurance. Norway (and every other member) made their *pledge* to help France (and any other member) *in case of attack* in exchange for a similar pledge to aid it in case of attack. This is a swap of promises that might never be called into play, and if it were, the exchange might not be equal. But it is based on a belief that others will feel morally obligated to comply.

---

[4] Keohane does not discuss trust but it is implied in the analysis.

Finally, generalized trust also facilitates cooperation with those about whom one has little information (Rotter 1980: 2). According to Yamagishi and Yamagishi, trust is a "springboard" in uncertain situations to leap into the "outside world," "emancipating" individuals from the secure confines of stable relationships and allowing them to seek other cooperative partners with whom there might be greater gains (1994: 141; also Messick and Kramer 2001: 108). Studies show that less trusting individuals rely more on committed relationships rather than seek out potentially more beneficial relationships with others they do not know (Cook and Cooper 2003: 215; Messick and Kramer 2001: 108; Uslaner 2002: 24–8; Yamagishi, Cook and Watabe 1998). Without generalized trust, individuals tend to limit their interactions to those about whom they have information and with whom they have long-term relationships. In an effort to avoid the uncertainty that comes with cooperation, they are led into isolation, cut off from the potential gains from cooperation by their fear of opportunism (Yamagishi 2001: 125). They under-cooperate. Generalized trust allows for a more inclusive community circle, one that remains relatively more open and therefore is easier for others to join. It facilitates new partnerships among states.

Those who lack generalized trust fall back on either strategic trust or what Uslaner (2002) calls *particularized* trust, moralistic trust of a particular other. The etymology is "A trusts B" (2002: 28). (What we could call particularized fear would be the opposite.) Uslaner describes it as trust in others who are like us, based on a shared identity (Brewer and Kramer 1986; Uslaner 1999). In this way it is different from generalized trust, which facilitates trust of outsiders rather than creating or reinforcing trust within groups. In differentiating generalized and particularized trust, Uslaner cites Putnam's (1993) distinction between "bridging" and "bonding" varieties of social capital. Even while the reciprocity circle in both varieties of trust is driven by a sense of inherent trustworthiness, the community circle of generalized trust is more open and encompassing than that of particularized trust, which is closed and more restricted. Nevertheless, particularized trust is far more substantial than strategic trust in that it serves as a form of social capital within a particular group.

Rationalists are of course acutely aware of the potential opportunity costs of non-cooperation highlighted by the emancipatory theory of trust. Indeed it is this problématique, known to them as

"market failure," that initially propelled what became known somewhat misleadingly as "neoliberal" institutionalism (Grieco 1988;
Keohane 1982; 1984). Rationalism is theoretically and empirically
important, but it is incomplete (Kramer et al. 2004: 284; Ostrom
2003: 45; Tyler 2001: 287). Both types of trust are empirically operative. However, by neglecting generalized trust, rationalists systematically understate the potential for cooperation in situations in which it
is difficult to assess strategically the interests of others. In an anarchic
environment, uncertainty is always an issue, making generalized trust
a potentially important resource for international cooperation.

   Generalized trust affects not only states' willingness to cooperate but
should also influence their preferences for and willingness to commit to
particular institutional forms. As argued in Chapter 1, rationalists have
a hard time explaining the creation of multilateral security institutions
unless states restrict membership, add some degree of hierarchical control, water down commitments or make them more flexible. Acceding
to qualitative multilateralism exposes states to entrapment, abandonment and exploitation. All of these solutions come with a price.

   Generalized trust helps resolve these dilemmas in a different way.
Concerns about opportunism are the expression of the distrust that
comes from placing one's fate partially in the hands of others. But this
is less worrisome when others are generally expected to reciprocate
cooperation and live by their commitments. Generalized trust encour-
ages states to build larger organizations to reap the benefit of numbers
even without the possibility of specific reciprocity. Even if interests
are not identical and do not fully overlap, a binding and indivisible
security guarantee might nevertheless operate in a larger group on the
basis of diffuse reciprocity if states feel assured that others will largely
live up to their moral obligations.

   This might be possible even without the imposition of hierarchy.
If organizations do not actually take physical control over policy
away from states, agreements among them are of course only moral
obligations. Yet generalized trust would leads states to believe such
commitments to be more credible than rationalism suspects. This
reveals a paradox. Generalized trust makes states more willing to
commit to hierarchy, as this type of trust ameliorates the fear of
placing one's fate in another's hands. However, it also makes states
less likely to see the need. A lack of generalized trust, in contrast,
would create a need for hierarchy to protect against opportunism; yet
without generalized trust, states cannot make such a commitment in

the first place. Hierarchy requires a solution to a second-order trust problem.

Nevertheless, some sort of international organization is still necessary because generalized trust is not total. If all could be trusted, there would be no need for an institution except to manage situations of inadvertent deleterious state behavior. The international system would resemble a large-N "harmony" situation, the naïve idealist position. But generalized trust would lead states to expect that breaches of trust will be relatively rare.

Generalized trust precedes and allows institutional creation of this kind, in contrast to the core assumptions of rationalism that distrust drives institutional creation and organizations produce trust. By lessening concerns about opportunism, it serves as a source of social capital to construct an anarchical society, a system of constraints placed on states that facilitates cooperation even while the international system remains anarchic (Bull 1977). If states make multilateral commitments in highly uncertain situations given the potential for opportunism, then relinquishing sovereignty does not reflect distrust but the opposite. It is placing a state's fate in the hands of others in situations that cannot be foreseen and in which it is not clear where a state's direct interests will lie.[5] It is the effect of generalized trust. Sovereignty, on the other hand, is the watchword of generalized trust's absence. States that do not trust will insist on retaining unilateral control.

Generalized trust allows institution building but it does not cause it. Institutions are instruments formed to solve collective problems. Generalized trust is often, I argue, a necessary condition, but not a sufficient one. Trusters do not create international organizations for their own sake, but rather when they are in their interests. In this book, those interests are the desire to preserve peace and security. However, part of that calculus rests on assumptions about what others will do, for which generalized trust is essential.

Dispositions to trust and social orientation: putting the "ism" in multilateralism

A general belief that others are generally trustworthy or untrustworthy, independent of the particular partner or situation one faces

---

[5] Hoffman (2006: 26–8) draws the same conclusions but does not recognize that granting discretion to others can also be a strategic way of circumventing others and reflect distrust, not only trust.

immediately, must by definition indicate a disposition. It is a quality endemic to the truster, not the relationship or even the characteristic of the specific target of distrust or trust (Sztompka 1999: 97). In this sense, generalized trust is radically different from strategic trust; it is not only moralistic, but also inherent to the individual rather than the situation.

Social psychologists have found overwhelming evidence that generalized trust improves cooperation levels in "social dilemmas" such as public goods and commons situations (Dawes 1980; Messick and Brewer 1983). Individuals with the same incentives are more likely to contribute to a public good or restrain from consumption of a common resource if they believe before the experiment that others will do so as well. This expectation of reciprocity is generalized in nature, based on assessments before an experiment begins of participants' general expectations of how others will play the game. Dawes et al. (1977) find that prior to experiments, defectors expect about four times as much defection as cooperators. Those playing have no prior history of interaction. Indeed, almost all experiments avoid direct human contact among research subjects, using computers instead (Alcock and Mansell 1977; Brann and Foddy 1987; Dawes 1980; Dawes et al. 1977; McClintock and Liebrand 1988; Messick and Brewer 1983; Parks 1994; Yamagishi and Cook 1993; Schlenker, Helm and Tedeschi 1973; Wrightsman 1966).

Studies show that less trusting individuals rely more on committed relationships than on seeking out potentially more beneficial relationships with others they do not know (Cook and Cooper 2003: 215; Uslaner 2002: 24–8; Yamagishi et al. 1998). That is, non-trusters behave as rationalists expect all to act in situations of great uncertainty. Experimental research also shows that in prisoner's dilemma games in which subjects are given the option to enter or leave the game, it is trusters who tend to play and keep playing (Orbell and Dawes 1993; Orbell, Schwartz-Shea and Simmons 1984). More important perhaps, trusters tend to do better (Orbell and Dawes 1993).

Anyone familiar with the cooperation debates in international relations will recognize these social dilemmas as the same problems of suboptimal cooperation and market failure that drive the rational institutionalist project. Yet with a few noteworthy exceptions (Cronin 1999; Larson 1997), work on cooperation in the international relations literature has virtually ignored almost a half century of work in social psychology on this subject. Instead rationalists have combed the more economistic, more formal and less empirical approach to these dilemmas for insights.

Differences in dispositions to trust are at the heart of the social psychological literature on "social orientations" (M. Deutsch 1960a; McClintock 1972; Messick and McClintock 1968). This line of research was driven by an interest in explaining the consistent finding that individuals demonstrate remarkably different levels of cooperation in the same structural circumstances. Social psychologists theorize that individuals transform objective decision matrices given by researchers into "effective" decision matrices that reflect their own subjective weights of particular outcomes (Hayashi et al. 1999; Kelley and Thibaut 1978; McClintock and Liebrand 1988; Parks 1994). They separate subjects into different types based on their subjective weights of game outcomes, typically measured by asking experimental subjects to rank-order a number of different own and others' outcomes before a game began. Most important for this book are the *competitive* and *cooperative* social orientations. Competitors specify a preference for maximizing the difference between their own and others' payoffs, whereas cooperators indicate a desire for joint gains.[6] In terms of behavior, competitors demonstrate consistently less cooperation in the same mixed-motive game situations than cooperators in line with the preferences they indicated before the game began (Kelley and Stahelski 1970; Kuhlman, Camac and Cunha 1986; Kuhlman and Marshello 1975; Kuhlman and Wimberley 1976; McClintock and Liebrand 1988).

The Kuhlman and Marshello study (1975) in particular and the social orientation program in general had an enormous impact on psychological research on cooperation. According to later researchers, this work "provided the basis for unraveling much of the theoretical and empirical confusion that followed from the often contradictory or insignificant findings obtained in the thousands of studies that used two-person, two-choice games as interdependence paradigms for investigating social decision making." Researchers had been puzzled by the high degree of cooperation in social dilemmas in which defection should have been the dominant strategy, but also by the fact that cooperation levels varied. "Kuhlman and Marshello demonstrated that

[6] "Individualists" lie somewhere in between.

what appeared as irrational choice behaviors in a Prisoner's Dilemma were in fact rational" (McClintock and Liebrand 1988: 396).

More important for the purposes of this book, subsequent studies consistently found that individuals' varying levels of cooperation could be attributed to their expectations prior to the experiment about what others will do (Kuhlman and Wimberley 1976). In other words, competitors and cooperators have different levels of generalized trust. Cooperators cooperate because they believe others will as well. Competitors compete because they believe they must. Later research found a direct link between cooperative social orientation and dispositions to trust (Kanagaretnam et al. 2009).

Competitors and cooperators have different views of the world (Kelley and Stahelski 1970). Competitors see a dangerous environment populated by other competitors. As a consequence, competitors convert repeated games with an assurance incentive matrix into an effective prisoner's dilemma, constantly defecting even against a strategy of 100 percent cooperation. In repeated prisoner's dilemmas, expecting defection they consistently defect against all strategies, including tit for tat, leaving potential gains on the table. In contrast, more trusting cooperators transform a repeated prisoner's dilemma given by researchers into an assurance game on the basis of their more optimistic assumptions about others' behavior. This framing leads them to begin games with cooperation with the expectation that it will be reciprocated (Kuhlman and Marshello 1975; Kuhlman and Wimberley 1976). Kuhlman and Marshello concluded on the basis of their famous experiment: "The most important point to be made in the present paper is that the effective structure of a Prisoner's Dilemma game ... varies from one person to the next, and a good deal of this variation may be understood in terms of ... motivational orientations" (1975: 930).

Research also shows that cooperators, as generalized trusters, are also moralistic trusters. Studies show that simple albeit unenforceable messages of cooperative intent induce higher cooperation on the part of cooperators but not competitors (Parks, Henager and Scamahorn 1996). Cooperators tend to attribute behavior by others during experiments to moral characteristics, holding cooperators to be more moral than defectors. They believe that honesty will have a greater effect on the level of cooperation of others than non-trusters do, and their own level of cooperation increases much more sharply against players identified as moral than does that of those who lack generalized trust (Kanagaretnam et al. 2009; Liebrand, Jansen, Rijken and Suhre 1986; Van Lange and Kuhlman 1994). Competitors in contrast attribute behavior to strength characteristics, viewing cooperators as weak and competitors as strong. It appears that competitors, believing that others are inherently self-interested and immoral, come to see their surroundings as an amoral environment in which only strength matters. The combination is called the "might versus morality effect."

However, cooperators are not altruistic. Studies show that cooperators demonstrate a greater degree of "compensatory" trust, willing to put up with a few defections in order to elicit reciprocity (Kramer et al. 2004). However, they will stop cooperating when faced with a partner who consistently defects (Kanagaretnam et al. 2009; Kelley and Stahelski 1970; Kuhlman and Marshello 1975; Kuhlman and Wimberley 1976; McClintock and Liebrand 1988; Rotter 1980). They feel particularly aggrieved because defection is seen as a moral failure, an act of dishonesty (Stouten, De Cremer and Van Dijk 2006). Cooperators' preference for joint gains is premised on an expectation of reciprocity.[7] Competitors, in contrast, demonstrate consistently low levels of cooperation irrespective of the other's strategy and the information that behavior provides (Van Lange and Kuhlman 1994). The combination of "behavioral assimilation" by cooperators and competitors' resistance to information leads to what Kelley and Stahleski (1970) call the "triangle effect," in which initially different predispositions to cooperate based on different dispositions to trust converge on non-cooperation over time in the face of defection.

---

[7] Cooperators do not differentiate, however, between the morality of 100 percent cooperative strategies and tit for tat, suggesting that self-interest is regarded as morally legitimate provided that it is predicated on reciprocity and mutual gain (McClintock and Liebrand 1988). The combination of a moral commitment to and expectation of reciprocity and a generalized sense of the trustworthiness of others explains why more trusting cooperators can be more aggressive in punishing defectors than their less trusting competitor counterparts (Oskamp 1971; Yamagishi 2001). There is evidence not only for behavioral assimilation but also for "overassimilation" (Kelley and Stahelski 1970). This makes sense since for generalized trusters, defectors have violated a moral norm that at least in their minds most others follow. Generalized trust mixed with strategic distrust of a specific other, based on his or her noncooperative behavior, makes for an explosive cocktail.

Nor are cooperators naïve or gullible.[8] Studies indicate that generalized trusters actually are more open to signs of the intentions of others (Rotter 1980). More trusting individuals have been shown to exhibit higher degrees of "social intelligence," an unfortunate term that captures the effort made and ability to judge the intentions of others (Yamagishi 2001). Similarly, Maki and McClintock (1983) find that cooperators are the best predictors of the social orientation of others, with competitors trailing behind.

Social psychological studies on cooperation therefore lead us away from a focus on the structure of the game towards the traits of individuals. Social orientation and generalized trust are particularly suited for explaining variation in cooperation in the same situational circumstances with the same information. Only non-structural factors or attributes of the players, what social psychologists call dispositional factors, can do so. For example, iterative prisoner's dilemma games offer the potential for mutual cooperation based on self-interest in a way that one-shot games do not. However, if we witness substantial individual variation in behavior among players in these situations, the explanation must lie in the traits of those playing. McClintock and Liebrand (1988) even find that social orientations are varied enough so that game structure itself had no statistically significant independent effect on the overall likelihood of the total population of subjects to cooperate or defect. For instance the overall level of cooperation of participants in an assurance game was not statistically significantly higher than that in prisoner's dilemma, even though the game structure would predict cooperation would be easier. Only the effect of social orientation was statistically significant.

Rationalists, with their focus on structure, cannot account for this. This suggests that political scientists have over-relied on structure in their theories concerning international organizations and cautions us to be more careful to integrate psychological insights and dispositional features of decision-makers that have been noticeably absent. Social orientation research paves the way for a distinctly *psychological* theory of international cooperation and international organization. Of

---

[8] Uslaner (2002: 23) and Kramer, Brewer and Hanna (1996: 376) blur the conceptual distinction between generalized trust and altruism. They write that the trusting behavior of generalized trusters is driven by the moral injunction to trust regardless of what the other does since this is the right thing to do. They miss that generalized trust rests on an assumption of reciprocity.

course, it is important to recognize that dispositions to trust are *relative* differences. High levels of generalized trust might be rare, particularly in international relations. And structure, of course, matters as well. However, generalized trust might nevertheless have an important additional effect on cooperation and explain variation in outcomes. The sole use of strategic trust leads us to understate not only the *level* of cooperation but also *variation* in cooperation. Elinor Ostrom, in her review of research on cooperation in experimental research, calls this variation the "really big puzzle in the social sciences" (2003: 39).

Social orientation will affect not only the likelihood of cooperation but also individuals' preferred design for international organizations. Martin (1992) argues that we can predict the type of institutional design that will arise by knowing the particular strategic circumstances decision-makers confront. Multilateralism, for instance, is an institutional form that solves a particular type of problem. It is not well suited to resolving collaboration problems such as prisoner's dilemmas in which there are significant incentives to defect (Martin 1992: 97). However, if political actors placed in the same structural circumstances understand their strategic situation differently based on different expectations about others' behavior, it complicates rational institutionalism at the very least.

Social orientation research implies that the emergence of multilateralism is not something we can simply assume from an objective game structure. Rather than it just being a strategic solution to particular problems, as rationalism assumes, we can think of multilateralism as a dispositional trait of cooperators, an inclination to trust others that allows them to seek out better opportunities through cooperation. Social orientation puts the "ism" in multilateralism. Cooperators see assurance games and therefore are consistently disposed towards multilateral cooperation. More fearful competitors are more unilateralist by disposition because they tend to see interactions as prisoner's dilemmas, something which multilateralism does not lend itself to solving.

More specifically, the social psychological argument expects cooperators to be more willing to make binding security commitments than competitors as the latter will be more concerned about opportunism even in the same structural circumstances with the same information and the same interests. They will be more likely than competitors to advocate more authoritative conflict resolution procedures as they are less likely to fear opportunism on the part of others, even in uncertain situations in which strategic calculation is more difficult or even impossible. They will be more inclined to believe that, even if they limit their sovereignty in this way and lose in particular cases, over time their long-term interests will be served based on their belief in diffuse reciprocity. They are qualitative multilateralists.

Generalized trusters will be more optimistic than non-trusters that these security commitments, which amount to moral obligations, can work effectively without hierarchical control. However, in the instance that pessimism prevails, cooperators will be more likely to consider hierarchy. Competitors will, seemingly paradoxically, be the most convinced that hierarchy is necessary to ensure compliance with obligations even while they advocate unilateralism because they expect more opportunism. Hierarchy poses a second-order trust problem that competitors cannot solve and cooperators do not see. Competitors will be systematically more concerned about opportunism of all types in comparison with cooperators.

Since cooperators have more confidence in diffuse reciprocity and moral obligations, they will consequently favor larger multilateral organizations with more members that add to the deterrent and pacifying effect. Competitors will prefer unilateralism or limited cooperation with a smaller number of other states who have a demonstrated record of trustworthiness and closely overlapping interests. In other words, there will be a direct and positive relationship between individual support for qualitative multilateralism and quantitative multilateralism. Fearing opportunism less, generalized trusters should also be more likely to promote the benefits of greater certainty and assurance by agreeing to organizations with longer terms and fewer provisions for opting out. Non-trusters will prefer flexible and non-onerous opt-out provisions and agreements of shorter duration. In short, the least willing to make strong commitments will be the most insistent on being able to walk away.

Constructivist theories of cooperation and international organizations: particularized trust and identity

A number of constructivist arguments explain preferences for multilateralism and unilateralism, and institutional choice in general, by reference to identity and culture (Ruggie 1997). The exact mechanisms by which identity leads to international cooperation and multilateralism in these accounts is often unclear. However, two are implied. The first is that a shared sense of identity leads to identification, at least a partial merging of the self with the other. For instance, Cronin (1999) argues that collective security is driven by a cosmopolitan identity, whereas traditional balance-of-power politics is characterized by states with only national identities. Patrick writes that identity leads states sometimes to pursue "ideal" interests other than power, wealth and survival (2009: xix). In this sense, cooperation and multilateralism are almost altruistic in nature. Gains for the other become gains for oneself. Relations are marked by a "we-feeling" and a willingness to treat others on equal terms despite disparities in power. If this is the case, trust is not an issue since trust is based on an expectation of reciprocity and we do not expect reciprocity from ourselves. If the other is part of the self, the very notion of opportunism loses any meaning.

Second, constructivist accounts sometimes imply a role for trust in international cooperation and multilateralism, but trust of the particularized variety (Hemmer and Katzenstein 2002). This is somewhat natural given its close relationship with identity. Constructivists understand particularized trust as being produced through a process of interaction. Trust for constructivists is relational and dyadic in nature, rather than dispositional. It is formed on the basis of common collective experiences (Cronin 1999; Wendt 1999). Relationships of particularized trust or fear are social constructions larger than the individuals who participate in them. They require a particular "other" to exist. These relationships are intersubjective rather than subjective. Trust is sociological rather than psychological.

On the basis of either of these mechanisms, constructivists might expect more cooperation than rationalists. Constructivism has more in common with social psychology than rational institutionalism. However, there are distinct differences. In constructivism, identity drives the process, as a source either of identification or of particularized trust. For instance, constructivists could argue that shared identity allows for the initiation of cooperation, diffuse reciprocity and binding multilateral commitments. This could be based on either a feeling of solidarity or the moralistic trust that comes from membership in a common group. Constructivists have difficulties accounting for significant cooperation with those with whom one does not identify, a problem that frequently emerges in international organizations when states attempt to collaborate with many diverse partners. As noted above, generalized trust provides not just a bond, but a bridge to cooperate with those whom one does not know.

Constructivists might object, arguing that support for multilateralism in more inclusive organizations is a function of the broadest possible identity, a cosmopolitan or humanistic conception of self. The opposite would be ethnocentrism, a general derogation of all outgroups. One of the core components measuring ethnocentrism is indeed the perceived trustworthiness of minorities unlike us. In international affairs, this ethnocentrism would express itself in greater nationalism or, in the terms used in this book, particularized trust of those within our country and distrust of those without.

However, research suggests that constructivists are reversing the causal arrow between identity and trust. Uslaner describes particularized trust, a suspicion of those who are different, as the fallback of those who lack generalized trust, consistent with the literature above indicating that non-trusters rely on those they know. Pessimists withdraw into their own communities, he finds (Uslaner 2002: 78, 106, 194). As reviewed below, studies in social psychology consistently indicate that prejudice and ethnocentrism are functions of a lack of generalized trust. Those who believe their environment is more threatening and dangerous are more inclined towards in-group solidarity and out-group derogation. The corollary in international relations is that the most fearful become nationalists and the most trusting become internationalists, rather than the reverse.

Research design

Hypotheses

On the basis of this theoretical review, we can draw the following contrasting rationalist, constructivist and social psychologically inspired hypotheses. One set pertains to the origins of cooperation, the other the design of international organizations. A key divide between the social psychological argument and rationalism is that the former expects variation in the same structural circumstances whereas the latter, as it relies on strategic trust, expects all decision-makers in the same position with the same information and preferences to make the same choices. Where individuals in the same structural circumstances with the same information differ in their willingness to cooperate based on different expectations about trustworthiness of others, the differences must be attributed to variations in generalized trust. Rationalists admit they cannot explain this. As Lake writes, variation in concern about opportunism on the part of those in the same structural circumstances is "something of a mystery" and lies "outside the current theory" (1999: 74–6).[9] The core difference with constructivists is that the latter claim that identity drives cooperation, either through a process of identification or by generating particularized trust.

Before organizations are created or designed, states must first decide on the potential merits of cooperation.

Origins of cooperation

- *Rationalists* expect the initiation of cooperation to be easier in reassurance situations than in prisoner's dilemma situations and in situations in which states form more of a privileged group and therefore will benefit regardless of opportunism. The nature of the strategic situation should be perceived similarly by those with similar interests and information.
- *Constructivists* would argue that shared identity allows for the initiation of the cooperative process, based on either a feeling of solidarity or the moralistic trust that comes from membership in a common group.
- The *social psychological argument* expects similarly situated actors to define strategic situations differently based on their expectations of reciprocity or opportunism, with cooperators, as generalized trusters, often seeing a reassurance situation where competitors see a prisoner's dilemma. Therefore cooperators will find it easier to take the first step. Competitors will be more likely to insist that others first demonstrate their trustworthiness.

The three arguments offer a number of different expectations concerning four aspects of institutional design – the degree of qualitative multilateralism in the security guarantee, the degree of qualitative multilateralism in conflict resolution mechanisms, the size of the organization (or "quantitative" multilateralism), and flexibility.

---

[9] Ikenberry confesses a similar weakness (2001: 119).

Institutional design

- *Rationalists* would expect that state preferences for qualitative multilateralism will be accompanied by preferences for organizations with a smaller number of members and/or the creation of supranational hierarchy. Where this is impossible or too costly, states will attempt to limit their exposure to untrustworthy behavior by insisting on control – unilateralism or its institutional equivalent – and/or flexibility.
- *Constructivists* expect stronger security guarantees and more authoritative conflict resolution in instances of shared identity, which mitigates concerns about opportunism or leads states to consider their interests as identical. A shared sense of self would lead to a preference for more durable institutions with less flexibility.
- The *social psychological argument* expects that in the same structural circumstances, generalized trusters will be more willing to make commitments to binding security guarantees and authoritative conflict-resolution procedures than non-trusters. Cooperators will be more optimistic than competitors that qualitative multilateralism can work effectively without supranational hierarchical control, although they will be more willing than competitors to consider this option when it seems necessary. They will simultaneously prefer larger organizations with less flexibility.

Case selection

My argument is validated if I can demonstrate the presence of, capture the impact of, and explain variation in dispositions to trust. Testing this argument requires country case studies in regard to preferences for the creation and design of international organizations. By analyzing the domestic politics of international institution-building, it is possible to hold constant other structural influences that might affect cooperation and to pinpoint more precisely the influence of variation in dispositions to trust.

However, other variables are at play. One factor affecting preferences for institutional design and cooperation other than trust is vulnerability. For instance, smaller or medium-sized states likely generally have a preference for more binding security guarantees and more authoritative conflict resolution mechanisms not because they are trusting, but simply because they are more reliant on others and better protected under institutions than if left to fend for themselves. The same might be true of states with historical rivals or who are geographically exposed as conflict is more likely for them (Snyder 1984). These states might also advocate hierarchical control to ensure that others live up to their agreements, which might be falsely taken as an indication of strategic distrust when in fact it is an expression of the greater *costs* of abandonment for them.[10] High vulnerability is not distrust.[11] They will also favor less flexibility and larger membership, but this is not the manifestation of trust. Rather it is a desire for greater predictability and more help. This describes France after WWI and Europe in general after WWII.

For this reason I focus on the United States and the United Kingdom. I nevertheless devote the bulk of my attention to the former for two reasons. First, it had the greatest bargaining leverage over the creation of these institutions. Second, because its domestic politics are not based on party loyalty and discipline in the way that is true of the British parliamentary system, it is possible to observe individual-level variation in dispositions to trust. The UK provides, however, a useful check on the generalizability of the argument, a test as to whether the United States again demonstrates its "exceptionalism."

In selecting particular IOs in which to evaluate American politics and policy, only those in which trust was a potential factor are relevant. I remove international economic institutions from analysis for reasons identified above. Reciprocity in these organizations, even of the diffuse variety, can be accounted for by a strategic trust mechanism. Also, international economic institutions have great domestic distributional implications, leading to divisions at home that have nothing to do with trust. By looking at security institutions, I can avoid those complications.

However, trust is not always in play, even in security institutions. Trust is a key consideration when there is the opportunity for reciprocal exchange and a possibility for opportunism that affects state

---

[10] For instance, the general European desire for a strong guarantee in the North Atlantic Treaty and a supranational command structure was the expression neither of trust nor of distrust. The Europeans wanted the most binding guarantee they could get in NATO not because they felt the US was untrustworthy or trustworthy, but because they could not afford to be abandoned.

[11] Hardin conflates the two, dismissing the idea that there might be a general tendency to trust others by arguing that there are always situations in which individuals will never trust or be trustworthy (Hardin 2001: 12). No one trusts anyone with everything (Hoffman 2006: 18).

decisions about whether or not to cooperate. If a state forms a "priv-ileged group" on its own, opportunism is not at issue because it will be willing to provide the public good of security regardless of whether others contribute. In these instances, a state will be perfectly willing to commit to a binding security guarantee of long length with as many members as resources permit, but for reasons that have nothing to do with trust.[12] Even in instances in which a state does not form a privileged group, trust is not in play when there is no real prospect of reciprocity. The social psychological argument is instrumental in nature. Generalized trust does not cause states to build institutions; rather it allows them to do so when there is the potential for mutu-ally beneficial cooperation. Therefore if a state has no real partner capable of contributing significantly to a security arrangement, even generalized trusters will not see the point.[13]

I focus therefore on the domestic politics of American consideration of the League of Nations, the United Nations and the North Atlantic Treaty. Structural circumstances vary in these settings in a way that makes them difficult cases for the social psychological argument in different ways. The first two institutions offer a difficult case for mul-tilateralism as they were designed to provide global security for many members without any specific adversary, cases in which, absent gener-alized trust, unilateralism or its institutional equivalent should be the default. If I can show that generalized trust led cooperators towards more cooperation than rationalists would have expected in what were inhospitable circumstances, that will demonstrate the social capital function of generalized trust more strongly. Generalized trust is also easier to identify in these circumstances. In smaller, bilateral or pluri-lateral settings, it becomes difficult to disentangle particularized trust (or distrust) from generalized trust. For instance, an individual's sup-port for a binding bilateral alliance between the United States and Britain might reflect generalized trust, but it might just as well indicate particularized trust.

---

[12] For this reason, the American decision to endorse collective security for the western hemisphere in the Rio Treaty in 1947 was not surprising; nor is the fact that it was virtually unanimous domestically. But it is not germane to this argument as trust was not involved.

[13] For this reason, I do not focus on American security policy in Asia after WWII as there was no real payoff for multilateral cooperation, and without this burden-sharing, the US would not actively consider a strong pact, trust aside.

The post-WWII cases should prove tough for a case stressing variation in generalized trust, as it is frequently maintained that the structural forces pushing the United States towards international cooperation were overwhelming after 1945. This should dampen differences in domestic politics emerging from generalized trust. If I can show that dispositions to trust still varied substantially in these seemingly overdetermined circumstances, the argument is strengthened immeasurably.

Measurement and data collection

Direct measures
Generalized trust is admittedly difficult to measure. Ideally we would have individual-level survey data for every politician, diplomat and bureaucrat involved in the creation of these institutions concerning their overall view of the world. This kind of data is of course not available, but I assemble relevant passages that reveal any information about the core beliefs of the most important participants in the process, those around whom the main coalitions for and against international cooperation formed. One example is explicit views about human nature. Studies indicate that those who believe that human nature is benign, altruistic or cooperative are generally more trusting (Wrightsman 1966).

Indirect measures: concern for opportunism and framing
Next I rely on proxies. A lack of generalized trust is manifested, I argue, in concerns about opportunism in international relations – exploitation, entrapment, abandonment and free riding. These are the indirect measures of the independent variable that lead individuals to their dependent variable – their preferred degree of cooperation and form of institutional design. I am looking for patterns. Assessments of the likelihood of opportunism should not vary systematically across individuals in the same structural situation with the same information and preferences, according to rationalism, whereas they will in a social psychological account. And concern for one type of opportunism should be correlated with concern about others. If an individual is relatively more anxious about entrapment, he should also be more worried about abandonment.

Framing is also an indication of the presence or absence of generalized trust. Cooperators are more likely, *ceteris paribus*, to frame the same structural situation as a reassurance game than competitors, who will be more likely to regard it as a prisoner's dilemma. If we see such variation in the same objective circumstances, we are confident that generalized trust is the cause of the framing, as structure cannot be. Again both private and public sources are important.

Indirect measures: political ideology
One might still object that concern for opportunism and framing could be a post hoc rationalization of a position based on a different set of interests, or a measure of views about the nature of foreign affairs independent of generalized trust. Therefore, I also look for correlations between the previous measures and *domestic* policy positions. If we can find a marker of generalized trust independent of the phenomenon under study – international cooperation – we become more comfortable drawing our conclusions.

Generalized trust is ideological, a core belief about the nature of the world. Therefore it is somewhat unsurprising that we should find remarkable parallels between the literature on social orientation and generalized trust on the one hand and the psychological literature on political ideology on the other. Binning (2007) finds a cluster of positive relationships between generalized distrust, conservatism and "competitive" foreign policy preferences. Democrats score more cooperative on scales of social orientations whereas Republicans are more competitive (Sheldon and Nichols 2009). This is because of the substantive differences between left and right in advanced democracies. All of the leading theorists in political psychology now agree that a general sense of threat is central for explaining the adoption of rightist political views. Duckitt (2001) and his colleagues argue that the right has a "motivational goal" of security, driven by a belief that the world is a dangerous place. Feldman claims that rightist ideology is a reflection of a pessimistic view of human nature, consistent with a longstanding observation about the nature of the right (Conover and Feldman 1981; M. Deutsch 1960b; Feldman 2003: 48; Tomkins and Izard 1965). Both are capturing the same core aspect of rightist thinking – that others cannot be trusted. Jost et al. (2003) call this the "existential motive," a common denominator that they find in a remarkable effort to synthesize the findings of hundreds of studies on the psychological correlates of political ideology with 88 different samples from a multitude of countries.[14]

This more threatening worldview finds a logical expression in an endorsement of coercive means to maintain societal order at home. Rightists are advocates of what Altemeyer (1988; 1998) calls "authoritarian aggression," a strong state to punish and deter transgressors. In the balancing act between individual freedom and autonomy on the one hand and the desire for social order on the other, rightists side with the latter. As Feldman (2003) explains, authoritarians believe that left to their own devices, individuals acting freely will not produce a safe and secure social order.[15] More trusting liberals, in contrast, come down in favor of greater political liberty, both in the United States and in other advanced democracies. This explains the stronger support of the right for more hierarchical policies in the areas of civil liberties and criminal justice (Inglehart 1977; Inglehart and Flanagan 1987; Kitschelt 1988a; 1988b; 1994; Kitschelt and McGann 1995).[16] Those

---

[14] There are dozens of other studies (Altemeyer 1988; Altemeyer 1998; Cohrs, Moschner and Maes 2005; Cohrs, Moschner, Maes and Kielmann 2005; Duckitt 2001; Duckitt and Fisher 2003; Duckitt and Sibley 2009; Feldman and Stenner 1997; Greenberg et al. 1990; Janoff-Bulman 2009a; 2009b; Jost et al. 2007; Jugert and Duckitt 2009; Van Leeuwen and Park 2009).

[15] One exception might seem to be the left's greater support for gun control, but a feeling of entitlement to protect oneself is the perfect expression of a sense that the world is a dangerous place. It is the manifestation of fear and distrust.

[16] This characterization of rightist views might raise the objection that the left is equally authoritarian. Totalitarian communist regimes systematically repress individual liberties (Rokeach 1973; Shils 1954). I concur with these opinions, but they are not germane to my argument, which is confined to democracies. Jost et al. (2007) have demonstrated the relative absence of left-wing authoritarians in democracies, something that is particularly true of the United States (Tetlock 1983). Left-wing authoritarianism as a regime type is something else entirely, premised on a completely different value system with a different conception of the relationship between political equality and liberty (Donnelly 1982; Howard and Donnelly 1986). Authoritarianism in those regimes might also reflect an antagonism and distrust of capitalist countries as well as the fact that a strong state is a necessary instrument for the radical appropriation of property and stifling of dissent under communism. In advanced democracies, authoritarianism is generally confined to the right side of the political spectrum and strongly associated with attitudes typically regarded as conservative or on the part of individuals who identify themselves as conservative. Conservative views, based on either attitudes generally associated with the right or self-identification measures, are correlated with perceptions of the world as a dangerous place (Altemeyer 1998; Duckitt 2001; Duckitt and Fisher 2003;

with a more threatening view of the world also believe in "submission" to this authority as the price to be paid to be protected (Duckitt 2001; Duckitt and Fisher 2003; Duckitt and Sibley 2009; Feldman and Stenner 1997; Janoff-Bulman 2009a; 2009b; Jugert and Duckitt 2009; Stenner 2009b).

While some might object that the left is less libertarian than conservatives, liberal and conservative support for state action has a different basis. Whereas conservatives' enthusiasm for government is almost exclusively premised on preventing negative outcomes through institutional restraints, liberal support for government action aims at positively providing for society, harnessing the power of the state to redistribute wealth or reach collectively more optimal resource allocation (Dworkin 1978; 1985). This was the basis of the progressive movement and the New Deal. Conservatives exhibit an "avoidance" tendency, using the state to provide physical security. Liberals demonstrate an "approach" tendency, using the state to guarantee economic welfare (Janoff-Bulman 2009a; 2009b).[17] However, even liberals advocate some coercive action, as generalized trust is never total. It is a question of degree.

The same tendencies are evident in foreign affairs. Generalized trust links domestic policy with foreign policy preferences. In international relations, the natural response to generalized distrust is the accumulation of power, hence the right's stronger support for national defense. A number of scholars have noted the correlation between conservative

---

Duckitt, Wagner, du Plessis, and Birum 2002; Peterson, Doty, and Winter 1993; Saucier 2000; van Leeuwen and Park 2009; G. D. Wilson 1973).

[17] Liberals are driven to provide for society not by their optimistic view of human nature, but by their broader altruism, another defining difference between left and right that is not germane to this study. Nevertheless, their more trusting disposition does help enable this concern for others. Rightists generally are more resistant to social spending on welfare and homelessness because they attribute the cause of these problems to a deficiency in moral standards and effort on the part of those lacking income and shelter. They fear that others will take advantage of government largesse. The lack of trust is implicit but obvious. Liberals in contrast tend to explain these problems in structural terms. People are trapped into poverty and crime by forces beyond their control. The implication is not that they suffer from moral weakness, but rather that there are situational factors that impede their development. This is a direct reflection of liberals' implicitly more optimistic and trusting assumptions regarding human behavior (Cozzarelli, Wilkinson and Tagler 2001; Feather 1985; Furnham 1982; Kluegel 1990; Kluegel and Smith 1986; Sniderman and Tetlock 1986).

self-placement and "militant internationalism" (Holsti and Rosenau 1988; 1996; Murray, Cowden and Russett, 1999).[18] My own survey work discovered a strong link between more authoritarian positions on domestic issues such as privacy, gay rights and decriminalization of drugs on the one hand and advocacy of preponderance of power and preemptive military strategies and a belief in the domino theory on the other. If others are inherently untrustworthy, cooperation is impossible. One must accumulate as much power as possible. As threats are sure to become reality, it is necessary to strike early. And as others are always testing one's limits, it is essential to demonstrate firm resolve lest one lose credibility and watch dominoes fall. Liberals in contrast demonstrate a predilection towards "cooperative internationalism," including greater support for multilateral institutions and relinquishing sovereignty to global governance structures (Rathbun 2007a; 2008).

The psychological literature indicates that sensitivity to threat induces the right to make more intense distinctions between in-groups and out-groups and to emphasize loyalty to the former (Duckitt 2006; Duckitt et al. 2002; Jugert and Duckitt 2009; Van Leeuwen and Park 2009). As Janoff-Bulman explains, "In their attunement to threats, they are essentially interested in who can be trusted, which is essentially a matter of knowing who is in your group and who is not" (2009b: 125). The solidarity that conservatives demand is a reflection of a general fear. Nationalism is a form of particularized trust driven by a lack of generalized trust. Stenner and Feldman find that threat activates the need for conformity and sameness among authoritarians, which might not be expressed in times of felt security (Feldman 2003; Feldman and Stenner 1997; Stenner 2009b). Jugert and Duckitt (2009) find that intense group identification does not lead to rightist political views, but rather is instead completely mediated by a greater motivational need for collective security (Duckitt 1989; Duckitt 2001).

The right's pessimism about human nature does not, however, make it immune to the importance of morality – indeed the opposite. Social and cultural norms are essential features for governing

---

[18] Liberals, however, might be more hawkish in particular circumstances, such as humanitarian interventions, despite this general tendency towards antimilitarist and institutionalist solutions, because they exhibit a greater degree of altruistic concern. See Rathbun (2004).

communal behavior that would otherwise degenerate into anarchy. They are another form of social control to protect society. Tomkins and Izard (1965) call this the "normativist" dimension of political ideology. Dworkin refers to it as "virtue" (Dworkin 1985). This explains the importance the right places on adherence to traditional morality in the personal sphere. The left, in contrast, takes more libertarian positions on these issues (Inglehart 1977; Inglehart and Flanagan 1987; Kitschelt 1988a; 1988b; 1994; Kitschelt and McGann 1995). Liberals see less threat to society from free expression and personal liberty. The left is more comfortable with and supportive of diversity. The right is more likely to sanction those regarded as deviating from the dictates of social conformity (Duckitt 2001; Duckitt and Fisher 2003; Feldman and Stenner 1997; Janoff-Bulman 2009b; Jugert and Duckitt 2009; Stenner 2009b; Van Leeuwen and Park 2009).[19]

This remarkable parallel between studies in social and political psychology indicates that we can use domestic policy positions as a proxy measure for generalized trust. More conservative politicians should be the least trusting, more liberal politicians the most trusting individuals. This allows us to bring more data points into the analysis: those individuals for whom we do not have expressions of generalized trust or its absence. We can use Keith Poole and Howard Rosenthal's quantitative measure of ideology, NOMINATE scores, as proxy measures for generalized trust in members of Congress.[20] Even though the issues in which generalized trust is indirectly expressed, such as opinions on law and order, are only a portion of the roll call votes on which these scores are based, Poole and Rosenthal find such high correlations between patterns of voting in different issue areas that a unidimensional model still outperforms more complex models, and explains 80 percent of individual voting decisions (Poole and Rosenthal 1991; 2001; 2007). A second dimension, based on differences over civil rights and race, adds only 3 percent more.

---

[19] One might argue that this focus on morality undermines the claim made above that generalized trusters feel that states can rely more on moral obligations. However, it demonstrates precisely the point I am trying to make. The left feels that morality is already present, the right feels that it is absent and must be actively promoted by reference to religion and tradition.

[20] Data found at www.voteview.com/DWNL.htm. An explanation of how the scores are calculated can be found in Poole and Rosenthal (2007). I use the D-NOMINATE variety.

Assuming that ideology structures domestic political divisions, the relationship between political ideology and trust also leads us to expect that there should be significant partisan divisions in American domestic politics over international cooperation and institutional design. We gain more confidence in this statement by qualitative evidence that reveals that the party of the right in the United States, the Republican Party, has consistently been the party of order, tradition and a strong defense (Gerring 1998). The Democrats have been supporters of civil liberties and international cooperation, even in eras in which these types of issues have gone relatively dormant (Gerring 1998: 94; Sinclair 1977). That is, there is an obvious parallel between contemporary studies of political psychology and the history of the American party system. While this certainly will not surprise observers of contemporary American politics, it has been the case for over a century. Qualitative and quantitative evidence indicates that even the New Deal did not fundamentally realign the party system but only grafted a new issue onto preexisting ideological contrasts (Brady and Stewart 1982; Poole and Rosenthal 1993; 2007; Sinclair 1977).[21] Core ideological differences between the parties have been generally the same for well over a hundred years.

Nevertheless, we can push the use of party as a proxy for ideology too far, particularly after WWII. The ideological distance between the parties decreased, which resulted in more overlap between the parties and a fair number of liberal Republicans and conservative Democrats. Most notably, the period marked the beginning of the growing conservatism of Southern Democrats who, even on non-civil rights issues, began to align with Republicans (Poole and Rosenthal 1991; 1993; 2001; 2007). In these post-WWII instances we should expect a general tendency of northern Democrats to support quantitative and qualitative multilateralism, and a general preference of Republicans and Southern Democrats to favor unilateralism.

---

[21] A reading of party platforms does as well. Gerring for instance argues that Republicans shifted from statism to individualism sometime around mid-century as a critique of big-government New Deal liberalism. However, this was a refrain long before. In 1908, they complained of Democratic populism as equivalent to socialism. They "would have the nation own the people" (Johnson 1978: 163). And in 1916, they complained that "business success . . . is apparently regarded by the Democratic party as in itself a crime" (Johnson 1978: 206).

However, where we find individuals largely out of step with their party based on ideological differences domestically, those same individuals should be out of step in foreign policy as well, since both sets of positions are largely expressions of generalized trust. I argue that ideology matters, not party, because only the former is a measure of generalized trust. We expect Republicans who are liberal to be more multilateralist than their fellow party members, and more conservative Democrats to be more unilateralist than their fellow Democrats. These outliers are actually extremely useful as they help dispel the notion that domestic politics is purely a matter of partisanship and party loyalty, something that quantitative research also discounts.[22]

In using ideology as an indirect measure of generalized trust, I am also careful to establish that domestic divisions are not reflections of another factor that also might structure political conflict. While the security literature, and my argument as well, presumes that decision-makers make choices based on their beliefs about the consequences of strategy for the nation-state as a whole, this might not be the case if there is more than security at stake. There is a prominent thread of rationalist research that traces domestic political differences in grand strategy, of which international organizations would be considered a part, to different material stakes in security in parts of the world in which they have economic interests. In short, what appears to be differences in trust could be the result of political economy (Fordham 1998a; 1998b; Narizny 2007; Trubowitz 1998). The assumption of much of this work is that politicians are not ideological, but rather vote-seekers whose preferences are simply reflections of their constituents' interests. This line of argumentation is prominent in the literature on American foreign policy and features the very different economic interests of particular regions of the country. I must be careful to distinguish the two logics empirically.

None of these three measures – statements on generalized trust, alternative framings and concerns about opportunism, and domestic ideology – are ideal by themselves, but we gain great confidence in them if they are systematically correlated, as nothing else would seem to explain that pattern. This is a triangulation strategy. Other studies

---

[22] Poole and Rosenthal's model outperforms one that simply uses party identification as a predictor of vote choice (Poole and Rosenthal 1985; 1987a; 1987b).

indicate that they should be. For instance, those who vote for right-leaning parties have been found to identify with prisoner's dilemma framings of conflicts while those who vote for left-leaning parties think of the same in assurance terms (Halevy et al. 2006).

Sources

My sources include statements, speeches, congressional debates, private diaries, party platforms, memoirs, biographies and formerly classified documents. I use both private and public sources as one might doubt the genuineness of the latter. It is also important to note that the domestic process by which these institutions were created affects the kinds and number of sources and data points available. There is no shortage of data of any type in the League case. There are fewer direct measures of generalized trust in the post-WWII cases when the main features of these IOs were negotiated behind the scenes, since it is public debate that tends to draw out fundamental ideological assumptions, not department planning documents in private settings. Also, expressions of concern by non-trusters about opportunism are rarer because, in anticipation of non-trusters' objections, proposals made by generalized trusters were watered down. This also affects the ability to use data on political ideology. Given that the only vote in both instances was on the finished treaty after a political compromise meant to alleviate concerns, congressional voting patterns on treaties reveals little information and is not of great use in testing the argument.

In these instances, I am forced to focus attention on the positions at the outset of particular individuals who serve as leaders of their parties or factions thereof, whether informally or formally. Their position of leadership is generally indicative of a broader acceptance of their views; they are speaking to a party or party faction's ideological inclinations. I measure their personal political ideology, their level of concern about opportunism and look for any direct statements on generalized trust. I supplement this focus on leaders with data on the positions and justifications of more rank-and-file members so as to establish that the leader's position is reflective of a broader ideological tendency in his or her party. Even if politicians do not vote, the way they talk can be used to gauge their level of generalized trust and their commitment to multilateralism.

Plan of the book

This chapter proposed a psychological theory of international cooperation and institution building. Theory is not enough, however; we
need evidence. In this way, I hope to improve upon some of the literature on trust in politics. Russell Hardin, the foremost advocate of
strategic trust, dismisses dispositional, generalized trust as "incoherent
and utterly implausible" and "openly absurd," so much so that studies putting forth the concept "must strike almost everyone but their
authors as odd" (Hardin 2001: 13; 2006: 25). Unfortunately, Hardin
cites little more than his personal experience, writing that "most of my
trust relationships are not grounded in such [moralistic] commitments
of others, and it seems unlikely that overriding moral commitments
make much of the social order or most ongoing relationships work"
(2001: 4). I hope to do better. In the chapters that follow, I seek to
demonstrate that generalized trust might play a role where we expect
it the least, in international relations where the stakes are high and the
protections are low. If generalized trust makes a difference in international relations, where its impact should be the lowest, we are forced
to take it seriously.

The next four chapters proceed chronologically, beginning with the
creation of (and the United States' aborted entry into) the League of
Nations in Chapter 3. The American President Woodrow Wilson conceived of the organization as an open circle in both senses, in which
a multitude of states would undertake a moral obligation to come to
the aid of others in case of aggression. Less trusting conservatives in
the Republican Party believed that such a design exposed the United
States to the risks of opportunism of all kinds and offered a number
of reservations that would have essentially converted the League into
a great-power concert of American allies based on mere consultation
without any binding commitments. Isolationists, marked by their particular disdain of opportunistic Europeans, refused participation even
in this type of organization. With American politicians unable to come
to a compromise, the Covenant failed to be ratified in the US Senate.
Similar divides were evident in British politics. Rationalists can explain
neither how Wilson and his Democratic allies would have proposed
an organization that combined quantitative and qualitative multilateralism without any supranational hierarchy, nor why there were such
intense ideological differences between the parties.

These same cleavages reemerged after WWII as the Roosevelt administration began to consider its position on a replacement for the League. Chapter 4 traces the origins of the United Nations, as the Democrats tried to square the circle between their preference for a more multilateral League and the Republicans' renewed desire for a great-power concert. Rationalists again cannot account for these differences, nor why the same positions manifested themselves in a completely different structural environment said to significantly constrain the United States. While trusting Democratic planners in the State Department expressed an early preference for a multilateral institution with an even more binding collective security guarantee than the League, they had to compromise their plans to gain the support of both the President and Republicans. Deferring to conservatives on issues such as the great-power veto later created dilemmas for the United States as relations with the Soviet Union fractured. Most notably the possibility that permanent members of the Security Council might vote on their own disputes and possess the ability to block action by regional bodies undermined qualitative and quantitative multilateralism respectively. The UK faced its own quandaries, such as how to reconcile the conservative demand for a concert with the Dominion preference for a more inclusive and egalitarian organization.

Chapter 5 considers the drafting of the North Atlantic Treaty. When compared to the League or the UN, the formation of the alliance amounted to a closing of the circle. There were fewer members and less of a need for diffuse reciprocity in light of the presence of a common adversary. Nevertheless, despite rationalist claims that the threat of the Soviet Union compelled American participation, American decision-makers would not make the commitment unless they were assured of reciprocity. Generalized trust was a necessary ingredient to begin the reciprocity circle. Whereas the Democratic Truman administration framed the issue as one of reassurance in which the United States would take the first steps towards cooperation, Republicans in both the moderate and conservative wings of the party were much more cautious. Rationalists cannot explain why differences between the two sides were at least as great as those between the United States and the Europeans. Needing to secure the consent of part of a Republican Party that feared free riding and entrapment, the Democrats engaged again in extensive behind-the-scenes consultations with the opposition. By compromising their multilateral vision in a number of ways, they ensured ratification in the Senate.

In Chapter 6, the book comes full circle to the issue raised at its beginning: the United States' unilateral decision to invade Iraq in 2003. I explore the role played by fear, the opposite of generalized trust, in convincing American political decision-makers of both parties of the need to use military force to disarm Saddam Hussein, as well as the partisan divisions that emerged over unilateralism as the memories of 9/11 began to subside. I argue that terrorism as an issue creates a sense of generalized distrust. Threats that formerly seemed unlikely and unimportant demand immediate attention. Threats that once seemed unconnected are thought to be part of a package. While the fear generated by terrorism has a structural effect across populations, it is particularly powerful for conservatives who already see the world as a more dangerous place than do others. The book concludes with an assessment of the current state of partisan divisions on unilateralism and multilateralism and the prospects for trust in international cooperation in the future.

3 | The open circle: the failure of the League of Nations

The League of Nations was a revolutionary attempt at international cooperation. Forever associated with its primary proponent, the American President Woodrow Wilson, the organization called on members to submit all of their disputes to some form of international conflict resolution before resorting to force and specified sanctions if they failed to comply. The institution's constitution, the Covenant, also contained a moral pledge promising that each member would come to the aid of other members so as to preserve their political independence and territorial integrity. The League's scope was to be global, encompassing most of the states of the world. The Covenant was negotiated with difficulty at the Versailles peace conference, only to be brought home by Wilson and defeated in the US Senate by those who believed it was a dangerous infringement of American sovereignty. The United States, whose president was the most strident advocate of the League of Nations, never joined. Ever since, scholars have contemplated the counterfactual of whether, had the United States been a part, the League for all its weaknesses might have served as an effective deterrent against Nazi aggression.

Rationalists have difficulty explaining Wilson's vision. Both in its dispute resolution mechanisms and its security guarantee, collective security rested on diffuse reciprocity among a large group of members with very different interests. Strategic trust cannot sustain qualitative multilateralism. Entrapment, abandonment and exploitation were all significant risks. Yet the Covenant bringing about the organization created no real supranational hierarchy to prevent opportunism. Lake concludes that for this reason it failed to garner the requisite American support in the Senate for ratification, but this begs several questions. How was Wilson able to make such a proposal in the first place and why did it garner such support in his Democratic Party? How could its supporters believe that the League would work? Rationalism also cannot account for why the League caused so much domestic

division given that the primary opponents in the internal political struggle had the same set of interests and the same information.

The standard answer to these puzzles is that Wilson was an idealist
and that he was opposed by various forms of non-idealists (Lake 1999:
95; Monten 2005; Patrick 2009: 12; Ruggie 1997: 93–8). Constructivist accounts note this ideological variation in the same structural
circumstances (Dueck 2006; Legro 2005). Yet this begs still another
question. What is an idealist, and what was the core of the objections
of Wilson's opponents? The detractors of collective security are given
various labels – isolationists, realists, unilateralists – that reveal their
alternative preferences but do not identify the substance of the beliefs
that led them to their different conclusions. Why were the unilateralists
unilateralist? And why were the isolationists isolationist?

Below I demonstrate that "idealism" was the expression of generalized trust. Wilson had a benevolent view of human nature that led
him to believe in the power of moral obligations. He framed the situation as an assurance game – if the United States decided to make
this sort of commitment to collective security and conflict resolution,
others would reciprocate. Entrapment and exploitation were not significant concerns. Indeed the League was a "disentangling alliance,"
a "Monroe Doctrine for the world" that would reduce opportunism
in international affairs. Although Wilson was the main protagonist,
he had the solid backing of his political party, the Democrats. The
liberal party in the United States expressed its generalized trust indirectly in the left-wing populism of its political program at the time.
The Democrats believed in the moral nature of the masses.

For Wilson and the Democrats, generalized trust served as a source
of social capital to construct an institution premised on an open circle
in two senses. First, in such an arrangement, cooperation would not be
immediately reciprocated, perhaps would never be. Collective security
is an open-ended commitment. The reciprocity circle is never closed.
Second, despite the binding commitments advocated by Wilsonians,
the community circle of the League was not closed like an alliance
but rather meant to be inclusive and encompassing, a truly global
organization (Ikenberry 2001: 145–6). Qualitative and quantitative
multilateralism went together.

That generalized trust served as a form of social capital necessary for
creating the League is perhaps best evident in the domestic and international opposition that the League provoked on the part of those with a

competitive social orientation. At home, Wilson's League drew the ire of two distinct groups who are often conflated – traditional isolationists and "conservative internationalists" (Knock 1992; Lake 1999). Isolationists eschewed any American participation in formal international organizations altogether, whereas conservative internationalists took issue with the precise design of the League of Nations.

Wilson's primary opponents at home were the latter, led by the powerful chairman of the Foreign Relations Committee, Henry Cabot Lodge. Conservatives believed that American interests were indeed served by political and military engagement in international politics but were much more concerned about opportunism than Wilson and his allies. These internationalists objected that the League of Nations dispute resolution procedures would expose the United States to exploitation in the western hemisphere, where it had vital interests, by undermining and neutralizing the Monroe Doctrine. They argued that any security guarantee was an "entangling alliance" that would entrap the United States into conflicts there were not in its interests. Nor, they claimed, could moral obligations properly provide for international security since countries would not be bound to them. States would abandon others in their time of need absent some type of hierarchical enforcement mechanism. Yet, because of their less trusting disposition, conservative internationalists were the least willing to countenance this type of supranational organization. Concern for each of these types of opportunism was correlated with the others, suggesting a generalized distrust of others. The conservatives who dominated the British Cabinet expressed similar worries.

This general concern about opportunism is symptomatic of a competitive social orientation, a lack of generalized trust also expressed directly in pessimistic statements about human nature by the factions' main leaders. It is also evident indirectly in the fact that conservative internationalists were, not surprisingly, conservative, a fact noted but not explained by the originators of the term. The most inveterate opponents of the League were also some of the most conservative legislators domestically, and were all Republicans. More moderate Republicans domestically tended to be milder critics.

Conservatives embraced various unilateral alternatives to the League that did not require generalized trust – a concert with wartime allies who had demonstrated their trustworthiness or whose interests overlapped with the United States, a bilateral alliance with France and/or

Britain, or a simple declaration of interest in the security of Europe akin
to the Monroe Doctrine that did not bind the United States in any way
in the future. In the Senate, this faction insisted on reservations to the
Covenant that would have limited its qualitatively multilateral character by exempting matters pertaining to the Monroe Doctrine and by
disavowing any obligation (moral or otherwise) to come to the aid of
others. The conservatives also sought to allow unilateral withdrawal
and to limit the jurisdiction of the League over matters considered
by the United States to be of solely domestic concern. In short, they
wanted limitation on both qualitative and quantitative multilateralism. They wanted to restrict the openness of both the reciprocity and
the community circles.

Traditional isolationists shared conservative fears about opportunism and also embraced their negative views about human nature.
What set them apart was a particularly vehement particularized distrust of Europeans. Isolationists saw themselves as the heirs to Washington and Monroe and their warning to maintain separation between
the Old World and the New. Whereas conservative internationalists
generally felt a kinship with at the least the "civilized" great powers, the isolationists defined America in opposition to them. Europe
was aristocratic, autocratic and imperialistic. Isolationists argued that
mere association with these great powers would habituate the United
States to the ways of power politics and destroy American democracy
in the process. Hence they opposed any form of association, even (perhaps especially) a purely consultative great-power concert, which they
described as a new Holy Alliance.

In this way, identity was important for explaining part of the topog-
raphy of American domestic politics over the League, as constructivists
might expect. However, traditional isolationists amounted to a tiny
fraction of League opponents in the Senate. And shared identity was
not enough to lead conservative internationalists to make a binding,
qualitatively multilateral commitment to even a handful of European
allies they trusted. Only Wilson and the Democrats, who did not identify with the Europeans, could embrace such an institution.

Therefore, the failure of the League Covenant in the American
Senate owes almost exclusively to the inability of Wilsonian multilateralists and Republican unilateralists to bridge their ideological differences (Lake 1999; Patrick 2009). After compromising on key elements
of his plan with a conservative British government that preferred a

great-power concert with no collective security commitment or compulsory arbitration, Wilson returned home from Paris and found himself unable to garner the necessary two-thirds vote in the Senate for ratification. The President could not reach enough Republicans to pass the treaty, irrespective of how the few isolationists voted.

In the pages that follow, I first lay out the domestic political landscape in the United States as regards collective security. I identify the three distinct groups that battled over the League of Nations and their fundamental beliefs, their concerns about opportunism, and their preferences for institutional design. I focus on a few key personalities but also demonstrate how their personal positions correlated with the domestic positions that also reveal something about generalized trust and attracted the support of other like-minded individuals. This forms the bulk of the chapter because, despite all of the historical attention paid to the League, few have attempted to get at the core of these ideological differences. As the League fight was so public and so intense, it offers an opportunity to capture how bedrock assumptions regarding trustworthiness explain positions on the organization.

After setting the scene at home, I turn to the international negotiations over the League Covenant, which amounted to a compromise between Britain and the United States. Wilson and the Democrats fought not only the conservatives in their own country but also those forming the bulk of the British government. Tories wanted to limit the League to just an informal concert of great powers. Britain was marked by the same domestic ideological divisions, which indicates that this was not the uniquely American debate that it is often made out to be and suggests a broader generalizability of the argument. Wilson prevailed in his efforts to preserve a moral obligation to guarantee the political independence and territorial integrity of League members and a pledge by members to engage in third-party conflict resolution through a variety of mechanisms, but the conservative British government was successful in reinserting numerous elements of unilateral control such as unanimous voting in the League Council and in limiting when states would be automatically obliged to apply sanctions to those disturbing the international peace.

The final section describes the process of domestic ratification after Wilson returned from Europe as the Republicans introduced and successfully passed reservations effectively limiting the League to the great-power concert they preferred, at least as concerned American participation. This forced the dramatic showdown between unilateralists and multilateralists. Simple quantitative analysis of voting patterns over reservations, amendments and the final treaty allows us to capture the ideological nature of domestic divisions in the full Senate, adding many more individual data points to the main historical protagonists. I finally consider alternative explanations of these largely partisan domestic divisions, such as debates over the separation of powers and differences in economic constituencies, and find them wanting.

The "disentangling alliance": Woodrow Wilson's conception of collective security

Woodrow Wilson's conception of collective security was based on two principles. First, members would submit matters of potential conflict to an international body for collective resolution. Second, participants would jointly commit to the use of some sort of sanctions to ensure that countries abided by those procedures and did not resort to military aggression to settle their disputes. Although the precise mechanisms by which the new League would function were vague in Wilson's mind and became more specific only over time, collective security entailed some loss of sovereignty in that states would allow others a role in mediating their disputes and all would make a pledge in advance to use some sort of coercion against those who resorted to force. In Ruggie's terms, it was qualitatively multilateral. "Some of our sovereignty would be surrendered," Wilson admitted. The enterprise could not succeed "without some sacrifice," (Knock 1992: 233), a sentiment he consistently expressed in public and private (Dueck 2006: 53; Knock 1992: 76, 97; Lake 1999: 112). States would, however, reap the self-interested gains of limits on their sovereignty. While "entangling alliances . . . would draw them into competitions of power, catch them in a net of intrigue and selfish rivalry, and disturb their own affairs with influences intruded from without," under collective security "when all unite to act in the same sense and with the same purpose all act in the common interest and are free to live their own lives under a common protection" (Ambrosius 1987: 29; Link 1966,[1] vol. XL, 539).

[1] Hereafter PWW (Papers of Woodrow Wilson).

Such an organization had to rest on diffuse reciprocity, and Wilson understood as much. For instance, the President recognized that the Americans might sometimes lose in conflict resolution proceedings and would "take our medicine" (Knock 1992: 266; Patrick 2009: 23). What America gave up in the short term would be paid back in the long run. Ikenberry takes this embrace of diffuse reciprocity as evidence for his argument that the United States was practicing "strategic restraint" to ameliorate other countries' concerns about American domination (2001: 117–19). This was indeed restraint, but Ikenberry misses the generalized nature and motivation behind it. All countries were to be similarly restrained.

Wilson's position is a puzzle for rationalism. Lake argues that the United States' objective interest in collective security after WWI was decidedly ambivalent; it had an interest in a mechanism to ensure peace, particularly in Europe, but not at any price as the United States still had a viable strategy of relative isolation and unilateralism given the nature of military technology and America's relative geographic remove. Even though the United States had a stake in deterring future global conflict, any binding commitments could lead to entrapment or free riding. Even had these issues been satisfactorily resolved, there was the question of abandonment. And hierarchy was too expensive. The default should have been, Lake claims, unilateralism (1999: 107).

The risk of opportunism of all kinds only increased with large numbers, in terms of not only the security guarantee but also the possibility of exploitation in third-party conflict resolution. Rationalists expect states to demand unilateral control in these highly uncertain situations. Yet, as we will see, Wilson advocated a relatively multilateral binding security commitment with authoritative dispute resolution in a large organization of global scale, so as to mobilize a greater deterrent power (Dueck 2006: 53). And he did not advocate any type of international hierarchy to ensure that states met their obligations, the only other protection against opportunism. Wilson conceived of the League as having an enormous scope, providing a system for global conflict resolution and a worldwide security guarantee.

Wilson's ideas were even bolder when we consider how radically they departed from America's traditional policy of isolation, whose foundations were best articulated by former presidents George Washington and James Monroe. Collective dispute resolution, which would have made any potential conflict in the western hemisphere an affair of relevance to the entire international community, ran afoul of the Monroe Doctrine, the unilateral declaration that the US would not tolerate any interference by others in its sphere of influence. Whereas Monroe had sought to separate predominantly American affairs from those of others, Wilson sought to intertwine them. By making the resolution of local conflicts an interest of the world, the power of the international community could be mobilized to prevent disputes from escalating. However this came with the risk of exploitation by others on issues of vital interest to the United States. Non-parties to a dispute might nevertheless have an ulterior motive other than peace at stake in the outcome and use their vote to American disadvantage. Whereas conflict resolution allowed others to interfere in America's business, any pledge to enforce collectively the will of the League to protect others against aggression obligated the US to meddle in others, a departure from Washington's warning in his farewell address to avoid "permanent alliances." This threatened free riding and entrapment.

The cooperative social orientation of Woodrow Wilson and the Democratic Party

How could Wilson propose such a scheme given America's structural position and interests? Had the initiative come solely from those who faced more immediate and obvious threats, such as the more vulnerable France and Belgium who wanted the League to serve as a dressed-up anti-German alliance, rationalists could easily explain collective security based on the strategic calculation of more vulnerable states. Yet the impetus came from Wilson, with support from ideological allies in the United States and Britain. The standard answer to these puzzles is that Wilson was an "idealist." Indeed the term itself has become synonymous with "Wilsonianism." This concept is generally left to stand on its own, or defined tautologically as a faith in multilateral institutions to create peace in international relations. I argue that Wilsonian idealism is a product of generalized trust.

Wilson framed the situation in assurance terms. If the United States made a pledge, it would keep it and others would follow. By joining a League, Wilson argued, the United States "steadies the whole world by its promise beforehand that it will stand with other nations of similar judgment to maintain right in the world." If it did not, "the world would not have the knowledge before it that there will be concerted action by all the responsible governments of the world in the protection of the peace of the world." The very promise of nation-states in advance to come to the aid of victims of aggression in the future amounts to a "centering upon it generally of the definite opinion of the world, expressed through the authoritative organs of the responsible governments" (PWW, vol. 45: 388–90).

Wilson's generalized trust found indirect expression in his lack of concern about opportunism of all kinds in his proposed League. In terms of abandonment, he stressed that states would meet their commitments even if there were no hierarchy in the organization, such as some supranational control (Knock 1992: 127). A belief in the power of moral obligations suggests moralistic trust, a belief that once states made commitments, they could be trusted to fulfill them. And Wilson did not make exceptions in his expectations of compliance. This was moralistic trust of a generalized variety. Wilson claimed, even privately, that he did "not think such a refusal [to comply with the security guarantee] would likely often occur" (PWW, vol. 45: 393). After the negotiation of the treaty, in response to a skeptic's query about what strength underlay Article X if it were only a moral obligation, he responded: "Why, Senator, it is surprising that question should be asked. If we undertake an obligation we are bound in the most solemn way to carry it out" (PWW, vol. 45: 361).

Entrapment was not a concern for Wilson either. He argued the League would help solve that problem of opportunism, not exacerbate it. The President claimed that the League was not an entangling but rather a "disentangling alliance ... which would disentangle the peoples of the world from those combinations in which they seek their own separate and private interests and unite the people of the world to preserve the peace of the world upon a basis of common right and justice" (PWW, vol. 37: 126). Only "special and limited alliances entangle," whereas he proposed a "general alliance" (Ambrosius 1987: 46). Washington, he argued, would surely agree (Cooper 2001: 21; Knock 1992: 113; Ambrosius 1987: 29; PWW, vol. 40: 539). Because collective security would successfully deter, entrapment would generally not be an issue.

Wilson was not worried about exploitation either. The League would prevent rather than increase distasteful interference in the internal affairs of other states. Wilson sought to reinvent the Monroe Doctrine, converting it from a statement declaring the boundaries of the American sphere of influence into a general statement of principle. A commitment to the territorial integrity and political independence of all members meant that the "nations with one accord adopt the doctrine of President Monroe as the doctrine of the world: that no nation should seek to extend its polity over any other nation or people, but that every people should be left free to determine its own polity, its own way of development, unhindered, unthreatened, unafraid, the little along with the great and powerful" (PWW, vol. 40: 539). He expressed this in private as well (Ambrosius 1987: 28–9; Cooper 2001: 21; Knock 1992; Patrick 2009: 13).

Wilson also expressed his generalized trust directly (Ambrosius 1987: 2). He once advised his daughter in a letter that "most people are fundamentally good – of that I am sure. Don't let a few cheap and dishonest ones hurt you" (Curti 1957: 6).[2] And generalized trust was indirectly evident in his domestic political agenda. Wilson was one of the great liberal reformers in American history. His progressive populism was based on his acceptance of the moral nature of the masses who had to be protected against the few entrenched interests. This was a common theme in his speeches and legislative agenda (PWW, vol. 38: 128; PWW, vol. 37: 191; PWW, vol. 38: 131).

Wilson was hardly unique in this regard. The era of Democratic, left-wing populism began before he became President and was a consistent refrain in the party's electoral platforms. Therefore it is not surprising that even though the President was the League's most forceful advocate, he had the complete backing of almost everyone in his party. And the intensity of support for his vision increased as one moved towards the left of the political spectrum, as will be seen quantitatively later. Other Democrats understood the League in the same terms as Wilson. Scholars note, but cannot explain this puzzle (Cooper 2001: 26; Ikenberry 2001: 119, 155; Lake 1999: 107). The little resistance Wilson encountered in his party was confined to its most conservative members, who also directly expressed a lack of generalized trust. Senator Reed referred to the "inherent evilness of men" (Ambrosius 1987:

---

[2] "So for him the latent causes of faction are *not* sown in the nature of man, or if they are, historical progress will overcome this human nature," writes Pestritto (2005: 6).

91). Thomas believed that "human nature is the same as it always has been. Man is a fighting animal. He is a selfish animal" (Stone 1970: 18–19). Five of the six consistent opponents of Wilson in his party ranked as among the top ten most conservative members based on their NOMINATE scores, and the average score of the six was 1.2 standard deviations from the party mean.[3]

The generalized nature of Wilson's trust is also evident by the fact that it extended beyond American borders. While Wilson claimed, as all American politicians did, that the United States was exceptional, unlike others he argued that American values were shared by almost everyone: "These are American principles, American policies. We could stand for no others. And they are also the principles and policies of forward looking men and women everywhere, of every modern nation, of every enlightened community. They are the principles of mankind and must prevail." The President believed that in his support for collective security, he was speaking for the "silent mass of mankind everywhere who have as yet had no place or opportunity to speak their real hearts out concerning the death and ruin they see to have come already upon the persons and the homes they hold most dear" (PWW, vol. 40: 538–9). As was the case in domestic politics, the masses were trustworthy. War was the result of the selfish interests of the few, whereas the masses were peaceful and could be expected to embrace international cooperation (PWW, vol. 41: 523).

It is this faith in the masses, an indirect expression of generalized trust, that explains Wilson's fixation on the spread of democracy as a precondition for the functioning of collective security. Autocracies, by protecting the privileges of a select few over the many, were inherently aggressive and could not be trusted to observe the commitments of collective security. "Only free peoples can hold their purpose and their honour steady to a common end and prefer the interests of mankind to any narrow interest of their own," he asserted (PWW, vol. 45: 525). This generalized trust is also evident in the weight that Wilson placed on the role of public opinion in the operation of collective security. It was the "searching light of conscience" (Ambrosius 1987: 51).[4]

---

[3] These were Walsh, Thomas, Shields, Gore and Smith (Cooper 2001: 242–3; Stone 1970: 18–19).

[4] Without mobilizing the force of public opinion, war would be "determined upon as wars used to be determined upon in the old, unhappy days when

Democracy would allow Wilson to circumvent obstructionist European leaders, practitioners of traditional power politics that Washington warned about (Ambrosius 1987: 9, 14–15, 28, 33; Ikenberry 2001: 156–7). The President wrote to a colleague, "Yes, I know that Europe is still governed by the same reactionary forces which controlled this country until a few years ago. But I am satisfied that if necessary I can reach the peoples of Europe over the heads of their Rulers" (Knock 1992: 162). In this way, the President believed that he could "convert" the Europeans (Ambrosius 1987: 82–4). Wilson remarked, "I discovered that what we called American principles had penetrated to the heart and understanding not only of the great peoples of Europe. But to the heads and understandings of the great men who were representing the peoples of Europe" (Ikenberry 2001: 158–9).

Alternative conceptions of idealism: cosmopolitanism and pacifism

It is important to note that Wilson's idealism was not inspired by two other notions often linked to his vision – cosmopolitanism and pacifism. Wilson's idealism was not a form of international altruism premised on a cosmopolitan identity in which the United States would put moral principle and the interests of the international community above its own narrower self-interests, as is often maintained by realist critics (Kupchan and Kupchan 1991; Mearsheimer 1994).[5] This is the implicit assumption behind Ruggie's (1997) and Patrick's (2009) accounts of Wilsonianism, that it reflected a uniquely American conception of nationalism based on inclusion in keeping with the United States' history as a melting pot.

While a feeling of common identity and an altruistic concern for weaker powers certainly would have helped collective security function more effectively, this was not the President's understanding. For

---

peoples were nowhere consulted by their rulers and wars were provoked and waged in the interest of dynasties or of little groups of ambitious men" (PWW, vol. 41: 523).

[5] In moments of hyperbole, Wilson would imply as much. This more altruistic justification was more common during Wilson's efforts to drum up public support for the League, such as his speaking tour of the United States by train after he returned home from Paris (Cooper 2001: 4; Lake 1999: 112; R. A. Stone 1970: 21, 59).

Wilson and his supporters, collective security was based not on a sense of community but rather on a belief in interdependence, that the United States, or any other nation-state for that matter, could only secure its own interests by cooperating with others. He declared: "No nation should be forced to take sides in any quarrel in which its own honour and the integrity of its own people are not involved; but no nation can any longer remain neutral as against any willful disturbance of the peace of the world. The effects of war can no longer be confined to the areas of battle" (PWW, vol. 38: 135). This was a persistent theme.[6] This interdependence was partially a function of the growth of American power and interests, something that the war had brought home.[7] Wilson had himself advocated non-engagement in his first years in office (Ambrosius 1987, Chapter 2; Cooper 2001, Chapter 1). Collective security was, for the President, a "demonstration of the needs of the time" (Knock 1992: 97). What was "once considered theoretical and idealistic, turns out to be practical and necessary," he declared (Knock 1992: 196).

This belief in the interdependent nature of world affairs made Wilson and his allies "internationalists" as opposed to isolationists. Of course, the President was not the only politician to recognize this; indeed, as we will see, this was the predominant opinion. What distinguished Wilson and the "idealists" was their solution to the problem – that the United States should and could coordinate with others to realize the joint gains of cooperation, in this case a lasting peace after WWI. This was not magnanimity on his part, but rather based on an expectation of reciprocity. "We are participants, whether we would or not, in the life of the world . . . We are *partners* with the rest," he argued (Knock 1992: 76 [emphasis added]).

---

[6] "The world is linked together in a common life and interest such as humanity never saw before, and the starting of wars can never again be a private and individual matter for the nations. What disturbs the life of the whole world is the concern of the whole world. And it is our duty to lend the full force of this nation – moral and physical – to a league of nations" (Knock 1992: 96; also Ambrosius 1987: 12); "All the peoples of the world are in effect partners in this interest, and for our own part we see very clearly that unless justice be done to others it will not be done to us" (PWW, vol. 45: 536).

[7] Wilson said, "The isolation of the United States is at an end not because we chose to go into the politics of the world, but because by the sheer genius of this people and the growth of our power, we have become a determining factor in the history of mankind, and after you have become a determining factor you cannot remain isolated, whether you want to or not" (Ambrosius 1987: 177).

Nor was Wilson less patriotic than his opponents. Wilson had a
strong belief in America's special providence (Knock 1992: 252).[8] It
was what the President did with his patriotism that made his position
distinct. He said, "the greatest nationalist is the man who wants his
nation to be the greatest nation, and the greatest nation is the nation
which penetrates to the heart of its duty and mission among the nations
of the world" (Ambrosius 1987: 176). As he described it, the US faced
a choice between "provincials – little Americans – or big Americans –
statesmen. You either have to be ostriches with your heads in the sand
or eagles" (Cooper 2001: 182).

And of course Wilson was not a pacifist. Wilson's idealism was
a function of generalized trust, not a greater commitment to antimili-
tarism. The President's cooperative social orientation led him to believe
that breaches to the peace would be relatively rare, especially given
the collective promise of countries to help one another (Knock 1992:
261). However, generalized trust is never total, and the international
community needed an answer to breaches of the peace. When presenting the first draft of the League Covenant to the Paris peace conference, Wilson stated that the threat of physical coercion was only "in
the background" as it would generally not be needed, "but it *is* in the
background . . . and if the moral force of the world will not suffice, the
physical force of the world shall" (Ambrosius 1987: 77; Cooper 2001:
55). Wilson stressed that a collective sanction would act as a greater
deterrent than the balance of power: "It will be absolutely necessary
that a force be created as a guarantor of the permanency of the settlement so much greater than the force of any nation now engaged or any
alliance hitherto formed or projected that no nation, no probable combination of nations could face or withstand it" (PWW, vol. 40: 535).

Generalized trust helps explain the paradox that Wilson, while he
asked more of the United States than others in his country were willing
to provide, did not see the need for a strong institution to guarantee
the meeting of that commitment. The League was to operate on the
basis not of a world state or supranational army but of a moral obligation. This is why Wilson used the term "covenant" (PWW, vol. 40:

---

[8] Wilson said, "The stage is set, the destiny disclosed. It has come about by no
plan of our conceiving, but by the hand of God who led us into this way. We
cannot turn back. We can only go forward, with lifted eyes and freshened spirit,
to follow the vision. It was of this that we dreamed at our birth. America shall
in truth show the way. The light streams upon the path ahead, and nowhere
else" (Knock 1992: 252).

535). The sense of moral obligation would suffice, both for the United States and other members of the League. For Wilson, collective security was "a very grave and solemn moral obligation." Even though such a moral obligation was "binding in conscience only, not in law" (PWW, vol. 45: 343), the President stressed in a closed-door meeting that a "moral obligation is of course superior to a legal obligation, and, if I may say so, has a greater binding force." "There is a national good conscience in such a matter," he declared to dubious senators and in other instances of private correspondence with his collaborators (PWW, vol. 45: 361). Hierarchy, therefore, wasn't necessary. Wilson wrote that he thought the League was "a matter of moral persuasion more than a problem of juridical organization" (Knock 1992: 127).[9] Lake tries to incorporate such moral commitments under the rubric of hierarchy, arguing that Wilson thought the Covenant would "control" states (1999: 78: 106). If this were true, it could only have been on the basis of the strength of moral obligations as there was no true hierarchical control in the League in the rationalist sense of the word.

In sum, Wilson and his allies, overwhelmingly in his Democratic Party, embraced a vision for international order of quantitative and qualitative multilateralism. It was based on generalized trust, which served as form of social capital, lessening concern about opportunism and thereby convincing its proponents that such an organization could succeed. That Wilson's approach was such a radical departure from American tradition is not surprising. George Washington's admonition to avoid any permanent alliances was premised on a negative view of the nature of international politics and human nature in general (Monten 2005). Washington cautioned the United States to avoid both friends and enemies in world affairs, as both were illusory and fleeting and would lead the United States into harm by making it a "slave."

The "open-ended commitment": conservative opposition to collective security

Although the fight in the United States over collective security is sometimes framed as pitting Wilsonian internationalists against

---

[9] Wilson wrote Colonel House, his confidant: "My own conviction . . . is that the administrative constitution of the League must grow and not be made; that we must begin with solemn covenants, covering mutual guarantees of political independence and territorial integrity" (Ambrosius 1987: 39; Knock 1992: 149).

isolationists, Wilson's primary antagonists were internationalists themselves, what Lake (1999) and Knock (1992) call "conservative internationalists."[10] Only a handful of senators were isolationists. The former group, exclusively Republican in party affiliation, believed that the United States had a role to play in international affairs but complained bitterly about Wilson's notion of collective security even before the precise contours were negotiated at the Versailles peace conference. It was led by the majority leader of the Republicans in the Senate, Henry Cabot Lodge, who also took up the position of chairman of the Foreign Relations Committee.

The competitive social orientation of the conservative internationalists

Although Lake claims that there was general agreement in the United States, across the political spectrum, as to the risks of opportunism inherent in international cooperation, this was hardly the case (1999: 80, 118). Compared with Wilson and his progressive, Democratic allies, conservative internationalists were systematically more concerned about opportunism of all forms. Where Wilson and the Democrats expected reciprocity, these Republicans expected defection. They framed the same situation as a prisoner's dilemma.

Conservatives' primary fear was the entrapment that might result from any security guarantee. Lodge and other Republicans held up the specter of other nations drawing Americans into foreign conflicts not necessarily of concern to them. The majority leader asked: "Will it not be worth while to pause a moment before we commit ourselves to an army of 500,000 men, to be held ready for war at the pleasure of other nations in whose councils we shall have but one vote if we are true to the President's policy of the equality of nations" (US Congress,[11] 65:2: 2,368).[12] Senator Philander Knox cautioned that

---

[10] These are Ruggie (1997) and Dueck's (2006) "realists," Legro's (2005) "unilateralists," and Patrick's (2009) "great power internationalists." Jackson (2006: 53–7) conflates them with isolationists and consequently vastly exaggerates the weight of the isolationists.

[11] Hereafter, CR for *Congressional Record.*

[12] "Are you ready to put your soldiers and your sailors at the disposition of other nations?" asked Lodge at another point (Knock 1992: 230). He complained, "I never for a moment contemplated that we were to be handed a document which bound us for all time, without any possible limit anywhere" (Cooper

the League would "presuppose the sending of American troops thousands of miles for some distant purpose perhaps of no great concern to American citizens" (CR, 65:3: 606; Cooper 2001: 41). They expressed these same sorts of concerns in private correspondence as well. In a letter to the elder Republican statesman, former Secretary of State Elihu Root, Lodge wrote that the League was "in the highest degree dangerous" . . . as it "requires us to guarantee the territorial integrity and political independence of every nation on earth" (Cooper 2001: 59). Conservative internationalists also were concerned that states would exploit the United States in conflict resolution institutions (Cooper 2001: 135; CR, 66: 1: 3,778–84). Even Lake admits that one cannot understand conservative internationalist objections to exploitation and entrapment separately (1999: 135). They were part of a package.

These same Republicans were the most skeptical that an agreement premised on moral commitments could function properly. They were convinced that states, including the United States, would abandon their pledges when a crisis ensued. Publicly, Lodge complained of "too many and too Utopian proposals . . . and too difficult obligations (Stone 1970: 26; CR 65:2: 11,485–8). Privately he said the same, that collective security would "bind us to all kinds of things which the country would not hold to" (Cooper 2001: 20). In a closed-door meeting with Wilson, for which a transcript is now available, Senator Warren Harding asked skeptically, "if there is nothing more than a moral obligation on the part of any member of the league, what avail [the security guarantee]?" He predicted to Wilson that others would "take advantage of the [moral] construction that you place upon these articles" and asked rhetorically, "[R]eally what do we get out of this international compact in the enforcement of any decree?" (PWW, vol. 45: 361, 388). Republican Senator Frank Brandegee felt the same, arguing that states would not fulfill their obligations. He forecasted that others would doubt the credibility of moral obligations as well, thereby undermining the ability of the League to deter (PWW, vol. 45: 391–3). If states would abandon others in case of attack, diffuse reciprocity could not function and the League would fail. The League could not work on the basis of "verbal adherence to general principle," declared Lodge. "You cannot make effective a league of

2001: 229). Brandegee preferred "not to have any entanglements or connections with European powers" (Cooper 2001: 144).

peace, 'supported by the organized force of mankind,' by language or high-sounding phrases" (Knock 1992: 124).

Conservative concerns about opportunism were the indirect expression of a lack of generalized trust, seen directly in their pessimistic statements about human nature, both in international relations and in life in general (Ambrosius 1987: 48; Patrick 2009: 17; Stone 1970: 10–11). Lodge cautioned, "We must deal with human nature as it is and not as it ought to be" (Ambrosius 1987: 28). Human nature is conflictual, Lodge believed, and therefore international relations are marked by discord. "There has been pretty constant fighting in this unhappy world ever since the time when history begins its records, and in speaking of lasting peace in terms of history we can only speak comparatively" (CR, 65:2: 2,365). Lodge expressed these same sentiments long before he became a leading Republican politician. Quoting Aldous Huxley, the Foreign Relations Committee chairman once said, "The world is very ignorant and very wretched, and the man who in his little corner makes less that ignorance and wretchedness does the highest work that it is given to man to do" (Widenor 1980: 65). Lodge's biographer concludes that he had a "conservative view of man – one which emphasized his shortcoming" (Widenor 1980: 64). This led him to embrace "realism" in foreign affairs, which Lodge contrasted with Jeffersonian idealism (Widenor 1980: 35–41).

Conservatives dismissed Wilson and his scheme as utopian. Knox said, "One must be visionary indeed to suppose that the heterogenous peoples of the earth could so completely overcome human nature as to combine now in the real internationalism of a world State or even in a league involving a great catalogue of unnatural self-restraints. Such conceptions to-day touch rather the postulates of religion than the facts of statesmanship" (CR, 65:2: 11,487; also Cooper 2001: 40). Lodge argued, "In the present state of human nature and public opinion is it probable that any nation will bind itself to go to war at the command of other nations and furnish its army and navy to be disposed of as the majority of other nations may see fit?" (CR, 65:2: 2,368).

These opponents of the League were among the most conservative members in the US Senate (Cooper 2001: 128; Lake 1999: 94; Stone 1970: 94). The prominent detractors mentioned above – Sherman, Knox, Moses, Brandegee, Lodge and Harding – all ranked in the top fifteen in their party in terms of their NOMINATE scores. Given the nature of Republican Party ideology, this is an indirect expression of a lack of generalized trust and a competitive social orientation. In an exhaustive review of the history of American party ideology, Gerring writes, "Perhaps more than any other value, order – and its antithesis, anarchy – defined...Republican ideology" (2001: 97). This was natural because Republicans "viewed human nature with an abiding mistrust," and feared that without order, society would degenerate into chaos (Gerring 1998: 103). "The significance of anarchism...can hardly be overstated," Gerring writes. "Anarchism was, logically speaking, the polar opposite of everything the party stood for – order, authority and tradition" (2001: 97).

Those who are less trusting by disposition stress the necessity of strong state authority and moral sanctions to protect against excessive individualism. They are more likely to rely on tradition and to be more resistant to change. Republicans viewed liberty with trepidation. Their 1908 platform read, the "Republican party stands for a *wise* and *regulated* individualism" (Johnson 1978: 162 [emphasis added]). Even the progressive Theodore Roosevelt believed that "harm comes from excessive individualism" (Gerring 1998: 102). Republicans did not stress "natural rights" like Democrats did beyond those of basic civil rights; individualism was contingent on duty to both society and the state. Republicans understood themselves as the party of law and order, of strong central institutions to protect society from danger. Moral values served as another check on dangerous individualism. The Republicans were the party of Yankee Protestantism, of almost Victorian self-restraint such as support for temperance and consumption laws. Even before evangelicalism and the rise of the religious right, the Republican Party was the home of social conservatives (Gerring 1998, Chapter 3). The value placed on maintaining order made the Republicans resistant to change even during the progressive era (Gerring 1998: 93–5). The party's presidential candidate in 1916, Charles Evan Hughes, promised that the "party of stability" would "look to the future but we are inspired by a consideration of the record of the past" (C. E. Hughes 1916: 3).

Republicans vigorously opposed the left-wing populism of the Democrats as both a threat to social order and a dangerous social experiment.[13] This fear of unchecked political participation was

---

[13] Even when the party chose Theodore Roosevelt as its nominee, Republican progressivism was conservatively motivated. Roosevelt's New Nationalism was based on nurturing national solidarity so as to create social cohesion and diminish social unrest in a way not unlike Bismarck's (Gerring 1998: 80; Widenor 1980: 50–3).

natural for a party that lacked generalized trust. The party's 1912 program stated, "We believe in our self-controlled representative democracy which is a government of laws, not of men, and in which order is the prerequisite of progress. The principles of constitutional government, which make provisions for *orderly* and effective expression of the popular will..." (Johnson 1978: 183 [emphasis added]). Republicans called Democratic populism a "sudden, dangerous and revolutionary assault upon law and order" and portrayed their opponents as "prone to dangerous experimentation" (A. M. Schlesinger 1971: 1,863, 1,870–71).

It is impossible to check these key ideological traits against all the personal beliefs of all the main protagonists in the conservative internationalist faction of League opponents, much less the entire Republican Party. However, a brief sketch of Henry Cabot Lodge's political philosophy indicates that these elements of rightist ideology do indeed characterize party members. Lodge was a standard conservative. He was a moral traditionalist with "reverence for the old Puritan values" (Garraty 1943: 59) and was concerned about progressive cultural relativism (Widenor 1980: 25–7). The senator also embraced strong state institutions to maintain order and was suspicious of unbridled mass participation in politics (Widenor 1980: 8, 28, 33, 49).

Given that conservative internationalists demonstrated a systematic lack of generalized trust measured both directly in their views about social relations and indirectly in their concerns about opportunism in international cooperation and their party's domestic political positions, what effect did this have on their views about the proper alternative to collective security? The conservatives did not endorse hierarchy. Fear of opportunism led the conservative internationalists towards the seeming paradox of arguing at the same time that the League required more force, yet asked too much of its members. Conservative internationalists questioned Wilson's mechanism, the sense of moral obligation embedded in a covenant. Lodge argued that to function effectively, given the presumption that states would not live up to their commitments, the League would need at its disposal some kind of international authority. Lodge said if the League was to be more than an "exposition of vague ideals," it must have "authority to issue decrees and force to sustain them" (Knock 1992: 230). He said, "There is no halfway house to stop at... The system must be either voluntary or there must be force behind the agreement"

(CR, 65:2: 2,367). Roosevelt claimed in a private letter that the League was "like a mass meeting abolishing vice but vice isn't abolished that way" (Cooper 2001: 42). Yet these conservative internationalists did not advocate any such kind of supranational authority. Indeed they were the greatest opponents of any such ideas (Stone 1970: 55).

Because they lacked generalized trust, conservative internationalists could not endorse Wilson's idea of limiting individual sovereignty to reach a better collective outcome that would over the long term benefit all of the League's individual members. A qualitatively multilateral organization could only function if countries made a general pledge to take action regardless of the particular circumstances. Conservatives understood the logic but did not accept Wilson's premises. For opponents of the President, the essence of American foreign policy was to separate America's sphere of vital interest from that of others, not to combine them. Lodge rejected Wilson's notion of a "Monroe Doctrine for the world":

The real essence of [the Monroe] doctrine is that American questions shall be settled by Americans alone; that the Americas shall be separated from Europe and from the interference of Europe in purely American questions... The Monroe Doctrine exists solely for the protection of the American hemisphere, and to that hemisphere it was limited. If you extend it to all the world, it ceases to exist, because it rests on nothing but the differentiation of the American hemisphere from the rest of the world. (CR, 65:3: 4,521; also CR, 65:2, 2,367)

Republican alternatives to collective security: closing the reciprocity and community circles

Lacking generalized trust, Republicans with a competitive social orientation fell back on arrangements relying on a smaller group with whom they shared experience, interests and even an identity. They sought to reduce quantitative multilateralism. Unlike many Wilsonian Democrats and even Wilson himself, this group felt a fundamental kinship with those European great powers with whom they had fought in the Great War, and unlike Wilson they understood them as fellow righteous defenders of civilization against German aggression (Cooper 2001: 11–22; Knock 1992: 109; Patrick 2009: 11). Knox declared, "We have now passed from a dangerous balance of power to a beneficent preponderance of power in the hands of the proved trustees of civilization" (CR, 65:3: 604). Lodge warned, "To encourage or even to permit any serious differences to arise between the United States and Great Britain, or with France, or Italy, or Belgium, would be a world calamity of the worst kind . . . Any thought of war among them would be as abominable as it is inconceivable" (CR, 65:3: 725). This indicates a kind of particularized trust predicated on a common identity with allied European powers.

Conservative internationalists called for a smaller League formed out of the present alliance of great powers thought to desire peace, that is, those who shared American interests and values (Ambrosius 1987: 138; Cooper 2001: 11–12; Stone 1970: 26, 55). Knox said, "The league of nations that now challenges our solicitude is the league of nations of which we are now a member – the glorious present alliance of the many powers with whom we are now fighting as a league to enforce and to maintain peace from disturbance by the German menace." He suggested: "Out of the present alliance . . . it would seem possible to perpetuate the league we have . . . as a league for one single purpose of enforcing peace" (CR, 65:2: 114,867). Lodge and former President Theodore Roosevelt agreed.[14] A more inclusive League would mean the participation of less civilized, and less trustworthy forces. Knox said, "A universal league of nations . . . would have the power to impose upon the peoples most advanced in honor, justice, truth, enlightenment, and humanity – that is, in civilization—the judgment and the verdict of peoples less advanced. Power in the hands of the defenders of civilization holds the best promise of an ultimate international order founded upon justice and good will, which all good men long to see" (CR, 65:3: 605).

This suggested a particular form of organization, a concert of great powers not unlike that formed after the Napoleonic wars, which would enforce the peace on behalf of the world. In Knox's view, the allies would examine controversies that threatened war and intervene to

---

[14] Lodge said, "We have now at this moment a league of nations. They have been engaged in compelling Germany to make peace and in restoring peace to the world" (CR, 65:3, 728). Lodge called this a "league of victors" (Knock 1992: 100) and expressed the same support privately (Ambrosius 1987: 48). Roosevelt pushed for "the league which we already have in existence, the league of the Allies who have fought this great war" (Cooper 2001: 42). He wanted the League limited "at the outset to the Allies . . . with whom we have been operating and with whom we are certain we can cooperate in the future" (Patrick 2009: 18).

stop them with overwhelming force. "[A]n entente of those powers, with their preponderant power on sea, in air, and in the economic field, can stand ready, in their wise discretion, to take measures together, when they believe it their duty to do so, if the peace of the world is seriously threatened from any other quarter" (CR, 65:3: 604).[15]

However, as much as the conservative internationalists identified with the other civilized powers, they were not willing to grant their partners any formal role in determining US policy. Contrary to constructivist expectations, particularized trust did not lead to support for qualitative multilateralism even among a smaller group of American allies with whom they felt a shared sense of community. Particularized trust had its limits. As conservative internationalists envisioned it, such a concert required no loss of sovereignty that might threaten opportunism. Knox advocated a "permanent entente of the English-speaking peoples and of the French, Italians and Japanese... each recognizing the other's leadership in its peculiar field, and to form a permanent committee for consultation on these subjects" (CR, 65:3: 605). The concert would be informal and ad hoc in nature without any general obligations or even voting procedures. It "entangles us in no way," reassured Knox (Cooper 2001: 41). The conservatives preferred a League that simply allowed great-power discussion (Cooper 2001: 8). Even among former allies, trust might not be possible. The arch-conservative Brandegee warned Wilson in their closed-door meeting: "I want to call your attention to the fact that this era of good feeling which exists between the allied and associated powers after their common experience and suffering in this great war may not always exist, in view of future commercial contests and separate interests of different nationalities which may occur in the future" (PWW, vol. 45: 401). At most, conservative internationalists could embrace a

---

[15] This was a common conservative conception for an international organization, and was featured in Roosevelt's acceptance speech for the Nobel Prize years before: "Surely the time ought to be ripe for the nations to consider a great world agreement among all the civilized world powers to back righteousness by force" (Knock 1992: 49). Roosevelt repeated this call during WWI, arguing that the civilized nations should "introduce some kind of police system in the weak and disorderly countries at their thresholds." It would include all "those great powers honestly bent on peace... not only to keep the peace among themselves, but to prevent, by force if necessary, its being broken by others" (Cooper 2001: 12) Lodge also endorsed a system in 1915 in which the great powers would unite to prevent others from going to war (Cooper 2001).

traditional alliance with France and Britain, those countries with whom they shared overlapping interests (Ambrosius 1987: 149; Cooper 2001: 76–9; Dueck 2006: 48–51; Lake 1999: 115).

Prominent conservative internationalists endorsed a number of other, more unilateral alternatives as well. Knox suggested, as an alternative to Wilson's notion of the League, a unilateral declaration of American concern for the security of Europe and a pledge that it would consult with its present allies if a threat to the continent's security reemerged (Cooper 2001: 101; Stone 1970: 45).[16] The senator noted that this new doctrine had "some correspondence to the Monroe doctrine – a declaration that a menace to the liberty of Europe is a menace to America, and that America will consult her friends and prepare for action if ever such menace shall again rise" (CR, 65:3: 606). As will be seen, this idea reemerged in the early Cold War as a unilateral alternative to NATO. All of these options indicated a preference for unilateralism given a lack of generalized trust.

Conservative internationalists concluded that the United States was better served by not putting its fate in the hands of others given their pessimistic view of the world. Republican presidential candidate Charles Evan Hughes asserted: "We must not involve ourselves in a League of Nations that may make us the pawn of selfish people in other lands and in the end destroy the peace and happiness of our own people" (Cooper 2001: 60). Sherman foretold a "Pandora's Box of evil to empty upon the American people the aggregated calamities of the world" should a collective security system be created (Cooper 2001: 66). Lodge maintained that the US could "serve the cause of peace best . . . by not permitting herself to be fettered by the dictates of other nations" (Cooper 2001: 167). He promised he "would keep America as she has been, master of her own fate" (Dueck 2006: 74).

---

[16] The United States would simply declare that if "the freedom and peace of Europe" were "again threatened by any power or combination of powers, [it] will regard such a situation with grave concern as a menace to its own peace and freedom, will consult with other powers affected with a view to devising means for the removal of such menace, and will, the necessity arising in the future, carry out the same complete accord and cooperation with our chief cobelligerents for the defense of civilization" (Cooper 2001: 101; Stone 1970: 45).

It is not surprising that part of Republican opposition to the League was its revolutionary nature. Less trusting conservatives were not able to draw on the social capital of generalized trust to construct new arrangements with new partners given the uncertainty that would create. Knox and others cautioned a more pragmatic, conservative approach: "Wise policy, as opposed to shallow empiricism, would seem to counsel us to solidify and build upon what we have tried rather than to plunge headlong into a universal experiment" (CR, 65:3: 604). Lake notes that the "open-ended nature of the commitment to the League" and the "high level of uncertainty about the future" bothered conservative internationalists (1999: 115).

A new holy alliance: isolationist objection to the League of Nations

In addition to the conservative internationalists, there was another notable and distinct group of League opponents – traditional isolationists. In many ways their concerns and their views were identical. Both groups feared opportunism more than Wilson and his allies did. Isolationists lamented that the League could both entrap the United States into wars not in its interests and allow others to interfere with matters of vital American concern in the western hemisphere (Cooper 2001: 61; Stone 1970: 16).[17] And like the conservatives, they matched this indirect expression of a competitive social orientation with a direct expression of their pessimism about human nature. Said William Borah, the spiritual leader of this faction, "[W]hile the ideal has its place, into that land of promise, like the patriarch of old, the legislator is not permitted to enter. He must deal with concrete things and things practical... His material is human nature as it is and as it always will be – struggling up and moving on, hoping, aspiring, but human nature still... you and I are to deal with a world tortured and twisted by selfishness and greed, vexed and driven by rivalry and ambition" (CR 65:3: 196). Another isolationist, Senator Miles Poindexter, claimed that collective security was "theoretically defensible upon some high plane of brotherly love; but we all know that international relations are not... determined by principles of brotherly love" (CR, 64:1: 11,377–8).

---

[17] See Borah in the Congressional Record (65:3: 189, 192, 3,912).

As a consequence, isolationists rejected Wilson's notion of collective security. Borah understood Wilson's aims correctly, as seeking to combine formerly separate spheres to reach collectively greater gains. However, he wanted them kept separate, just as Lodge did (CR 65:3: 3,912). Isolationists expressed the same seemingly paradoxical position as the conservative internationalists. The League would need more hierarchy in order to prove effective, but this group was as adamantly opposed as the conservatives to providing it. Borah believed that the League needed control over the armed forces of members or it would be "nothing more than an old ladies' international quilting society" (Stone 1970: 51).[18] Yet he complained bitterly of any infringement of American sovereignty.

What distinguished the isolationists from conservative internationalists was their particularized distrust of Europe (Jackson 2006: 57; Monten 2005; Patrick 2009: 3, 20). Whereas the latter felt a kinship with America's wartime allies, the former were the custodians of Washington's farewell address and the Monroe Doctrine (Cooper 2001: 5, 124; Knock 1992: 124; Stone 1970: 41–2). In response to the argument that the international situation was different than that which existed at the time of American independence, Borah responded, "Europe's primary interests are just as distinct in a multitude of the nations of Europe to-day as they were when Washington was upon the earth" (CR 65:3: 195). He complained that if the US joined the League, American foreign policy would not be left "to the judgment and sense of the American people, but to the diplomats of Europe" (CR 65:3: 3,913). Of course, it was not only that European interests were antagonistic to American interests; Europeans were immoral. Invoking and paraphrasing Washington, Borah asked rhetorically, "Are there people in this day who believe that Europe now and in the future shall be free of selfishness, of rivalry, of humor, of ambition, of caprice? . . . Why should we interweave our destiny with the European destiny?" (CR 65:3: 3,912). "European statesmen," according to Joseph France, were dominated by "bigotry, hatred, and intolerance" (Cooper 2001: 217).

Isolationists were concerned about opportunism in general, but they were particularly convinced of European untrustworthiness. The

---

18 Borah asked rhetorically, "If the council has no authority, no power, no
    reserve force until it consults with Congress, what reason have we to believe
    that its authority will preserve peace any more than the actions of Congress
    itself, without any contract binding us?" (Cooper 2001: 227).

League would thrust America "to the very storm center of European politics," according to Borah (Cooper 2001: 19; Lake 1999: 117). He complained "that the Army and the navy of the United States...will be at the command of any plan agreed upon between the Government and the nations of Europe for the protection of the small nations of that country [*sic*]" (Czernin 1964: 410; Stone 1970: 16).[19] Isolationists were most adamant about separating the European and American systems so that neither could or would interfere with the other (Cooper 2001: 61; CR 65:3: 3,912; Stone 1970: 55).

Particularized distrust of Europeans was driven by identity. For isolationists, Europe was the antithesis of the United States – aristocratic, anti-democratic and imperialistic. The Monroe Doctrine was more than a warning to Europeans to remain out of the American sphere of influence; it was a statement of difference between the Old World and the New World. It was the "Republic's bold challenge to this unconscionable conspiracy bent upon the destruction of free governments," explained Borah (CR, 65:3: 195).

Isolationists directed particular ire at Britain, never because of any specific conflict of geopolitical interest but as the quintessential example of an Old World, European state (CR, 65:3: 3,914; Ambrosius 1987: 90). The League would "give back to George V what it took away from George III," lamented Borah (Stone 1970: 83). As Marguiles describes it, isolationists saw Britain as "the world's bastion of aristocracy and imperial domination" (1989: 111). Borah called the League the "greatest triumph for English diplomacy in three centuries" (Knock 1992: 232).

Even while all American politicians paid lip service to American exceptionalism, the isolationists were the great American "exemplarists," those who maintained that America should lead primarily by its unique example (Jackson 2006: 53–7; Monten 2005). Borah promised America would "continue her mission in the cause of peace, of

[19] Borah asked scornfully, "Do you say that you propose that American citizens shall be called into military action at the bidding of a tribunal composed almost entirely of members from Europe and Asia and wholly beyond the selective or elective control of our people?... Are we to have our security determined by the 57 varieties of nations in Europe?" (CR, 65:3: 189, 192). He said Americans were "pledging ourselves, our honor, our sacred lives, to the preservation of the territorial possessions the world over and not leaving it to the judgment and sense of the American people but to the diplomats of Europe" (Lake 1999: 117).

freedom, and of civilization" (Cooper 2001: 265). This explains the otherwise anomalous relationship between their domestic and foreign policy ideas. While the isolationists maintained that the rest of the world, particularly Europe, was wicked and untrustworthy, the United States was different. Therefore, they were not conservative domestically. A general distrust characterized their foreign but not their domestic agenda. They practiced "populist nationalism" (K. A. J. Miller 1999). This handful of politicians was made up of Republican "insurgents" who continually challenged the leadership of the party and regularly crossed party lines to vote with the Democrats' more populist domestic agenda (Cooper 2001: 19). Poole and Rosenthal note that the group was different enough from mainstream conservatives that it briefly defined a second dimension of party politics during this period, a true rarity in the history of American congressional voting (Poole and Rosenthal 2001: 19; 2007: 57).

Like conservative internationalists, isolationists embraced unilateralism. Borah explained, "What we want is... a free, untrammeled Nation, imbued anew and inspired again with the national spirit; not isolation but freedom to do as our own people think wise and just; not isolation but simply the unembarrassed and untentangled freedom of a great Nation to determine for itself and in its own way where duty lies and where wisdom calls" (Stone 1970: 57). Poindexter cautioned, "There is abroad in the land a strange, new doctrine of internationalism, which would surrender the national independence and sovereignty which our fathers fought to establish and preserve" (Stone 1970: 23).

However, isolationists also opposed any American participation in any League of any form. All isolationists were unilateralists, but not all unilateralists were isolationists. As a consequence of their unique distrust of Europe, isolationists believed that irrespective of the voting procedures of the League of Nations, Europeans would dominate it and use it for their nefarious purposes (CR, 65:3: 3,913; Stone 1970: 51, 58). Isolationists attributed to Europeans an almost mythical ability to lead the United States astray. Hiram Johnson referred to the "sordid, cunning, secret and crafty designs of European governments" (Cooper 2001: 100). Therefore the specific design of the League mattered little. It was the very presence of the United States in the League that would do the damage. "Close the doors upon the diplomats of Europe, let them sit in secret, give them the material to trade on, and there always will be unanimous consent," cautioned Borah (Czernin 1964: 408).

Isolationists believed that the League would function as a new Holy Alliance, a dictatorship of great powers repressing democracy across the world (also CR, 65: 2: 11,622–5; 65:3: 87–8, 189; Stone 1970: 42). "And if anything would stir to uncommon activity and fire with unwonted zeal a Richelieu, a Metternich, a Bismarck," Borah claimed, "it would be just such an engine of power as that which is to mold and direct not alone a nation or a single people, but all other nations and all peoples" (CR, 65:3: 191–2). By participating in this new Holy Alliance, the United States would become a European-like power, losing its democratic character and identity. "These distinguishing virtues of a real republic you cannot commingle with discordant and destructive forces of the Old World and still preserve them," Borah argued. "We will in time become inured to its inhuman precepts and its soulless methods, strange as this doctrine now seems to a free people" (Czernin 1964: 411). The League would draw the United States into the "rapacious power of the imperial system of Europe," he warned. "I know that instead of Americanizing Europe, Europe will Europeanize America" (Cooper 2001: 227).[20]

Since the very act of participating threatened to change the United States, isolationists instead advocated maintaining the traditional touchstones of American foreign policy – the Monroe Doctrine and Washington's admonition against entangling alliances. Indeed the two were interdependent. Borah said, "[D]o you think that you can intermeddle in European affairs and never permit Europe to intervene in our affairs? We cannot protect the Monroe doctrine unless we protect the basic principle upon which it rests, and that is the Washington policy" (Czernin 1964: 410). Isolationists also stridently opposed the Knox doctrine as it foresaw involvement in Europe (Cooper 2001: 101; Stone 1970: 110–11). Johnson called it "as obnoxious as the League of Nations itself" (Cooper 2001: 102).

The unique position of the isolationists does indicate the importance of identity in explaining trust relations among nation-states, as constructivists maintain. However, this isolationist group, although it appealed more to the traditions of American foreign policy than any other, was a tiny minority in the Senate and was vastly outnumbered

---

[20] Similarly, Borah claimed, "[I]f we assume the task of effectuating a change, save as in the past by whatever power of precept and example we may exert, we will . . . fall into disintegration and as a Republic die" (Patrick 2009: 23).

among opponents by more traditional conservatives (Cooper 2001: 5).[21] Identity mattered, but only marginally.

A new concert of Europe: British Conservatives and the League

President Wilson's scheme also faced opposition from the right-leaning government in Britain. The Prime Minister, David Lloyd George, was a Liberal but could only govern with support of the Conservatives who formed the majority of the coalition. The war had provoked a serious split in Lloyd George's centrist party, and the Prime Minister could only count on the backing of about a third of Liberals, predominantly their right wing. The rest went into opposition, the most vocal opponents being the party's left-wing Radical faction. Nearly all Conservative leaders held cabinet positions in his government, whereas the most notable Liberals sat on the opposition benches. Even after the war ended, Lloyd George decided to throw his lot in with the Tories and continue the wartime coalition rather than attempt to heal party divisions. In the first election after the cessation of hostilities, he and the Conservative party leader, Bonar Law, co-signed letters of endorsement for the overwhelming majority of Conservative members of parliament and about a third of Liberals. The real effect was to prevent Conservative challengers to Liberals loyal to Lloyd George. Those Liberals receiving the "coupon" ran largely unopposed on their right. As the coalition was enormously popular following the allied victory, the result of the "khaki" election was a parliamentary swing to the right. Lloyd George's choice decimated the party, accelerating its decline as a serious force in British politics (David 1970; T. Wilson 1964).

The Lloyd George government's preference was similar to that of more conservative, and therefore less trusting, internationalist Republicans – to form a concert (Cooper 2001: 51; Egerton 1978: 17; Wolfers 1940: 326). Indeed there was frequent contact between conservative Republicans and British Tories (Cooper 2001: 39). The Prime Minister commented that "if only the leaders of the different nations could meet

---

[21] At most, the isolationists numbered nine, and this includes three more idealistic isolationists – Norris, LaFollette and Gronna – whose reasons for opposition were very different. See n. 26 below.

it would make all the difference in international relations" (Egerton 1978: 105). Lloyd George and Conservatives in the Cabinet were warm to a number of proposals, such as regular system of conferences among the major powers or an agreement to meet whenever a crisis threatened international stability, with smaller powers brought in only when they were directly affected (Egerton 1978: 122).

There was a consensus in the British government for a "negative covenant," a pledge by countries not to resort first to force to settle disputes. However, this did not include any positive obligations to take action in case of aggression except to meet to discuss the situation. Such a concert could be built out of structures that had proved successful in coordinating policy among the allies during the war. The Imperial War Cabinet, which organized the contributions and strategy of the Dominions and colonies, and the Supreme War Council, which brought together representatives of the four major allies, were held up as examples. The concert was seen as a continuation of the alliance after the war, an organization of only a limited number of members – those allies who shared interests and who had proved trustworthy during the war (Egerton 1978: 57, 70, 105, 123). This was the fallback for those who lacked generalized trust.

There were a few advocates in the British government for an organization with more formal procedures, greater obligations and more coercive sanctions, the most important being Sir Robert Cecil, who served in a variety of powerful positions in wartime and postwar governments. Cecil set out his vision for a League in a number of memoranda, which were subsequently reflected in the scheme recommended by the Phillimore Committee. The British began formal planning on this question much earlier than the Americans, and the committee was charged by the government with developing ideas for a postwar international organization. It submitted its report in March 1918.

Under the committee's plan, members of a new organization would pledge not to resort to force before first submitting disputes to either arbitration or a conference of allied states and waiting for a judgment (Miller, 1928: 3–7).[22] In the instance that a state did not submit its dispute before using force, went to war before the appropriate body's

---

[22] Miller (1928) contains the full text of the various draft plans offered by the British and Americans.

deliberations were concluded, or used force against any allied state complying with the judgment of that body, it would be "'ipso facto' at war with all the other Allied States." Members of the organization would then sever all relations of trade and finance with the subjects of the covenant-breaking state, and take the means necessary to restrain the offender, which might include a blockade or even military means (Egerton 1978: 37–8, 65–9, 89, 100). The "Cecil Plan," drafted just prior to the convocation of the Versailles conference, included the same mechanism (Miller 1928: 61–4).

The Phillimore Committee report and the Cecil Plan went further than the arrangement favored by most in the British government. Nevertheless, both attempted to capture the spirit of a concert in a number of ways. The former referred to the organization as one of "allied states." The Cecil Plan went further in this direction. Cecil stressed "that whatever happens peace shall be preserved between members of the Alliance"(Egerton 1978: 67). The League would be governed by a Council of only the five great powers – Britain, the United States, France, Italy and Japan. The organization was merely a system of regular conferences dealing with matters threatening world peace. Smaller members would only participate in a meeting every four years (Ambrosius 1987: 41–3, 55; D. H. Miller 1928: 3–7, 61–5). In short it was low in quantitative multilateralism.

It was also low in qualitative multilateralism. In Cecil's scheme, members were primarily bound by a negative covenant, and even this had significant loopholes. A state was perfectly entitled to use force legally after a judgment was rendered, even if that decision went against it, provided it did not use force against third parties complying with the award. If no decision could be reached, states were also free to pursue whatever remedy they chose. Moreover, members were not obligated to submit their disputes to an international body in the first place, only not to use force before doing so. There was no compulsory dispute resolution, either through arbitration or League Council consideration. Nor was there any generic obligation to preserve the independence or territorial integrity of other members. Obligations to participate in sanctions only emerged when a state violated the relatively loose terms of the negative covenant. Cecil instead put much faith in the "cooling off" period, that by forcing states to the table deals could be struck diplomatically (Ambrosius 1987: 41–3, 55; D. H. Miller 1928: 3–7, 61–5).

Despite these various provisions preserving unilateralism, Cecil's various plans were received coolly by the right-leaning government (Ambrosius 1987: 55; Egerton 1978: 47–8, 89, 104). Conservatives were skeptical of the power of moral obligations and expected abandonment. Lloyd George argued that if the League were to succeed, "it will not be because the nations enter into solemn covenants to guarantee one another's territories, or to go to war with rebellious powers on certain stated conditions, but because it constitutes the machinery by which the nations of the world can remain in continual consultation with one another and through which they can arrive promptly at great decisions for dealing with all international problems as they arise" (Egerton 1978: 122). He dismissed any covenant as mere "paper obligations" (Ikenberry 2001: 146). The Prime Minister predicted that states would not meet their commitments, which would destroy the League entirely (Egerton 1978: 122; Knock 1992: 214). Conservatives only wanted a concert. As negotiations became more specific, a memorandum by a senior civil servant summarized the British consensus: "The function of the Executive Council shall be to secure agreement among all nations in the conduct of international affairs by means of a constant consultation and deliberation together" (Egerton 1978: 124).

I do not devote my attention here to a careful parsing of British Tory ideology or its party platform since the parallels to American conservatives are so obvious. However, I do note that Wolfers believes the conservative position reflected a "pessimistic point of view" among British conservatives that assumed "that man is incapable in the present state of world society of enforcing his ideals ... and must therefore accept the tragedy of international conflict as something beyond the power of nations to terminate" (1940: 228). Conservatives did not want to become entrapped in conflicts not in their interests and did not believe they could count on others to meet their obligations. They "like to think of themselves as realists," in opposition to the utopian ideas of their political opponents (Wolfers 1940: 227).

British Conservatives and right-leaning Liberals consequently exhibited the same seeming paradox as American Republicans, a belief that real collective security required greater hierarchy combined with intense hostility to consenting to it. Sir Eyre Crowe, a senior diplomat in the Foreign Office, doubted states' willingness to agree to and to honor any commitments to arbitrate their disputes or to take coercive action against those who did not: "Arbitrations and conferences have their uses, and serve their limited purposes . . . But it is a necessary and preliminary condition of the proper functioning of general conferences as the guarantors of peace, that the community of nations has effectively organized force for the defence of the right." Yet there was no endorsement of British participation in such a force. The Prime Minister described the memorandum as a "powerfully written document" (Egerton 1978: 41).

Leftist support for Woodrow Wilson's ideas abroad

The Conservative position was not unanimous opinion in Britain. As the social psychological argument expects, the leftist Labour Party and the Radical faction of the Liberals that had gone into opposition were much more receptive to Cecil's schemes and even more enthusiastic about Wilson's (Mayer 1969: 9, 42–4). The American President's conception of a League of Nations facilitated the healing of a division in the Labour Party that had arisen over whether to back Britain's entry into the war, and the party's resolutions made allusions to Wilson's ideas and phrases (Egerton 1978: 54–7; Mayer 1969: 317). Labour ministers, who had a marginal role in the wartime coalition, gave Cecil the most support in the Cabinet. Conservatives offered the least (Egerton 1978: 124). The same was true in parliament as a whole, evident in the responses to questionnaires distributed by the League of Nations Union, a civil society pressure group devoted to creating a League (Egerton 1978: 92). Wilson understood as much: "I hope that I am in effect speaking for liberals . . . in every nation," he said (Mayer 1969: 159).

Scholars attribute Labour's support to its belief in the masses, one that was identical to that of American Democrats. Supporters of the League in Britain, primarily on the left, had an "almost religious faith that the mass of the common people was intensely international-minded and was only waiting for courageous leadership to throw off the restraining influence of reactionary nationalistic governments and vested interests," according to Wolfers (1940: 335). Since the masses were inherently good, international relations would be different if diplomacy were made transparent and the public were put in control. Therefore, if Britain were to lead on the basis of a commitment to a moral obligation to assist others, other nations would follow. Mayer concludes, "Like Woodrow Wilson, Europe's progressives also assumed that the politically emerging masses of workers and peasants were equipped with sufficient reason and rationality to enable them to judge and support an enlightened foreign policy for their nation" (1969: 56).

Nevertheless Labour was a minority in the Cabinet as well as in parliament. Cecil complained privately that it is "only too evident that some of my colleagues do not want this scheme put forward." Of the Prime Minister, he said, "His whole attitude is inconsistent with any belief in the importance of the League, and if that is really his feeling in the matter I doubt very much whether the League can be made a success *as long as this government remains in office*" (Egerton 1978: 161 [emphasis added]). This suggests that Cecil himself believed things would have been different had the government leaned to the left rather than the right.

Since domestic political ideology is an indirect expression of the presence or absence of generalized trust, this largely partisan alignment in the US and the UK over the League speaks for the argument. Generalized trust explains the positions of both American *and* British politicians on the merits of collective security, lending some generalizability to my claims. In both countries more trusting liberals embraced multilateralism while less trusting conservatives adopted the same fallback option, a concert limited in number with no binding obligations either in terms of conflict resolution or a security guarantee. The exception to that pattern, Lord Cecil, found practically no support within his conservative government. And even Cecil's plans were noticeably less radical than Wilson's. Rationalism again cannot explain this variation in party positions. This additional case also undermines Ruggie's (1997) and Patrick's (2009: xxii) claims that collective security and multilateralism were the expression of the unique nature of American civic nationalism with roots in the country's founding ideals. Neither can explain why in his own country Wilson's ideas only found resonance among liberals, and why they did find significant support well beyond American shores.

International negotiations over the League of Nations Covenant: reconciling American and British visions

The conservative British Cabinet would not officially endorse Cecil's plans as the basis for Anglo-American discussion prior to the Versailles peace conference (David 1970; Egerton 1978: 76). Even publicly before parliament, the Secretary of State for War, Winston Churchill, argued that the League was at best a supplement to British security and that Britain could not reduce its armed forces (Egerton 1978: 113). This was a common conservative theme (Wolfers 1940: 322). The British ambassador to the United States was given instructions to talk to Wilson about Cecil's ideas but was also told that this "in no way committed His Majesty's government to any agreement on the subject, or to any definite line of action" (Egerton 1978: 78).

Nevertheless, Cecil had considerable influence, if only because Lloyd George paid little attention to the League question throughout his tenure, focusing instead on winning the war. Cecil was the lead negotiator on the aspects of the peace deal pertaining to the League of Nations. He complained that Lloyd George "did not want to talk about the League of Nations at all in which he takes no real interest" but this afforded Cecil significant room for maneuver (Ambrosius 1987: 66; Egerton 1978: 57, 121; Knock 1992: 214).[23]

As much as Cecil's preferences departed from those of the conservative British Cabinet, there were still major differences between his vision and that of Wilson, and the two sides began work to find a compromise even before the conference began. The President was slow in articulating the specifics of his plan for collective security. His first draft of a League of Nations Covenant came just before the peace conference and was much more qualitatively and quantitatively multilateral than the British. In contrast to Cecil, Wilson foresaw a positive commitment among members to "unite in guaranteeing to each other political independence and territorial integrity." The President was

---

[23] Lloyd George also gave Cecil a wide berth for two other reasons. First, the Prime Minister and other British leaders might have been inclined to compromise because it was more likely to guarantee American participation in any postwar organization, which was in Britain's interest (Egerton 1978: 33; Ikenberry 2001: 143). A Foreign Office memorandum on the postwar situation read, "If America could be persuaded to associate itself to such a League of Nations, a weight and influence might be secured for its decisions that would materially promote the object for which it had been created" (Egerton 1978: 36). Second, Lloyd George knew that Wilson's primary interest at Versailles was creating the League he envisioned, and the prime minister could and did use this as a source of leverage for "the things to which we attached importance," namely the terms on territorial settlement, and arms manufacture that would determine the balance of power (Egerton 1978: 201; Ikenberry 2001: 144).

confident enough that this procedure would provide security that his "Magnolia" draft also asked states to reduce their national armaments and to abolish the private manufacture of armaments.

The President's ideas for the League also came with a much stronger negative covenant and stricter positive obligations to sanction noncompliance. He complained of the British diplomat's scheme: "It has no teeth" (Ambrosius 1987: 44; Knock 1992: 151). In his version, states would be required to submit all disputes between them "of whatever nature, which shall not be satisfactorily settled by diplomacy . . . for arbitration." States would be obligated to cut off economic intercourse with states that refused as well as with those that did not comply with the arbitration body's decision. If a state were to use force, it would face the additional sanction of a total blockade (PWW, vol. 49: 467–71). By making arbitration compulsory, Wilson's notion of the League was much more encompassing as it would have made almost all international disputes matters of concern for the League, not merely those in which force was employed (Knock 1992: 153). Later, in his second draft, Wilson strengthened the sanctions, referring to the potential use of military or naval forces against aggressor states, defined as those who refused to submit their disputes to international conciliation, or used force before or after their case was mediated. The President added a provision allowing the League's Council, its most important branch, to consider disputes as well.

The President's preference for qualitative multilateralism was matched by a commitment to quantitative multilateralism, contrary to rationalist expectations (Miller 1928: 65–93). Wilson bristled at any conception of the League that revived a Concert of Europe. He pushed for a larger community circle. The President imagined that the Council would contain nine members, including four "minor states." And decisions would be based on two thirds of the body's members. There was to be no veto, great-power or otherwise (Ambrosius 1987: 64; Knock 1992: 205).

Cecil in contrast produced a British draft covenant that more resembled a great-power concert (Miller, 1928: 106–16). Membership in a Council was reserved to the five great powers. The plan restated Cecil's favorite sanctioning mechanism, used simply to prevent states from resorting to force before submitting their disputes to mediation. Cecil opposed compulsory arbitration and instructed senior diplomat Eyre Crowe to write a memorandum listing the major points against it. As Crowe was on the record in opposing any form of collective security, Cecil's reliance on him is an indication of the gulf between the trusting American and less trusting British visions for the League. The British consistently opposed any positive guarantee of security against aggression. Although the British draft added a pledge to their negative covenant to "respect the territorial integrity of members of the League and to protect them from foreign aggression," states would simply "undertake" to provide such security (Ambrosius 1987: 64, 73; Egerton 1978: 31, 114–17; Knock 1992: 220). The British proposals were much less binding and inclusive. They were less qualitatively and quantitatively multilateral.

Wilson recognized that American power was not so great as to obviate the need for an ally in the negotiations at Versailles, and he also understood that Cecil's more tepid plans did not even command the support of much of the British Cabinet. The President's close adviser, Colonel House, wrote to advise the President that Cecil "was the only man connected with the British Government who really had the League of Nations at heart" (Egerton 1978: 128). Wilson tasked members of his delegation to harmonize the British and American proposals and develop a unified draft that could serve as the basis of deliberations for the committee composing the covenant of the League at Versailles (Knock 1992: 217). This new version stripped out requirements for mandatory arbitration or any requirement on the League to enforce compliance with arbitral awards or Council recommendations for resolving disputes, essentially reverting to Cecil's initial scheme. Sanctions would apply automatically only when states used force in lieu of first submitting disputes to some sort of international mediation.[24] What became known as the "Cecil–Miller" draft also sided with Cecil's conception of Council membership as a great-power prerogative (Ambrosius 1987: 68–9; D. H. Miller 1928: 131–42). Wilson thought it important enough to draft another version that restored smaller members, one that again included qualified majority voting (Miller 1928: 145–54). However, he abandoned it for fear of alienating a necessary ally (Knock 1992: 217).

---

[24] In addition to securing British agreement, Wilson had concluded, correctly, that the Senate would reject any kind of compulsory arbitration or enforced compliance (Knock 1992: 221).

This common draft served as the basis for beginning negotiations in Paris. However, as the peace conference convened, the British themselves reopened debate on key provisions, attempting to strip out the security guarantee. Cecil proposed an amendment removing the obligation to "preserve as against external aggression" the territorial integrity of members, leaving only an obligation to "respect" it, converting the positive guarantee to a negative one (Ambrosius 1987: 73; Egerton 1978: 116–17). Wilson's compromise formula, adopted by the committee, was that the guarantee to "respect and preserve as against external aggression the territorial integrity and existing political independence of all Members of the League" would remain but that "in case of any such aggression, the Executive Council shall advise the plan and the means by which this obligation shall be fulfilled." This restored a degree of discretion that preserved more sovereignty, especially after negotiators, in contrast to Wilson's initial plans, adopted a unanimity rule for the Council (Ambrosius 1987: 113–15; Egerton 1978: 131; Knock 1992: 220). It also, not incidentally, squared the guarantee with the American constitution. But the first line nevertheless indicated that members were under some moral obligation to take some steps to protect other states. Sovereignty was not complete. Wilson won his most important battle.

However, the British lost when it came to the Council's composition. When smaller members of the committee noted the exclusiveness of the Anglo-American draft, they were outraged. The Belgian foreign minister, Paul Hymans, accused Cecil of creating "nothing else than the Holy Alliance" (Egerton 1978: 130; Knock 1992: 218). The British were outnumbered by all of the smaller countries and even Italy and France. Cecil was mindful of potential objections from his Cabinet but conceded (Egerton 1978: 131). The committee settled on Wilson's earlier formula, restoring more quantitative multilateralism. The President recounted that he concealed his glee to preserve good relations with the British (Knock 1992: 218–19).

During the multilateral negotiations, Wilson was explicit, both privately and publicly, on the role that trust would play in the organization. He assured fellow negotiators that a moral obligation would suffice:

It must not be supposed that any of the members of the League will remain isolated if it is attacked, that is the direct contrary of the thought of all of us.

We are ready to fly to the assistance of those who are attacked ... The only method by which we can achieve [peace] lies in our having confidence in the good faith of the nations who belong to the League. When danger comes, we too will come, and we will help you, but you must trust us. (Czernin 1964: 102; Knock 1992: 222)

As he placed the newly drafted covenant before delegates in Paris, he declared that "people that were suspicious of one another can now live as friends and comrades in a single family, and desire to do so. The miasma of distrust, intrigue, is cleared away. Men are looking eye to eye and saying, 'We are brothers and have a common purpose. We did not realize it before, but now we do realize it, and this is our covenant of fraternity and friendship'" (Stone 1970: 53–4).

In the final document, the Council consisted of five permanent members, the "principal allied powers," as well as four other members selected periodically by an Assembly. The Council would make decisions on the basis of unanimity, with parties to a dispute forced to abstain. States were obligated to submit their disputes to arbitration, judicial settlement if justicable, or Council consideration, and were obligated not to resort to war until three months after conclusion of those proceedings. Members pledged to sever all commercial ties with states who used force prior to submission or before the "cooling off" period. The League would "undertake to respect and preserve as against external aggression the territorial integrity and existing political independence" of all members, Wilson's moral obligation, but the Council would have to decide unanimously on the specific actions to be taken.

"Irreconcilable" differences: the domestic politics of ratification in the United States

The Republican reservations

After the delegates to the peace conference completed their first draft of the Covenant, Wilson returned home to the United States to take the pulse of political opinion, most importantly that of Congress. He needed the support of two thirds of senators to ratify the Covenant, which was to be attached to the peace treaty indicating the terms of the postwar settlement to be negotiated in the peace conference's second session. Republicans did not receive the document well. It was at this time that Lodge raised what would become the four major points of debate. In a speech before the Senate, he demanded four interpretative reservations be attached to the final version of the Covenant: a right of withdrawal; an exemption from League consideration of matters considered by the US to be of solely domestic jurisdiction, in particular sensitive questions such as immigration and tariffs; an exemption from the League's jurisdiction in matters covered by the Monroe Doctrine; and a disavowal of any obligation under the League's collective security guarantee (Ambrosius 1987: 75; CR, 65:3: 4,521–7; Knock 1992: 240–41). Lodge spoke for the other conservative internationalists in the party (Ambrosius 1987: 97, 103–4; Cooper 2001: 72, 79; Knock 1992: 243; Stone 1970: 87).

These reservations were aimed at eliminating any risk of opportunism by releasing the United States from multilateral obligations. By freeing the United States of a commitment to submit many matters of vital interest to the dispute resolution procedures of the League, an exemption for the Monroe Doctrine would prevent exploitation of the United States by countries outside the western hemisphere who might use their vote to undermine American interests in regional disputes. Disavowing any American pre-commitment to the security of member states removed the threat of entrapment. Withdrawal provided a further layer of protection by allowing the United States to exit at any point in time. And a restriction of the League's jurisdiction solely to international questions demonstrated the common denominator of conservative objections – a desire to maintain untrammeled American sovereignty given the potential for opportunism by other states. All reservations were designed to ensure unilateralism for the United States in an otherwise relatively qualitatively multilateral institution.

The first two reservations amounted to a preservation of two geographic spheres of influence, as Monroe and Washington had long cautioned, although with one critical difference – the United States would be a permanent member of the League's council. They eliminated Wilson's notion of combining forces so as to mobilize collectively against aggression. The changes requested by conservative internationalists, if made, would have meant that at least for the United States, membership in the League would have effectively amounted to participation in a great-power concert. The United States would have a seat at the great-power table by virtue of its participation in the League

Council but with very few obligations. Republican changes would have converted the League into what they always wanted it to be. Lodge wrote to Root: "If we can take the United States out by reservations my purposes are fulfilled" (Cooper 2001: 114). Conservative internationalists preferred reservations, as opposed to amendments, as the latter would require a renegotiation of the peace treaty and might endanger the creation of the League in this reduced form.

Isolationists opposed reservations to the treaty since they would not be enough to prevent American participation in a concert of great powers. Even with these protections, Borah stated in a private letter: "I am opposed to any league of nations. With me it is not a question of amendments of any kind... It is a deliberate attempt to sell our country to the domination of foreign powers. If my country is to be sold, I am not interested in the details of the bill of sale" (Ambrosius 1987: 139; Cooper 2001: 114; Stone 1970: 114). In isolationist eyes, even with institutional protections America would lose control of its foreign policy (and lose itself) in the League of Nations. Isolationists agreed to vote with conservative internationalists on reservations and amendments to the Covenant in an effort to weaken it but stated from the beginning of the ratification process that they would ultimately vote against any treaty in which the United States would join the organization, regardless of the type of modifications (Margulies 1989: 27; Stone 1970: 141).

Even without the isolationists, conservative internationalists amounted to a force easily capable of preventing the ratification of the covenant, a fact that became clear with the publication of a round-robin letter just as Wilson was returning to Europe. Lodge, Brandegee and Knox collaborated in gaining thirty-nine signatures from senators to a document declaring that the League could not be accepted in the form now proposed (Ambrosius 1987: 96; Knock 1992: 241). This was more than enough to torpedo the League in the Senate. Gilbert Hitchcock, the Democratic majority leader, urged Wilson to secure the four changes identified as essential by Lodge when the President returned to Paris (Ambrosius 1987: 97; Cooper 2001: 71; Egerton 1978: 148; Stone 1970: 73–4).

Wilson pursued three of these items in Paris with some degree of success, although the President had to offer side payments on issues of the postwar settlement in return. Withdrawal was allowed for a member after two years' notice, "provided that all international obligations and all its obligations under this Covenant shall have been fulfilled at the time of its withdrawal." The Monroe Doctrine was given sanction but not as a unilateral American doctrine. The new constitution of the League stated: "Nothing in this Covenant shall be deemed to affect the validity of international engagements, such as treaties of arbitration or regional understandings like the Monroe doctrine, for securing the maintenance of peace." Finally, disputes over domestic matters were exempt from League consideration provided that one of the parties identified an issue as such and the Council agreed (Ambrosius 1987: 115–18; Cooper 2001: 86; Knock 1992: 247–8).

Wilson would not, however, countenance any changes to Article X, or even Article XVI on economic sanctions, in cases of a resort to war before mediation. Wilson would continually stress that the guarantee was the "heart of the covenant," without which the League would merely be an "influential debating society" (Cooper 2001: 118, 142; Knock 1992: 261). It was the difference between a concert and collective security. Wilson told Hitchcock privately, "Without it, the Covenant would mean nothing. If the Senate will not accept that, it will have to reject the whole treaty" (Ambrosius 1987: 142).

Conservatives were dissatisfied with the amendments that Wilson secured, and even more so with his unwillingness to consider any modification of Article X. The three changes shared a common defect – they implied that others had some say in determining their use or meaning. These provisions restoring the exercise of unilateralism were not unilateral enough because they still placed American interests in the hands of others. Republicans argued that the Monroe Doctrine was not a "regional understanding" but rather, as Knox explained, "merely a policy . . . Its precise character, the extent, method, and time of its application, all are matters of our high and uncontrolled will and sovereign prerogative" (Stone 1970: 112). Lodge asserted that the doctrine was a "purely American policy" with the United States serving as "sole judge of what it means" (Cooper 2001: 135). They also maintained that the United States must have unhampered ability to withdraw from the League of Nations by deciding itself whether it had met its League obligations. Similarly, it was also up to the United States to determine itself what constituted domestic matters, with no involvement of the League Council. Immigration and tariffs were "purely American questions" (Ambrosius 1987: 148; Cooper 2001: 135).

Republicans vowed to add reservations to the instrument of ratification to safeguard properly American sovereignty on these three issues,
as well as the security guarantee. Former Republican presidential candidate Charles Evan Hughes, Republican national party chairman Will
Hays and Root all considered these the four most important issues
(Cooper 2001: 197; Margulies 1989: 26; Stone 1970: 113). Following
the legislative elections of 1918 that gave the Republicans a majority
of two in the Senate, Lodge took over as both majority leader and
chairman of the Foreign Relations Committee. He proceeded to stack
the committee with inveterate opponents of the League, including isolationists like Hiram Johnson as well as staunch conservatives such as
Republicans Moses of New Hampshire, New of Indiana and Harding
of Ohio, passing over Republican moderates and "mild reservationists" such as Kellogg. Given that Borah and other opponents were
already on the committee, there were six "irreconcilables" in the body
that would consider reservations and amendments to the treaty before
it came before the full Senate (Ambrosius 1987: 138; Margulies 1989:
31; Stone 1970: 97–8). "Irreconcilables" was the moniker associated
with the staunchest League detractors.

Lodge set to work on drafting specific reservations. To protect
against entrapment, the majority leader said he wanted a reservation
that made it "perfectly clear that no American soldiers, not even a
corporal's guard, that no American sailors, not even the crew of a
submarine, can ever be ordered anywhere except by the constitutional
authorities of the United States" (Cooper 2001: 135). His first version
of the exception to Articles X and XVI stated that:

The United States *decline to assume, under the provisions of article 10, or
under any other article, any obligation to preserve the territorial integrity or
political independence of any other country*, or to interfere in controversies
between other nations, members of the league or not, or to employ the
military or naval forces of the United States in such controversies, or to
adopt economic measures for the protection of any other country, whether a
member of the league or not, against external aggression or for the purpose
of intervention in the internal conflicts or other controversies which may
arise in any other ... *except by action of the Congress of the United States.*
(Cooper 2001: 166; Margulies 1989: 85 [emphasis added])

The position was one of default non-observance with both Article
X and Article XVI on the use of economic sanctions. Although a

subsequent modification, designed to gain the support of more moderately conservative members of the party whose position resembled that of Cecil, removed the reference to American non-participation in economic sanctions, the construction otherwise stood (Cooper 2001: 194; Margulies 1989: 103–4).

With voting falling along ideological lines, the Senate Foreign Relations committee approved this and a number of reservations to the Covenant, the most important of which were the four that Lodge had proposed before the treaty negotiations were completed (Ambrosius 1987: 173; Cooper 2001: 166, 226; Margulies 1989: 78). The reservation pertaining to the Monroe Doctrine proclaimed that the "United States will not submit to arbitration or to inquiry by the assembly or by the council of the league of nations, provided for in said treaty of peace, any questions which in the judgment of the United States depend upon or relate to its long-established policy commonly known as the Monroe doctrine; said doctrine is to be interpreted by the United States alone" (CR 66:1: 5,114).

The United States also reserved "to itself exclusively the right to decide what questions are within its domestic jurisdiction, and declares that all domestic and political questions relating wholly or in part to its internal affairs ... are solely within the jurisdiction of the United States and are not under this treaty to be submitted in any way either to arbitration or to the consideration of the council or of the assembly of the league of nations" (CR 66:1: 5,114). The reservation specifically mentioned immigration, labor, tariffs and a number of other issues. On withdrawal, the final reservation read: "The United States shall be sole judge as to whether all its international obligations under the said covenant have been fulfilled" (CR 66:1: 5,113).

The failure to compromise

Lodge's program of reservations had almost the complete support of the Republicans in the Senate, even if isolationists vowed to eventually vote against the treaty in any form. Lodge wrote to Root early in the League fight to inform him that perhaps all but two Republicans would support the four reservations they both sought (Ambrosius 1987: 150–3; Cooper 2001: 114). With Republicans so firmly behind Lodge, the onus was on the Democrats to compromise. However, Wilson and the Democrats were intransigent. Wilson continually urged

Democratic senators to resist any compromise that meant reservations. While the Democrats did not have two-thirds support in the Senate for a treaty without reservations, the Lodge Republicans could not muster a supermajority for their reservation program either, provided that Democrats held firm. Therefore, Wilson proposed that the Democrats let both versions of the treaty fail in the Senate, at which time he hypothesized that the pressure would mount on those "mild reservationists" in the Republican Party who preferred a compromise over no American membership in the League of Nations at all (Cooper 2001: 215, 250; Margulies 1989: 128). Meanwhile, in keeping with his faith in the masses, Wilson set out on a cross-country speaking tour, convinced that he could appeal over the heads of senators directly to their constituents and create a groundswell of support from the grassroots up. The President's gambit failed, however, and the strain contributed to a debilitating stroke.

A common refrain in the history of the League is its tragic quality, that the absence of the United States during the crises of the 1930s was avoidable given that more than two thirds of the Senate believed in US membership in some sort of League. Most cite Wilson's stubbornness, particularly over Article X, as the reason for the failure. Ikenberry writes, "The Lodge reservation deflated the moral authority that Wilson could wield after the war in the building of the League of Nations, but it did not necessarily alter the underlying terms of America's membership in the League . . . Lodge's reservations were politically objectionable to Wilson, but they were not a fundamental revision of the treaty" (2001: 154). Cooper laments that Wilson did not seize the opportunity at this point to compromise with the "mild reservationists" and secure an American place in the League, even if it came with limitations (Cooper 2001: 147–9). Wilson instead set out on an inflexible course.

Ideologically, however, the two sides were too far apart, as Knock notes (1992: 264). For Wilson and the Democrats, a revision of the collective security guarantee in particular fundamentally changed the nature of the organization. The President believed that a disavowal of Article X would amount to "nullification" (Cooper 2001: 260). Wilson saw the reservation as undermining the assurance on which his conception of collective security was based, and that he, as a generalized truster, was willing to make: "That we should make no general promise, but leave the nations associated with us to guess in each instance what we were going to consider ourselves bound to do, and what we were not going to consider ourselves bound to do" (Cooper 2001: 185). Any compromise with the Republicans would have meant a League that was, for the United States at least, essentially a concert, and Wilson could not come to terms with that.

The position of conservative internationalists was similarly deeply held. Lodge wrote privately to Borah, "We have votes that kill the treaty if proper reservations are not put on – I mean the real thing, such as you and I believe in" (Margulies 1989: 55). He promised, "I mean to kill Article X or kill the treaty" (Cooper 2001: 166). Borah noted privately that he believed that Lodge was as opposed to the League as he was (Stone 1970: 9).

Democrats placed their hopes in a deal with "mild reservationists," those senators who preferred some treaty to no treaty at all. This group was crucial in blocking any attempt by Lodge to amend the treaty, which would have reopened negotiations, something tantamount to sinking the League entirely (Cooper 2001: 147; Margulies 1989: 166–8). Not surprisingly they were domestically more moderate, and therefore more trusting, than their conservative counterparts in their party. The senators identified as mild reservationists by Marguiles in the most comprehensive study of this group had average NOMINATE scores that were almost a half of a standard deviation from the Republican Party's average and almost three quarters of a standard deviation if one removes the party's populist and progressive isolationists.

However, even the mild reservationists were not terribly mild. Substantively they were in agreement with Lodge's program of reservations (Margulies 1989: 62–3). Indeed they were co-authors of all of them (Margulies 1989: 96–101). The true test of the moderation of the mild reservationists of course was in the voting. Cooper has compiled a table of the percentage of votes in which individual senators sided with the Wilson administration's position (2001: 237). The data includes 90 roll calls, including amendments and reservations, all of which aimed at weakening the treaty. All of Lodge's four reservations garnered more than 50 votes, with almost total Republican support. Even Senator McCumber, the most softline of the Republicans, voted for the administration only two thirds of the time. After him, the most willing to compromise was Nelson, who voted with Wilson only 49 percent of the time. Overall, mild reservationists voted against Wilson's conception of the League 63 percent of the time. Democrats in contrast voted for the League as Wilson preferred it over 90 percent of the time. There was probably not any compromise that would have garnered two thirds of the votes in the Senate (Cooper 2001: 225; Margulies 1989: 65).

The final vote on the treaty with all of its reservations failed with 55 supporting and 39 against. Four of the most conservative Democrats defected to the Republican side and isolationists joined in opposition as they opposed a League of any kind.[25] A subsequent vote on the treaty as brought home from Wilson from Paris without reservations failed on a vote of 38 to 53. Of the supporting votes, 37 were from Democrats. The isolationists joined this time with conservatives in opposition. However, they numbered fewer than ten and were hardly decisive. The Covenant did not die an immediate death, but bipartisan efforts to forge a centrist compromise did not bear fruit (Cooper 2001: 305; Stone 1970: 153–8). The sticking point continued to be Article X. Moderate Republicans and Democrats considered the idea of a reservation that neither affirmed nor denied the obligation but rather would let Congress decide. However, this position could not muster enough support on either side to reach two thirds. As Lodge recalled, the issue was whether there would be some sort of obligation. The Democrats "went pretty far in offering exceptions to the obligation but they kept the obligation alive," he said (Cooper 2001: 308).

As discussed in Chapter 1, we can use NOMINATE ideology scores as an indirect proxy measure for generalized trust. The statistical correlation between this variable and the percentage of times in which a given senator voted with the administration is 0.83. If we remove the few isolationists, the result is 0.88. One might attribute this simply to party loyalty. However, there are strong associations between the two variables even if we break the data down by party. Within the Democratic Party, the correlation is still 0.42. In the Republicans, it is only 0.18, but this jumps to 0.49 if the handful of "insurgent" isolationists are removed. Even Lake attributes these partisan divisions to genuine ideological differences: "Parties were not just fighting, they were fighting over issues that they, at least, deemed important to the future of American foreign policy" (Cooper 2001: 1; Lake 1999: 93).

These numbers, and a correct reading of the history, also undermine Legro's (2005) claim that Wilson's failure lay in his inability to

---

[25] These Democrats were Gore, Shields, Smith and Walsh.

bring along the progressive constituencies in his party. He argues that the lessons of WWI undermined the premises of traditional isolationism, but that the early postwar experience, most notably the shameful peace settlement, convinced idealists that Wilson's new internationalism was a sham. The result was a reversion to isolation. While this might explain the disillusion that crept into the progressive ranks during the 1920s, it cannot account for the failure of the League in 1919 (Osgood 1953). There were only three senators in the entire Senate who voted against the League because of the faulty peace, all Republicans.[26] Democratic progressives held firm. The defeat of the League Covenant owed to the inability of liberals and conservatives, with their very different levels of generalized trust, to come to an agreement.

Alternative arguments: political economy and the institutional balance of power

Democrats and Republicans might have endorsed different visions for postwar order based on the unique economic nature of their constituencies' interests. The analysis up to this point is premised on the idea that both parties were primarily thinking of the national interest. However, the shape of the postwar system might have had distributional implications within the country. Narizny (2007) argues that given the contrasting profiles of the economic interests that American parties represented, they had very different preferences for grand strategy. He claims that Democrats favored the creation of a cooperative,

[26] They were Gronna, LaFollette and Norris, all more idealistic and cosmopolitan progressives. They ranked as three of the five most liberal Republican senators. Their issues were less with the League than with the peace settlement it was called to uphold, which they believed demonstrated that the evils of power politics and imperialism had not been eradicated. These senators were also American exemplarists but had more of a humanitarian streak and were more genuinely interested in the fate of other countries. They opposed the fact that the League relied on military means to ensure peace. They leaned towards pacifism, having been the only senators never to embrace American participation in the war. They called for the abolition of the draft, a world legislature, restrictions on the production of arms, and an end to secret diplomacy. The Republicans generally shunned them, as a consequence, except when it was not politically expedient, and sometimes even then. For instance, they were not even invited to sign the round-robin letter opposing collective security. Norris and LaFollette eventually left the party (Cooper 2001: 8, 13–14, 21, 95–97, 125–7, 219, 244; Knock 1992: 253 257; Stone 1970: 3–10, 13–14, 18, 30–1, 48–9, 85, 119–20, 135–140).

law-based, internationalist system in security because they represented Southern agricultural producers who exported large amounts of cotton and tobacco to Europe. More than Republicans, Democrats had an interest in maintaining peaceful relations with the great powers so as to minimize the political and military conflict that would disrupt trade ties with these important export markets. Republican constituencies, predominantly northeastern manufacturing, were largely shut out of Europe, and therefore the party embraced a more unilateral and coercive grand strategy (Narizny 2007: 39–55). Although Narizny applies the argument more broadly, he explicitly claims that it could explain the pattern of support for the League (Narizny 2007: 139–41).

Narizny's argument has a number of logical and empirical problems. First, Narizny argues that midwestern farming interests were extremely reliant on European markets and therefore supportive of a more cooperative international order. However, politicians from these areas had largely unilateralist or even isolationist preferences during the League fight, as we have seen. This is because the Midwest was solidly Republican, conservative, and therefore less trusting (Cooper 2001: 58; Rieselbach 1966: 107). And Republican populists such as Borah from farming states in the Great Plains detested Europe, despite their constituencies' interests, and wanted no institution at all. In support of his argument Narizny mentions those more idealistic midwestern peace progressives of both parties such as William Jennings Bryan, Gronna and Norris, but they also opposed the League (2007: 66). Some sort of American security arrangement with Europe, whether it be a concert or a small alliance, attracted much more support from conservative internationalist Republicans who largely represented the northeast manufacturing core of the United States. Yet they had little to gain in terms of political economy. In short, those factions of the Republican Party who should have supported a security commitment to Europe didn't, and those that shouldn't have, did.

The argument does not stand up when applied to Democratic preferences either. Wilson's interest in the League, as we have seen, was not to create a system of managing conflicts between great powers, but rather a global system of collective security. Had he been driven by political economic motives, he would have tailored his vision to Europe. In actuality, only the conservative internationalists did.

A reading of the historical record reveals that key business constituencies had an interest in bringing about a resolution of the League issue as soon as possible, but they had no particular preference as to the precise design. It was only after the extended delay resulting from the inability to bridge the chasm between unilateralists and multilateralists that business became involved, although there is no evidence that they had any real influence (Margulies 1989: 128). Banks, agricultural interests and manufacturers all grew exasperated at the inability of the government to ratify some peace treaty that would allow them to return to business as usual (Margulies 1989: 45, 64). All were lobbying Wilson, as well as Republicans, furiously, as private letters show (PWW, vol. 61: 526). The Treasury Department put pressure on Wilson to resolve the issue, as until the uncertainty was resolved, private banks were reluctant to make any loans to war-torn Europe, which would in turn be used to buy American machinery, food and agricultural products, (PWW, vol. 62: 266–7). The President drew the particular ire of the constituency to whom Narizny argues he should have been the most subservient – Southern cotton growers. As long as the United States was technically at war, there were numerous export embargoes that cut off cotton exports to the markets of enemies and neutrals (PWW, vol. 53: 78–89; vol. 55: 297; vol. 57, 511–12). Cotton manufacturers cared far more about lifting these wartime restrictions than the form the League took, or whether it was created at all. They stressed that if the League as Wilson envisioned it were defeated, they should "promptly" look for a deal based on mild reservations (PWW, vol. 63: 266).

Wilson decided to use this as leverage against the cotton interests (Margulies 1989: 45, 64). Rather than the economic constituencies of the Democrats driving security policy, as Narizny expects, Wilson used political economic interests to forge a coalition in favor of his ideological goals. An adviser to the President noted that "the fact that the market for about three million bales of cotton will continue to be closed until the treaty is ratified affords a lever that should be utilized. Steps can be taken without knowledge of where the motif emanates to start the movement on this issue" (PWW, vol. 63: 266). In order to bring them in line, the administration stressed to cotton growers directly that Europe could not buy cotton until they secured American credit, credit from private borrowers "cannot be arranged until the Peace Treaty is ratified and the League of Nations becomes a fact" as the situation was too uncertain for them, and the US government was not going to loan any more money to allies to buy cotton as they had during the war as a stopgap measure. "We hope for good results from this," the President's aide wrote cheerfully (PWW, vol. 63: 442–3).

The last argument stressing domestic politics centers not on the issue of ideological differences but domestic institutional prerogatives. The Article X reservation disavowed any obligation to comply with the League's moral obligation to guarantee political independence and territorial integrity unless Congress decided otherwise, leading some to conclude that the Republicans were defending the legislature's authority to declare war (Cooper 2001: 6). Of course, this could have been done without attaching this provision to a policy of default non-intervention. Protectors of the constitution could have simply required congressional approval in every case. And the Republicans were the party of strong central government and executive privilege, set out against the Jeffersonian defenders of states' rights and the separation of powers in the Democratic Party (Gerring 1998). Republican efforts to link the question of congressional authority to the League were disingenuous, something which Republicans themselves admitted privately (Margulies 1989: 104). Even if we were to grant that Republicans were genuinely concerned about congressional rights, this cannot explain their position on withdrawal and the Monroe Doctrine, which had nothing to do with legislative prerogatives. And we cannot account for why there was not a cross-party consensus in opposition to the President that included Democratic senators as well, since all legislators had an institutional interest in maintaining congressional influence over foreign policy (Lake and Powell 1999: 114).

From the League of Nations to the United Nations

It is tempting to conclude that passing the League Covenant was a pipe dream, that even if there were some generalized trusters, they were small in number. In this interpretation, Wilson was an anomaly, a dreamer, and the distribution of realists is always more than that of idealists. However, the votes in the Senate suggest that the two forces were roughly equally matched. As Ikenberry notes, Wilson's vision attracted even (perhaps, especially) the enthusiastic support of center-left and progressive forces across the world (2001: 119). The failure of the Covenant as drafted owes to the peculiarity of the American constitution that requires two thirds of senators to assent to any treaty.

A realist might counter that regardless of whether the United States joined the League, it is no matter; the organization could never have prevented the rise of Nazi Germany. This is likely true, but any institution would have had difficulty restraining perhaps the most militaristic and aggressive regime in history. This is not a fair counterfactual test. The example in the minds of Wilson and his allies was WWI, the war that no one wanted, a strategic situation for which the League might have been well suited. Nevertheless, one might still argue that the League would have fared far better had its deterrent effect, however limited, contained a moral obligation to defend the status quo by the tremendously powerful United States. After WWII, the heirs of Wilson took this as an article of faith, and it drove them to create the United Nations. They had more success, but only because they learned from Wilson's mistakes about how to handle domestic politics. They had to square the circle between their vision and that of less trusting conservatives. That is the story of the next chapter.

4 | Squaring the circle: the birth of the United Nations

The United Nations is often seen as the inevitable by-product of the failure of both isolationism and idealism. In the conventional account, both Democrats and Republicans realized after Pearl Harbor that the United States could no longer remain aloof from world affairs and needed to commit to postwar international cooperation to lay the foundations of a stable peace. However, at the same time the League had been powerless to stop aggression in the 1930s. A more realistic view of international organizations was necessary, and President Roosevelt was not the idealist that Wilson was. The United Nations was therefore based on the realities of power politics, preserving a special role for the great powers and eschewing any generic commitment to territorial integrity as the League had in Article X. FDR advocated for a United Nations based on the continuation of the wartime alliance of the same name, in which the great powers would serve as "four policeman" enforcing the postwar peace.

In certain respects, this standard account is correct (Legro 2005; Patrick 2009). Isolationism as an ideology, the belief that the United States could avoid political engagement with other great powers, particularly malevolent European ones, was weakened (although not destroyed) by the war. Pure geographical isolation was impossible, and the prostrate Europeans were hardly dangerous rivals of the United States after 1945. However, as seen in Chapter 3, isolationism was not a significant force even in 1919. Conservative internationalists, predominantly in the Republican Party, continued to have objections to any form of international cooperation that required any significant transfer of American sovereignty. Again their competitive social orientation forbade them from surrendering any discretion over American foreign policy for fear of entrapment and exploitation. Conservatives again preferred a kind of concert for great-power consultation without any significant limitations on American discretion. Those who lacked generalized trust exhibited the same seeming paradox as the conservative internationalists of the interwar years. They were systematically more concerned about opportunism, but they opposed the creation of some sort of international hierarchy, either an international police force or elements of a world government, to prevent it. Dissenting voices from the liberal side of the Republican Party were completely marginalized. Indeed they often struggled to have the party officially endorse the creation of an international organization at all.

The war had shaken the more idealistic and trusting Democrats. References to the benign nature of humankind were almost unheard of in light of Hitler's transgressions. A common refrain was that the new organization needed greater teeth to better deter future aggressors (Hilderbrand 1990: 122; Russell 1958: 209). However, generalized trust was much more resilient than most accounts allow. FDR's objections notwithstanding, the Democrats were still far more optimistic than Republicans, a consequence of their more trusting, cooperative social orientation. And FDR, unlike Wilson, largely delegated planning for the "new League" to more idealistic State Department officials. They embedded his "four policeman" concept in an institutional framework that showed remarkable similarities to the League, including a binding collective security commitment to act against aggression. These avowed Wilsonians even considered an organization without an American veto to prevent against exploitation. They successfully modified the President's scheme to allow for a more inclusive, quantitatively multilateral institution. And generalized trust served as a source of social capital that allowed them to consider elements of international hierarchy in light of the recent failure of moral obligations.

Therefore the divisions over foreign policy seen in American domestic politics after WWI reasserted themselves after WWII. Although generally recognized as a watershed, the war had changed little in terms of domestic political alignments on international cooperation, something that confounds both structural and ideational accounts of American foreign policy (Lake 1999; Legro 2005). And again rationalism cannot explain different propensities to cooperate in the same structural circumstances. The real lesson of the League for Roosevelt and his colleagues was the need to solicit Republican input and to modify their plans to ensure conservative support early on, so as to avoid a repetition of the pitched battle of 1919 over ratification.

Administration officials perhaps devoted more effort negotiating the UN Charter with Republicans in the Senate than with the Soviets and the British. Anticipating Republican criticism, the Democrats instituted perhaps the most familiar features of the United Nations, the great-power veto, and removed a security guarantee, opting instead for an arrangement in which the Security Council would assess each potential or actual conflict on a case-by-case basis with no commitment in advance on how to respond. This meant that when the UN Charter eventually reached the Senate, it passed almost unanimously. The result was a great-power concert embedded in the formal trappings of a more universal security organization, the United Nations as we still know it today.[1]

Therefore, the overwhelming cross-party support for the UN in the American Senate does not indicate the inevitability of international cooperation after the war or an absence of ideological differences. Rather it reflects the fact that the executive branch's proposals incorporated potential Republican objections in advance. Even Jeffrey Legro (2005), who claims that the post-WWII period was marked by a new cultural consensus on international engagement, notes that this was a coalition of two distinct types of "internationalists."

Those provisions inserted to assuage Republican concerns, particularly the great-power veto, created dilemmas for postwar planners. While Democrats recognized the veto's necessity for gaining bipartisan support, they were reluctant to allow permanent members of the Security Council to apply it in cases in which they themselves were party to a dispute, the so-called "absolute veto." Even though a more qualitatively multilateral arrangement might encumber the United States in particular instances, it would lead to collectively more optimal outcomes over the long run. They had faith in diffuse reciprocity.

It is of course possible to view this concern about the absolute veto as an expression of strategic distrust of the Soviet Union. Rationalists might argue Americans were forecasting the likely alignment of voting patterns after the war and attempting to isolate the Soviet Union by denying it this power of obstruction. However, the discussions

---

[1] Campbell writes that the UN amounted to "allied power politics with a Wilsonian coating" (1973a: 2; US Senate 1973: 330). The British diplomat Webster wrote of "harmonizing the Great Power Alliance theory and the League theory," noting that ultimately the "Charter . . . is an Alliance of the Great Powers embedded in a universal organization" (Jebb 1990: 36).

within the State Department were framed around the general problem of how to create an organization more capable of acting quickly and decisively. It was only in the last year of the war that strategic distrust of the Soviet Union arose as a consequence of concerns about Russian designs in Eastern Europe and the Soviets' very insistence on preserving the absolute veto. However, this merely reinforced the preexisting tendency of most in the State Department towards a more qualitatively multilateral institution.

Even though conservatives were more strategically distrustful of the Soviet Union, their lack of generalized trust meant that they were not willing to pay the price of relinquishing the absolute veto for the United States. As a compromise to ensure both international agreement and domestic ratification in the United States, the Roosevelt administration settled on a separation of peaceful settlement and enforcement issues in the Charter, in which the great powers, when party to a dispute, would surrender their veto in the former instances but not the latter.

The great-power veto also threatened effectively to undermine quantitative multilateralism. The Roosevelt administration was insistent on a powerful universal organization that could more effectively mobilize global power against breaches to the peace. Regional security organizations were to be subservient to the United Nations so as to prevent an American return to isolationism and the creation of spheres of influence. Therefore, in the Roosevelt administration's conception of the UN, all peace enforcement actions by smaller organizations required Security Council approval. However, as the Cold War began to brew, concern grew that the Soviet Union might use its veto to block American or regional efforts to restore peace in instances of communist aggression in the western hemisphere, thus undermining the Monroe Doctrine. As they had during the League fight, conservatives insisted on an explicit exemption for the Latin American area, but Democrats resisted. The ingenious solution was Article 51, which preserved the authority of the UN but permitted collective action for self-defense in the case of Security Council deadlock.

The administration's key allies in this process were the British, who themselves converged on the same design for the international organization, albeit along a different path. Unlike the Wilsonians in the State Department, the Conservative-dominated wartime coalition always preferred a great-power concert that would preserve the wartime alliance, subjugate its former enemies, preserve great-power unity, and act as a trustee on behalf of the international community. As they had after WWI, the Conservatives explicitly disavowed collective security, focusing instead on the international organization's role in allowing for conference diplomacy. The Labour and Liberal parties had more multilateral preferences. A review of the domestic politics of international cooperation in the United Kingdom bolsters the generalizability of the social psychological argument. However, this conservative scheme was diluted, not by the need to gain bipartisan support, but by the political necessity of carrying the Dominions. These former colonies wanted a more qualitatively and quantitatively multilateral organization that protected against the abuse of great powers by including more smaller countries in the Security Council and limiting the special prerogatives of its permanent members.

The story of the creation of the United Nations is one of squaring circles. The State Department had to reconcile its multilateral vision with FDR's "four policemen" formula. The Democratic administration had to ensure the support of more unilateral Republicans in the Senate. Republicans had to find the proper tradeoff between their strategic distrust of the Soviets and their overall preference for sovereignty based on generalized distrust. The veto created problems with the universal nature of the League. The British walked the line between their preferences for a concert and their role as spokesperson for the smaller countries of the Commonwealth (Hilderbrand 1990: 3, 14, 123; Hoopes and Brinkley 1997: 115; Patrick 2009: 41, 50, 55–6; Russell 1958: 228; S. C. Schlesinger 2003: 40). Indeed the President himself was conflicted, torn between the demands of the "dreamer and the practical politician" (Gaddis 2000: 27).

This chapter begins by reviewing the early American planning, demonstrating how the Democratic administration was inclined towards collective security, but that Wilsonians were forced to walk back those plans as they began to anticipate Republican objections identical to those in 1919. The Democrats then began bipartisan consultation so that American conservatives were on board with the administration's ideas before international negotiations began. I then trace the British decision-making process, showing how their early planning demonstrated a marked difference in preferences for organizational design given the conservative make-up of the wartime coalition.[2] At this point, I switch to the international negotiations, first the tripartite talks at Dumbarton Oaks where the controversy over the absolute veto came to a head, and then the San Francisco conference where countries worked out the relationship between regional bodies and the UN. The chapter ends with a review of the ratification debates in the United States and Britain. Given the care the administration took in soliciting Republican views, approval was assured in the United States, but examining the Senate's debate shows again how that domestic cooperation was essential for success and allows us to test whether the ideological differences evident in the behind-the-scenes elites are representative, evident and widespread in the parties as a whole. By adding the British debate, it becomes possible to establish that ideological differences in the United States were not unique but rather similar to those in other countries, reflecting a generalizable difference in dispositions to trust across the political spectrum.

Reconciling the "four policemen" and collective security: generalized trust in early State Department planning

Just as Wilson's notion of collective security served as the core around which the League was built, the United Nations was also built around a central Presidential concept, that of the "four policemen." Roosevelt believed that peace could be maintained by maintaining the wartime

---

[2] I do not review Soviet decision making in depth, treating it as exogenous for a number of reasons. First, the Soviets dedicated little time to planning for the United Nations, much less than the Americans and the British. Therefore their impact on the treaty is evident in only a few areas, and this on the basis of obstructionism during international negotiations. The Soviets were the most consistent supporters of a four-power alliance with few limitations on sovereignty and even fewer smaller-power rights. This policy was in many ways overdetermined, theoretically uninteresting and empirically unsurprising, a second reason for not analyzing it in depth. Soviet behavior was marked by strategic distrust, particularized distrust and generalized distrust. The Russians approached the international organization in terms of what it meant for creating security in Europe where they required a buffer zone of compliant states. Their instincts told them that countries with a capitalistic identity were inherently untrustworthy. And their authoritarian nature also led them to a "realistic" belief in power politics in general. Even so, we can never be sure of what exactly drove Soviet policy as documentation is not readily available, the third reason for not addressing it at length (Hilderbrand 1990: 46ff., 130ff.).

alliance and creating a concert of the great powers. Their combined force would serve as an overwhelming deterrent to any future aggressor, stamping out in particular any attempt at revanche by the defeated Axis. Roosevelt thought of the UN as a "sheriff's posse to break up the gang in order that gangsterism may be eliminated in the community of Nations" (Divine 1967: 137). The very name of the new organization was taken from the "Declaration by the United Nations" signed on January 1, 1942, which pledged unwavering commitment to the fight against a common enemy. The United Nations were wartime allies before they were members of an international organization.[3]

In many ways, Roosevelt's ideas resembled a new Holy Alliance even more than a concert (Hoopes and Brinkley 1997: 46, 108; Hull 1948: 1,238, 1,692). The President initially mused that all countries except the Soviet Union, the US, Britain and China would be completely disarmed after the war (FRUS 1942, vol. III: 568). Roosevelt argued,

There should be a meeting place of nations for the purpose of full discussion, but for management there seems no reason why the principle of trusteeship in private affairs should not be extended to the international field. Trusteeship is based on the principle of unselfish service. For a time at least there are many minor children among the peoples of the world who need trustees in their relations with other nations and peoples, just as there are many adult nations or peoples which must be led back into a spirit of good conduct. (Gaddis 2000: 24; Hilderbrand 1990: 15–16)

The success of such a plan, as with all concerts, depended on great-power unity.[4] Most American officials were optimistic about cooperation with the Soviet Union until at least late 1944, and Roosevelt remained hopeful up to his death in spring 1945. As American

[3] As Secretary of State Hull explained after the conclusion of the conference creating the United Nations Charter, the "delegation took the position that the war had been successfully prosecuted under the banner of the United Nations, that good fortune attaches to this name, and that we should go forward under it to realize our dreams of the peace planned by the President who conceived the phrase" (Senate 1945: 50).

[4] In a radio address on April 9, 1944, Secretary of State Cordell Hull declared: "However difficult the road may be, there is no hope of turning victory into enduring peace unless the real interests of this country, the British Commonwealth, the Soviet Union, and China are harmonized and unless they agree and act together. This is the solid framework upon which all future policy and international organization must be built" (Hull 1948: 1,322–3; Notter 1949: 234).

postwar planning commenced, cooperation with Britain and the Soviet Union was taken for granted. Roosevelt was not naïve. He understood that relations with the Soviets would always be difficult. They were not inherently untrustworthy. However, if cultivated, he and others believed that they could be won over to the cause of peace (Campbell 1973a: 89; Hilderbrand 1990: 1, 16; S. C. Schlesinger 2003: 72).

Unlike with Wilson, I do not attempt to elicit Roosevelt's level of generalized trust, since the President's core beliefs are notoriously difficult to pin down (Ruggie 1997: 98–102; Widenor 1992). I do not pretend to succeed where historians have failed. The President described himself as "the juggler," the consummate politician without any fixed ideological compass (Kimball 1991). Roosevelt's preferences for order after the war – ad hoc collaboration among a few allies – are consistent with his more pessimistic views about the prospects for international cooperation, which seem to reflect an understanding of the world as a dangerous and threatening place. This provides some evidence that FDR's position is in keeping with my argument. He dismissed the League of Nations as a "formula . . . based on magnificent idealism" and claimed that the world needed more than "good intentions alone." The war seems to have affected him: "We . . . have learned that if we do not pull the fangs of the predatory animals of this world, they will multiply and grow in strength – and they will be at our throats again once more in a short generation" (Divine 1967: 84). Publicly he said, "For too many years we lived on pious hopes that aggressor and warlike nations would learn and understand and carry out the doctrine of purely voluntary peace" (Patrick 2009: 58). Nevertheless, I am not comfortable drawing any firm conclusions on the basis of the data. I treat the President's position as exogenous to the story that follows.

What is clear is that Roosevelt's position was very much a minority view in his Democratic administration. The President himself understood that his vision would disappoint his more idealistic party (Divine 1967: 44). However, unlike Wilson, who managed the League matter almost single-handedly, Roosevelt was not actively engaged in the administration planning for the organization. Instead the process was managed almost exclusively in the State Department, without even active Pentagon involvement until the very end stages (Campbell 1973a: 3; 1973b). The President would only weigh in periodically on momentous decisions and often without a firm understanding of the issues. This gave more trusting State Department officials with a cooperative social orientation freer reign to design an institution more in keeping with their core beliefs but within the broad parameters set by Roosevelt. According to Schlesinger, Roosevelt "had stacked his own State Department and embassies abroad with passionate Wilsonians" (S. C. Schlesinger 2003: 29). Future Secretary of State Dean Acheson described planners as engaged in "platonic planning of a utopia, a sort of mechanistic idealism" (Acheson 1969: 88).

Three officials consistently stand out as the most important in all accounts of the UN's creation – Secretary of State Cordell Hull, his trusted aide Leo Pasvolsky and Undersecretary of State Sumner Welles. As the two latter individuals were never elected officials, operating largely privately and producing mostly dry policy memos, it is difficult to elicit their levels of generalized trust.[5] However, we do know that all three were devoted Wilsonians committed to collective security (Campbell 1973a: 3, 14; Divine 1967: 45; Hilderbrand 1990: 7; S. C. Schlesinger 2003: 34, 39). Hull "worshipped Woodrow Wilson" and "believed passionately in [his] ideals" (Divine 1967). In his term as a senator from Tennessee, Hull was its tenth most liberal member, with a voting record that stands 0.9 standard deviations towards the left of the political spectrum from the party mean.

Any administration planning had to revolve around Roosevelt's great-power concert concept (Hilderbrand 1990: 15; Russell 1958: 229). The first major planning document from the State Department was the "Draft Constitution of International Organization" of July 1943 (Russell 1958: 472–85).[6] In accordance with FDR's wishes, the four policemen enjoyed pride of place, constituting an Executive Committee with "responsibility in matters of international security." All were represented permanently in a larger Executive Council of eleven members, the germ of what would become the Security Council. Although the language was vague, the document suggested that the Executive Council could compel settlement of all disputes. If it was decided that a dispute might threaten the peace, the "Council shall cause an investigation to be made and shall cause such action

[5] Pasvolsky was perhaps the most important. After the UN was created, Senator Tom Connally, chairman of the Foreign Relations Committee wrote, "Certainly he had more to do with writing the framework of the charter than anyone else" (S. C. Schlesinger 2003: 45).
[6] Full text of all the American plans can be found in the appendices in Russell (1958).

to be taken as it may deem necessary to facilitate a settlement." In case of a breach of the peace, all members of the organization were to make available "armaments, facilities, installations, strategic areas and contingents of armed forces" that the Executive Committee and the Council regarded as necessary for the mission, as well as to "afford . . . freedom of passage through their territories."

However, State Department planners began to situate the "four policemen" idea within a broader framework more consistent with the generalized trust that generally characterized the Democratic Party, to square the circle of a great-power concert and a collective security arrangement (Hilderbrand 1990: 3). Pasvolsky in particular was the driving force behind the Draft Constitution. While it envisioned an organization dominated by the great powers as Roosevelt preferred, the rest was Wilsonian in nature. This is completely overlooked in almost all studies of the origins of the United Nations, which focus on the later stages of the planning. It contained a negative covenant, by which members would pledge to resolve their disputes peacefully, either by traditional diplomatic means, judicial decision, or through the mediation of the Council. In that way it resembled Cecil's British plan of twenty-five years earlier. However, if disputes threatened to lead to a "breach, or imminently threatened breach, of the peace between nations," the Council would request the parties to restore the position before the onset of conflict. States failing to comply were "presumed to intend a violation of the peace of nations" at which time the Council "shall apply all the measures necessary to restore or maintain the peace." The use of "shall" was telling, as it was not left up to the Council's discretion as to whether it would act. This was almost an automatic collective security guarantee, and much stronger than the one eventually included in the Covenant. And as Wilson's early plans in the League planning process had envisioned, sanctions would be used to force states to resolve their conflicts even if war had not yet broken out (Hoopes and Brinkley 1997: 68–9; Russell 1958: 229–33, 472–85). Surely coincidentally, given the American experience with the League, the "Security and Armaments" provisions fell under Article 10 of the Draft Constitution.

The guarantee was all the more striking in light of the Draft Constitution's voting provisions for the Council. The great powers would enjoy veto power in matters pertaining to the peaceful settlement of disputes but not in the enforcement of breaches to the peace. In these instances, decisions would require a two-thirds majority vote of the Council including only three quarters of the Executive Committee, who would be permanent members of the former body. This meant that on the most important issues, at least theoretically and legally, great powers would not have a veto over the use of their own armed forces (Hoopes and Brinkley 1997: 68–9; Russell 1958: 229–33, 472–85).

The combination of the requirement for peaceful settlement, automatic sanctions in case of non-compliance, and the lack of great-power veto meant that the United States could be called upon to enforce any breaches to the peace without any loopholes that restored unilateralism. This raised the same risks of opportunism through entrapment as the League's Article X. From the beginning, planners recognized this but due to their cooperative social orientation believed that these limitations on sovereignty were necessary in order to ensure the success of the organization. They embraced qualitative multilateralism. The earliest plans in the State Department stressed the necessity of some "derogation" of sovereignty to permit decisive action by the institution (Hilderbrand 1990: 9). The costs to national sovereignty were recognized, but would be outweighed by the automaticity and the speed with which such a force could be used. The need for unanimity in every instance would inhibit the institution's effectiveness. These planners recognized the difficulties in securing congressional assent to such a scheme but thought it was worth the risk (Hilderbrand 1990: 22–6; Russell 1958: 231–4, 243).

These more trusting Wilsonians also wanted a more inclusive organization than the concert proposed by FDR. They favored quantitative multilateralism. In their deliberations over the Draft Constitution, State Department officials considered but rejected an arrangement more consistent with Roosevelt's four policemen in which all enforcement functions would be placed in the hands of the Executive Committee alone with the requirement of unanimous voting in all situations (Russell 1958: 231–4). The next draft of a constitution for a postwar organization, the Staff Charter of August 1943, eliminated the Executive Committee altogether, leaving only an Executive Council (Russell 1958: 229, 240–50, 286–9). The Secretary of State in particular was uncomfortable with the "naked expression of four power dominance" in the Draft Constitution (Hilderbrand 1990: 25–7; Hoopes and Brinkley 1997: 77). Planners were trying to make the framework less repugnant to "internationalists who feared a new Quadruple Alliance" (Russell 1958: 206). Members would be consulted about their contributions although the Council could still compel participation (Russell, 1958: 526–34, appendix 23).

The Staff Charter also aimed at constructing a more centralized organization in order to bring the power of the entire world to bear on potential breaches of the peace. Hull and Pasvolsky in particular disliked the oblique reference of the Draft Constitution to regional institutions. In the earlier plan, non-permanent seats on the Council were to be divided among different regions of the world. Although the document did not state so, a prominent idea at the time was that regional organizations would select rotating members of the Council. Hull and Pasvolsky opposed regional organizations playing any significant role as they feared that would lead to a devolution of functions to smaller bodies, pulling apart the global organization. Under the new plan, a "General Conference" of the organization, what would become the General Assembly, would fill the rotating seats, ensuring a more universal approach (Gaddis 2000: 26; Hilderbrand 1990: 24–5; Hull 1948: 1,645; Russell 1958: 108, 220, 241–3, 526–34; S. C. Schlesinger 2003: 39, 43).

The Staff Charter did not, however, change the voting procedure, the obligations of members to resolve disputes peacefully, and the sanctions they would face, or the obligations on the part of members to enforce the peace. States refusing to submit to peaceful settlement "shall be regarded as intending a breach of the peace." This would activate the security guarantee of the Staff Charter, which was even stronger, while still specifying all the same actions that the Council "shall" take. It explicitly mentioned "measures of force" to be applied "forthwith" (Russell 1958: 526–34).

Therefore, even at the highest levels of the State Department, there was support at the time for an organization with a binding security guarantee and the requirement of peaceful conflict resolution, all without the protection of an American veto. And those who advocated this qualitative multilateralism, self-professed Wilsonians with higher levels of generalized trust, were also the greatest proponents of a more universal and inclusive, quantitatively multilateral League. Rationalism cannot explain this combination since qualitative multilateralism is made much more difficult as quantitative multilateralism increases, without the presence of generalized trust.

A rationalist account of the creation of the United Nations might suspect that the three-fourths requirement for permanent members in the Draft Constitution and the Staff Charter was based on an assessment of likely alignment of voting patterns after the war, that is, on an early prognosis of the Cold War. Of course by 1948 Soviet Union vetoes would hamstring the Security Council from taking action. It is theoretically possible that the US predicted that any danger in giving up an American veto over enforcement by the United Nations was made up for by the gain in preventing Soviet obstruction, particularly as it could count on cooperation from the other permanent members, particularly Britain. China was of course not yet communist. Perhaps the lack of a veto is reflective of strategic distrust, not generalized trust.

As noted above, however, the top-secret discussions within the State Department were framed around the general problem of how to create an organization more flexible and therefore more effective than the League of Nations, without any specific mention of potential problem countries. A veto would inhibit effective action, as it had in the operation of the League (Russell 1958: 232–3). The American willingness to countenance an institution without an American veto is an expression of generalized trust rather than strategic distrust. Acheson, who would later become Secretary of State, described this process as largely "theoretical," "detached from the practicalities of current problems and power relationships" (Acheson 1969: 88).

Moreover, these plans predate deep suspicions of Soviet intentions. American officials expected and were even somewhat understanding of Soviet desires for some kind of buffer in Eastern Europe after the war, even if they did not envisage the extent to which Russian influence would penetrate. Historians have concluded that up until fall 1944 there was, however misplaced in retrospect, a strong feeling that the Soviets would be cooperative if their security concerns were met (Campbell 1973a: 18; Gaddis 2000: 6–7, 15; Hilderbrand 1990: 1, 16; Widenor 1992). Harry Hopkins, Roosevelt's trusted aide who often served as a go-between between the President and Stalin, recalled that the "Russians had proved that they could be reasonable and farseeing and there wasn't any doubt in the minds of the President or any of us that we could live with them and get along with them peacefully for as far into the future as any of us could imagine" (Gaddis 2000: 164).

Planning at the time explicitly mentions two "assumptions": "*First*, that the four major powers will pledge themselves and will consider themselves morally bound not to go to war against each other or against any other nation, and to cooperate with each other and with other peace-loving states in maintaining the peace. *Second*, that each of them will maintain adequate forces and will be willing to use such forces as circumstances require to prevent or suppress all cases of aggression" (Russell 1958: 576–81). Patrick concludes that these guidelines "betray optimism, even naivete, about the ease of achieving and preserving such great power comity" (2009: 57).

The return of Republican reservations: conservative unilateralism and the Connally resolution

The war experience had not led to any significant reevaluation of the preferences of mainstream Republicans in regards to international organization (Campbell 1973a: 7). Republicans had become less isolationist but not less unilateralist. The conservative internationalists remained the core of the party. This meant familiar divides with the Democrats. The war was not the break it is often believed to be. Contrary to rationalist expectations, in the same structural circumstances, while the Democratic administration was generally contemplating an institution with significant multilateral elements, most Republicans were advocating forms of cooperation that protected American unilateralism. That the differences mapped onto the liberal–conservative spectrum domestically suggests that generalized trust was the source of the difference.

The former Republican President, the staunch conservative Herbert Hoover, called for an organization that might attempt to settle disputes peacefully but no more. The enforcement of the peace would rest with a separate military alliance, "trustees of peace" composed of the major allied powers who would disarm and crush aggressors (Divine 1967: 60–62). He fell back on particularized trust, as those with a less trusting disposition do. Hoover called for a realism based on a more pessimistic view of human nature. He derided idealists: "To many people, global planning is a field where imagination can engage in unrestrained play. It is indeed a playground where they may blow gigantic bubbles by dipping their pipes in suds of human kindness" (Divine 1967: 123). Thomas Dewey, the Governor of New York and presumptive presidential nominee, also resisted quantitative multilateralism, favoring a permanent, bilateral alliance with the British to police the peace. Many Republicans would not even endorse participation in a formal organization. Before the 1942 elections, 115 Republican congressmen signed a postwar manifesto, pledging only that the "United States has an obligation and responsibility to work with other nations to bring about a world understanding and cooperative spirit which will have for its supreme objective the continued maintenance of peace," cautioning that "in so doing we must not endanger our own independence, weaken our American way of life or our system of government" (Divine 1967: 71).

Prominent dissenters in the party, such as Warren Austin, Harold Stassen and Wendell Willkie, called for some form of international police force. However, they were among the most liberal members of the party domestically. Austin had the second most liberal voting record of the Republicans in the Senate. Nine Democrats were more conservative. Stassen was a liberal Republican as well, a former progressive governor of Minnesota. Willkie, the surprise presidential nominee of the party in 1940, had formerly been a Democrat (Divine 1967: 62–3, 70, 78; S. C. Schlesinger 2003: 63).

In the fall of 1943, the Republicans began to formulate an official position. A policy committee laid down a marker of their expectations for the postwar organization at a September 1943 conference of party leaders at Mackinac Island. The Republican Advisory Council included all Republican governors, fifteen members of the House and the Senate and ten members of the Republican National Committee. No one was more important in this meeting, and in the bipartisan consultation process as a whole, than Senator Arthur Vandenberg of Michigan. Vandenberg had been a staunch proponent of non-interventionism prior to American entry into World War II.[7] However, Vandenberg had a change of heart after Pearl Harbor, which he would famously claim in his diary "ended isolationism for any realist" (Vandenberg 1952: 1). He insisted that his party must dispel the notion that it "will

---

[7] He was the preferred candidate of the isolationists for the Republican presidential nomination, fought for the Neutrality Law of 1937 and against its repeal in 1939. However, he did not exhibit the ideological traits of a true isolationist, such as an antipathy to Europeans (Doenecke 1979: 45). He was an "insulationist," a "realist," who thought that America's geographical position afforded it the luxury of independence. WWII disabused him of this notion.

retire to its foxhole when the last shot in this war has been fired and will blindly let the world rot in its own anarchy" (Hoopes and Brinkley 1997: 126; Vandenberg 1952: 56).

Vandenberg's personal epiphany only took him so far, however. While the war was damaging for traditional isolationism, it did not have the same effect on mainstream Republican unilateralists. Even as an internationalist, Vandenberg was deeply skeptical of collective security: "I doubt whether any hard and fast international contracts looking toward the automatic use of cooperative force in unforeseeable emergencies ahead will be worth any more, when the time comes, than the national consciences of the contracting parties when the hour of acid test arrives," he wrote privately (Vandenberg 1952: 114). Vandenberg was as skeptical of the power of moral obligations as Lodge and the conservative internationalists of the interwar years. He expected abandonment. The Senator's consistent mantra was consistent with this competitive social orientation. The difference between his party and "New Deal foreign policy" was, in his words, that the Republicans would ensure "that we shall remain a totally sovereign country" (Vandenberg 1952: 57).

Most important, even though Vandenberg diagnosed the problem of international cooperation as one of opportunism, he greatly feared the creation of some sort of hierarchy, such as an international police force or elements of a world state. He exhibited the same seeming paradox as his conservative predecessors twenty years before. Vandenberg was deeply suspicious of "World Staters," and he saw himself as guaranteeing the "continuance of the American Flag over the Capitol" (Vandenberg 1952: 45). Privately, Vandenberg wrote:

I am hunting for the middle ground between those extremists at one end of the line who would cheerfully give America away and those extremists at the other end of the line who would attempt a total isolation which has come to be an impossibility. I am sure we can frankly assert our purpose to participate in post-war cooperation to prevent by any necessary means the recurrence of military aggression and to establish permanent peace with justice in a free world so far as this is humanly obtainable. But I am equally sure that this has to be paralleled by equally forthright reassurance to our own American people that we intend to be...vigilant in the preservation of our legitimate American interests...I think we must maintain our own sovereignty in the final analysis. (Hoopes and Brinkley 1997: 86; Vandenberg 1952: 55–6)

Vandenberg spoke for the vast majority of Republicans. He noted that the sovereignty argument has great importance to "conservative portions of the party" (Campbell 1973a: 20). The Republican Senate steering committee claimed that his "views respond more completely to the composite judgment and conscience of Republicans in this international field than do those of any other Senators" (Campbell 1973a: 148; Hilderbrand 1990: 22–6). The party completely marginalized those amongst them pushing for more dramatic plans based on pooling sovereignty, such as Wendell Willkie (Campbell 1973a: 20; Divine 1967: 63, 106; Hoopes and Brinkley 1997: 62; Patrick 2009: 63). Even though he had been the surprise Republican presidential candidate in 1940, he was denied any prominent role in later party gatherings (Hoopes and Brinkley 1997: 161). He called on Republican candidates to Congress in 1942 to endorse a pledge to work towards "some system of joint international force," but not a single politician followed his lead (Divine 1967: 71).

On the basis of Vandenberg's drafts, the Republican conference at Mackinac endorsed a resolution in favor of only "responsible participation by the United States in a postwar co-operation organization among sovereign nations to prevent military aggression and to attain permanent peace with organized justice in a free world" (Russell 1958: 126; Vandenberg 1952: 58). Vandenberg was particularly insistent on the mention of sovereignty and took great pride in its inclusion (Vandenberg 1952: 61). This phrase later formed the basis of the party's 1944 presidential campaign platform (Notter 1949: 286). It was only at the insistence of the liberal senator Austin that the plank even mentioned an organization. Vandenberg's preference was only to endorse international "cooperation." FDR's responded sarcastically to this noncommittal resolution: "Well, I always have my thesaurus handy on my desk" (Divine 1967: 132).[8]

---

[8] The same divisions occurred in the politics surrounding the drafting of the electoral manifesto in 1944. Willkie and Austin pushed for an endorsement of an institution with greater teeth, in which sovereignty would have to be surrendered, but Vandenberg enlisted the support of the more conservative presidential candidates, Dewey and Bricker, to soundly defeat them. The Republican platform paraphrased the Mackinac resolution with its emphasis on the maintenance of sovereignty. In his acceptance speech, Dewey simply pledged to "participate with other sovereign nations in a co-operative effort to prevent future wars" (Divine 1967: 209–10).

Conservative unilateralism was also evident in the first congressional deliberations over a postwar peace organization. A bipartisan group composed of senators Joseph Ball, Harold Burton, Carl Hatch and Lister Hill (subsequently known collectively as "B2H2") was eager to pass a congressional resolution indicating American support for a new postwar international organization so as to reassure American allies that the US would not retreat into isolation after the war. Only a resolution endorsed by most of the Senate could give such an indication, they argued, given the American failure to pass the Covenant in 1919. More controversially, however, their draft explicitly mentioned a "United Nations military force . . . to suppress by immediate use of such force any future attempt at military aggression by any nation" (Divine 1967: 107; Hilderbrand 1990: 27–8; Hoopes and Brinkley 1997: 65–6; Patrick 2009: 62; Vandenberg 1952: 45). Burton and Ball were not coincidentally two of the most liberal Republicans.[9]

This provoked objections from more conservative Republicans but also administration officials terrified of any repeat of the League disaster. The latter were consistently wary about any precipitous public statement in favor of American membership in a postwar security organization (Campbell 1973a: 3–4; Divine 1967: 96; Gaddis 2000: 30; Hilderbrand 1990: 27; S. C. Schlesinger 2003: 45; Vandenberg 1952: 47). Even while the State Department had been planning for an international organization since before the United States entered the war, it feared that public discussion was premature and might lead to an isolationist or unilateralist backlash. Hull in particular, as a former senator who had also worked for the Wilson administration to promote the League, believed that the Congress had to be carefully managed (Divine 1967: 51, 67, 81, 115). The administration also feared that floor discussion on any resolution would potentially lead to acrimonious debate, the offering of amendments, and even turn the mood against postwar cooperation. The notion of an international force in particular conjured up images that could damage the prospects for an international organization both with isolationists who feared

---

[9] Burton and Ball were the ninth and twelfth most liberal senators in their party. Burton was more liberal than four Democratic senators. His voting record is 0.82 standard deviations from the party's more conservative mean, Ball's 0.51 standard deviations. See www.voteview.com/DWNL.htm. Ball was a protégé of Governor Stassen, the liberal Republican governor of his home state (Divine 1967: 91). Hill and Hatch were Democrats.

American involvement in a new Holy Alliance and mainstream Republicans opposed to any delegation of American sovereignty. And it would not command enough votes in the Senate, creating the prospect of a devastating defeat. The administration turned to the Democratic Chairman of the Foreign Relations Committee, the conservative Democrat Tom Connally, for help. He bottled up the B2H2 resolution at Hull's request (Divine 1967: 95; Hoopes and Brinkley 1997: 67; Patrick 2009: 62).

When the four sponsors refused to let the issue die, Connally set about work on an alternative to appease them that would also capture the views of both sides of the aisle. If the Congress was going to go down this road, Hull wanted to ensure that any resolution passed overwhelmingly, which required Republican support (Hoopes and Brinkley 1997: 91; Russell 1958: 93–4; Vandenberg 1952: 43). This required a much more generic resolution. Initial versions did not even mention an "organization" at all, which pleased Vandenberg (Divine 1967: 145–6). The Republican senator used his Mackinac resolution as a template for what Republicans were looking for, the most important being references to "sovereignty and constitutional process" (Hull 1948: 1,261; Vandenberg 1952: 43–4). The Foreign Relations Committee beat back amendments offered by Claude Pepper, one of the most liberal senators, to mention military force explicitly, but the Florida senator was successful in inserting a reference to an actual organization. When the resolution emerged from the committee, Senator Gillette declared, "A child is born." But when asked if it were a boy or a girl, he drolly responded: "Neuter" (Divine 1967: 146).

The "Connally resolution" passed 85 to 5 on November 5, 1943. Only traditional isolationists opposed.[10] It expressed Senate support for the United States to "join with free and sovereign nations in the establishment and maintenance of international authority with power to prevent aggression and to preserve the peace of the world" and recognized "the necessity of there being established at the earliest practicable date a general international organization, based on the principle of the sovereign equality of all peace-loving states . . . for the maintenance of international peace and security." Vandenberg took great pride that

---

[10] Johnson, Langer, Shipstead, Reynolds and Wheeler voted against. The latter two ranked among the ten most conservative Democrats. The first three were Republicans. Johnson had been a prominent League detractor.

the final resolution would "bow to our Republican 'Mackinac' statement" in these regards, and noted derisively that the House equivalent, drafted by up-and-coming Democratic congressman William Fulbright, did not mention sovereignty at all (Vandenberg 1952: 61–2). Several Republicans indicated in the debate that the omission of any reference to an international police force was a precondition for their consent (Divine 1967: 152).

Reconciling Republican and Democratic Party differences: The "Possible Plan for a General International Organization"

Even as it served as a signal to the wider world that the United States might emerge from its interwar isolation, the Connally resolution also showed that ensuring two-thirds Senate support for the UN Charter would require significant attention to sovereignty given the less trusting disposition of Republicans and conservative Democrats (Hoopes and Brinkley 1997: 65–7, 124–6; Russell 1958: 93–4; Vandenberg 1952: 61–2). Early State Department planning had not yet given active consideration to the likely reaction of Congress, most importantly Republicans. It is no coincidence that at precisely this time, the Democratic administration began to rethink the lack of a great-power (and therefore American) veto on enforcement action by the United Nations as well as the nature of the security guarantee (Hilderbrand 1990: 29). The Secretary of State became more intimately involved in the planning after the Draft Constitution and Staff Charter, as he knew that he was "entirely responsible for the outcome" (S. C. Schlesinger 2003: 42). A former senator himself, Hull saw himself as best equipped to deal with the concerns of senators. The President recognized the Secretary of State was indispensable in helping win the legislators' approval (S. C. Schlesinger 2003: 41–3).

As a consequence, policy-makers stripped the binding security guarantee from their drafts, inserting more unilateralism into their plans. A memorandum from the Secretary of State transmitted to the President on December 23, 1943 explained State Department planning at that point. There was no positive guarantee akin to Article X. The section of the document entitled "Principal Obligations of a Member State" only mentioned a negative covenant, "to refrain from the use of force or the threat to use force in its relations with other states" and "to settle all disputes with other states by pacific means." The Security

Council could, but was not obligated, to enforce the peaceful settlement of disputes in case of a breach of or potential threat to the peace (Russell 1958: 576–81, appendix 33).

The Secretary of State wanted to preempt conservative objections to entrapment. He later wrote:

As for our own country, we recalled the insistent demand made in Woodrow Wilson's period for veto privileges in the League of Nations. Bitter opposition had been raised to the United States' entry into the League on the basis of erroneous assumptions that, if we became a member of the League, the Covenant allowed an agency of the League to give orders to our military forces in preserving peace. The biggest stumbling block that sent the Wilson movement in support of the League to utter destruction in 1920 was the argument over this point and no other political controversy during our time has been accompanied by more deep-seated antagonisms. The hint in 1919 – however false that it was – that we were in any sense surrendering or impairing Congress's prerogative to declare war or the President's prerogative to direct the movements of our armed forces proved fatal. I had not forgotten this fact. (Hull 1948: 1,622–3)

This was the real difference between the post-WWI and post-WWII cases, a willingness to compromise based on the vivid memory of the League failure. The ideological alignment was virtually identical despite the intervening war experience. It was a matter of process, not preferences. Roosevelt and Hull were haunted by the specter of 1919 and determined to take into account conservative objections before the treaty reached the Senate (Campbell 1973a: 3, 6, 17; Notter 1949: 195–6; Vandenberg 1952: 95–6). The administration was laying the groundwork for future Senate approval.

Still Hull and his advisers were hoping to limit the exercise of the veto. In their memorandum, they asked FDR to choose between a requirement for three-quarters or unanimous voting among the permanent members of the Council (without a distinction between peaceful settlement and enforcement) (Russell 1958: 576–81). Pasvolsky and Hull, suspecting that Roosevelt would choose the former, also offered some alternatives that might make it more likely for him to assent to a degree of sovereignty derogation. They proposed that permanent council members might free themselves from any obligations to enforce the peace by abstaining or dissenting, allowing the institution to move forward while not requiring any great power to participate against its will. They were keen to retain some restrictions on the veto so as not to inhibit the organization's effectiveness (Hilderbrand 1990: 32–6).

When shown the memorandum, Roosevelt concluded that Council action should indeed require unanimity of all major powers. He was concerned that the US could otherwise be called upon to furnish armed forces without its consent. The evidence available does not allow us to know whether Roosevelt was expressing his own personal reservations or his fears that Congress would never consent to such an arrangement, a sentiment he also expressed at that time (Hilderbrand 1990: 36). However, with Hull it was clearer. The Secretary of State was not pleased with the veto provision but was willing to compromise: "We might as well recognize that this is about the best that can be done as a beginning," he stated. The United States "should not be deterred for an instant from pursuing the sole course that is open, the alternative being international chaos as we have had heretofore" (Hull 1948: 1662). Hull also was coming to the conclusion that without the veto, Congress would not approve and the US "would not remain there a day" (Russell 1958: 275).

In another way, however, Roosevelt was moving away from a preference for a pure four-power concert towards a more quantitatively multilateral organization. State Department officials were careful to hew to FDR's "four policemen" concept in their justification for the Executive Council's prerogatives, stressing the great powers' "exceptional responsibilities for the maintenance of international security." And in deference to his views they even gave Roosevelt the option of choosing an Executive Council consisting of only the four wartime allies. However, State Department planners preferred a larger council with between seven and fifteen members and convinced Roosevelt of the desirability of such a scheme (Hilderbrand 1990: 31–6; Russell 1958: 250–51; S. C. Schlesinger 2003: 46). By the time the Dumbarton Oaks conference began, the United States supported a council of eleven, with five permanent and six rotating members. Hull had made Roosevelt into a "universalist," concludes Campbell (1973b: 26).

It is also at this point that the administration decided against endorsing any kind of international military force to be placed under the control of the Security Council. State Department officials had considered various options for such units because they wanted to build in some mechanism to ensure that the new institution could act quickly in the event of a threat to peace and security, something the League was never able to do. Ad hoc contributions on a case-by-case basis would not provide the assurance that adequate forces would be available at the time of crisis.

Records show that one of the most important factors weighing against such an option was the anticipation of objection from Republicans to any element of institutional hierarchy on the grounds of national sovereignty. This had led to the dilution of the B2H2 resolution the previous year. Vandenberg consistently expressed opposition to such a force and any type of world state in general (Hilderbrand 1990: 140–42; Hoopes and Brinkley 1997: 118; Russell 1958: 471; Vandenberg 1952: 114, 120). Roosevelt thought the Republicans would use fears about such an army against him in the 1944 elections (Campbell 1973a: 44). It is not clear whether, absent fears of congressional opposition, administration officials would have endorsed some sort of international force. The armed services were opposed, and there were significant problems of practicalities and logistics (Campbell 1973a: 44ff.; Hilderbrand 1990: 140ff.). Nevertheless, it can be said that the administration gave active consideration to various ideas creating some sort of hierarchy, including the creation of an international air force, something that only generalized trusters could do.

The administration settled instead on a plan in which members would negotiate agreements with the United Nations Security Council as to the forces they would delegate for use in enforcement actions. These national contingents would serve as a dependable reservoir, without creating a standing international army (Campbell 1973a: 21, 42; Hoopes and Brinkley 1997: 118; Russell 1958: 100, 253–5, 964). The plan squared the circle between the need for reliable, rapid and decisive action and concerns about sovereignty. As it was to be based on prior agreement with, rather than compulsion by, the Council, it also had the advantage of making the Security Council less of a great-power dictatorship, something State Department officials were keen on. It did, however, disappoint some of the most liberal members of the party who later advocated for a party plank endorsing an international air force. Pepper and Hatch tried unsuccessfully to insert this into the 1944 Democratic Party platform, but the more conservative Connally successfully worked behind the scenes to undermine their efforts (Divine 1967: 212).

By late April 1944 the nature of the international organizations was largely set, laid out in a paper entitled the "Possible Plan for a

General International Organization" (Russell, 1958: 582–91, appendix 35). Its vision closely resembled the eventual form of the United Nations, essentially fusing a great-power concert with a universal security organization. Member states would agree to a negative guarantee, a promise to refrain from the threat or use of force. If parties to a conflict could not reach agreement, they were obligated to refer the matter to the Council for a just and equitable settlement. The great powers, along with a number of smaller member states, would consider potential flashpoints in the international system, deciding what to do on a case-by-case basis and thereby preserving unilateralism. If the Council determined that any dispute threatened international peace and security it could assume jurisdiction, impose settlements and enforce its decisions. However, there was no general obligation for it to take any particular action in case of aggression or threats to international peace and security. The great-power veto also protected sovereignty. Nevertheless, a more inclusive Executive Council would include four permanent and four rotating members, the latter elected by a General Assembly. And the process was to be formal in nature, based on voting rather than informal consultation. Council decisions required a majority vote including the votes of all permanent members except on simple procedural questions.

The "Possible Plan" was shared with a Committee of Eight convened by the administration to build congressional support prior to the Dumbarton Oaks conference of the Big Three (the Soviet Union, the United States and Britain), who would work out a common position on an international security organization. The committee was composed of four Democratic, one Progressive and three Republican senators who began active consultations in April 1944 (Campbell 1973a: 3, 6, 17; Hull 1948: 1,622–3, 1,677; Notter 1949: 195–6; Russell 1958: 273–5; Vandenberg 1952: 95–6). Vandenberg was by far the most important of the three Republicans, as the others were very liberal and multilateralist Republicans, something the Senator himself did not fail to note (Vandenberg 1952: 95).

Hull was careful to point out features that would appeal to less trusting Republicans concerned about sovereignty, particularly the veto. Domestic politics were foremost on his mind. The Secretary of State had been so concerned about the veto that before his congressional consultations he asked Pasvolsky to draft a memorandum outlining how it would safeguard American interests (Hilderbrand 1990: 186).

"The veto power is in the document primarily on account of the United States," he told the senators. "Without it the United States would not have anywhere near the popular support for the postwar organization as with it in, any more so perhaps than in 1920." Hull presented the veto in a way that would resonate with conservatives, as a "necessary safeguard in dealing with a new and untried world arrangement" (Hull 1948: 1,662). He acknowledged and spoke to their fear of uncertainty.

Hull's pitch was perfect. In his diary, Vandenberg claimed that the most "striking thing about it is that it is so *conservative* from a nationalist standpoint." By "conservative," Vandenberg seems to have meant unilateral. His diary entry hit on all the preferences of those with a less trusting disposition. The "Possible Plan" limited the potential for entrapment. "To [Hull's] credit," wrote Vandenberg, "he recognizes that the United States will never permit itself to be ordered into war against its own consent." The Senator liked other guarantees of American unilateralism: "I am deeply impressed (and surprised) to find Hull so carefully guarding our American veto in his scheme of things." There was also no hierarchy. "This is anything but a wild-eyed internationalist dream of a world State," he wrote. "On the contrary, it is a frame-work...to which I can and do heartily subscribe." Vandenberg was also pleased not to find any reference to a "standing 'international police force.'" The Senator appreciated the limitations on quantitative multilateralism as well. "It is based virtually on a four-power alliance...the real authority is in a Council of eight upon which America, England, Russia and China shall always be represented; and no action looking toward the use of force can be taken if any one of the Big Four dissents." Vandenberg recognized that Hull was "manifestly eager to avoid Wilson's mistake of attempting commitments destined for ultimate congressional rejection." He concluded, "All in all...I think his preliminary scheme is excellent" (Vandenberg 1952: 95–8).

Generalized trust or strategic distrust?: the absolute veto controversy and the domestic politics of qualitative multilateralism

Hull had not put everything on the table, however. The plan shown to Roosevelt in December 1943, which the President had endorsed, stated that "In no decision of the Executive Council should the vote of a party directly involved in a dispute and represented on the Executive

Council be counted" (Russell 1958: 578). This raised the question of the "absolute veto," whether the ability of the permanent members to block action both in peaceful settlement and enforcement action could apply to their own conflicts with other members. Without such a veto, the United States would expose itself to potential exploitation, a key fear of less trusting conservatives. Other members of the Council could agree on and even enforce decisions on matters of vital American interest without this protection. The issue was regarded as too politically controversial to broach with the Committee of Eight, and Hull purposively omitted it from the "Possible Plan" (Campbell 1973a: 39; Hilderbrand 1990: 48; Hoopes and Brinkley 1997: 117; Hull 1948: 1,671; Russell 1958: 273–5). The Secretary of State suspected that an absolute veto might be necessary to get the United States into the United Nations because it would be indispensable for conservatives, but he did not want to broach the subject yet.

The absolute veto became the focus of intensive scrutiny in the run-up to the Dumbarton Oaks conference of August 1944 in Washington, DC. The faction lobbying against the absolute veto for the great powers was led by the Wilsonian Pasvolsky and others who had opposed the great-power veto as a whole earlier in the planning process. They based their objections on multilateral grounds. The group argued that such a provision would undermine the universal nature of the institution, making it more of a concert of great powers. More important, however, was the fear that such a veto would hamstring the organization. The institution would function better if there were general procedures that all would abide by, regardless of the particular case. It was a question of qualitative multilateralism versus the institutional equivalent of unilateralism. With the veto, the United Nations would be as powerless to stop a potential aggressor as the League was to stop Germany and Japan. The Pasvolsky group was willing to risk a loss of American sovereignty, placing the United States' fate in the hands of others, to reach a potentially greater gain in peace and security (Campbell 1973a: 39; Hilderbrand 1990: 184–6; Russell 1958: 274, 403).

The other side's position, at least initially, was influenced primarily by considerations concerning ratification. Not surprisingly one of the three members of the faction supporting an absolute veto was the State Department's liaison with Congress, Assistant Secretary of State Breckenridge Long (Campbell 1973a: 39; Hilderbrand 1990: 184–6; Russell

1958: 274, 403). Another was the only Republican in the American planning group (Hilderbrand 1990: 196). They were outnumbered, but Secretary Hull was torn between his domestic political instincts about what the Senate would accept and his impulse towards qualitative multilateralism. The official US position was left unresolved and ambiguous. The "Tentative Proposals," the American blueprint for an international organization sent to the British and Soviets for consideration before the conference, explicitly stated that "provisions will need to be worked out with respect to the voting procedure in the event of a dispute in which one or more of the members of the council having continuing tenure are directly involved" (Russell 1958: 299, 599).

It is important to note that this discussion was originally framed almost completely in general terms, not in reference to beliefs about the likely alignment of interests among the wartime allies as future permanent members of the Council. The Democratic administration's decision making was always oriented towards the future in somewhat abstract terms, something which puzzled the British (Campbell 1973a: 32; WP [44] 220).[11] Even if this would not remain the case, there was initially no discussion at this point on either side about how to design institutions that would enable, for instance, the isolation of the Soviet Union. To the extent there was concern about the Soviets, it was couched in terms of how to preserve great-power unity, not how to circumvent it. In fact, Hull defended the Soviets in the Committee of Eight consultations with the senators, some of whom asked if the veto might not allow the Soviets to obstruct Council action (Campbell 1973a: 18; Stettinius 1975: 141). Republicans expressed the most skepticism about the reliability of the Soviets (Hoopes and Brinkley 1997: 127). Robert Taft, an up-and-coming senator from Ohio, criticized the Democratic administration for basing policy on the "delightful theory that Mr Stalin in the end will turn out to have an angelic nature" (Gaddis 2000: 153).

Also, the arguments for an absolute veto were initially based on what the Senate might accept, not what the British and Soviets would want. This was a dispute between those with a cooperative social orientation and others more concerned about the Republican senators'

[11] Items designated by WP are memoranda considered by the War Cabinet. The first number indicates the year, the second the number of the paper. Every memorandum considered in the War Cabinet is numbered sequentially throughout the year.

less trusting disposition. For instance, when the American diplomat Bowman conferred with his British colleague on the issue, he "admitted that [the Americans] thought only of the Senate and had never discussed the effect on Commonwealth or Latin America" (Reynolds and Hughes 1976: 42).

Pasvolsky knew that Hull's own personal ideological inclination was to oppose the absolute veto, and he continued to solicit and advance alternative proposals in an effort to win over the Secretary of State (Hilderbrand 1990: 187; Russell 1958: 407). However, it was a turn in domestic politics that eventually changed Hull's mind. In the only real injection of partisan politics into the 1944 election campaign, Republican presidential candidate Thomas Dewey, Governor of New York, expressed his dismay that recent press reports indicated the proposed international security organization would "subject the nations of the world, great and small, permanently to the coercive power of the four nations holding this conference . . . proposals which amount merely to a permanent four power alliance to control the world" (Campbell 1973a: 22; Hilderbrand 1990: 189; Hoopes and Brinkley 1997: 161; Notter 1949: 287). This was the more traditional isolationist critique, likely made by a candidate trying to unite his party and looking for something to criticize in a plan to which conservative internationalists could not really object. This line of criticism played to a lingering sense of anti-imperialistic and anti-European identity in the United States, small but still present.[12] Vandenberg had identified this, not sovereignty, to Dewey as Roosevelt's chief vulnerability on the issue (Gaddis 2000: 146). The criticism was almost certainly electorally motivated, as Dewey's chief foreign policy adviser, John Foster Dulles, publicly backed a great-power concert to police the peace and, after finally formally reviewing the administration's plan on Dewey's behalf, praised it (Divine 1967: 218). This led to an agreement between the two camps to keep foreign policy out of the presidential campaign (Campbell 1973a: 23; Notter 1949: 289, 316; Patrick 2009: 66; Russell 1958: 200).

---

[12] Roosevelt had recently stoked these fears in an interview with the *Saturday Evening Post* in which he outlined publicly for the first time his vision of the four policemen imposing a kind of Pax Britannica with scarcely a mention of an international institution at all, except to deride a "heavily organized, bureaucratic world organization" (Hilderbrand 1990: 64; Hoopes and Brinkley 1997: 127–9; S. C. Schlesinger 2003: 40).

Nevertheless, Dewey's intervention seems to have given Hull the domestic political cover to go with his instincts: restrictions on great-power sovereignty in the United Nations. The UN was surely not a great-power alliance ruling the world if the great powers could themselves become the targets of its actions. After Dewey's criticism, it would be politically difficult for a period of time for the Republicans to complain about the lack of an absolute veto. This combined with help from the British, who had recently arrived for consultations prior to the great-power conference and who had their own reasons for restricting the great-power veto reviewed below. Hull reinstated the old position before the conference began, that the US would oppose the absolute veto (Hilderbrand 1990: 187–8; Notter 1949: 285–7). The British diplomat Alexander Cadogan claimed that Dewey had "set the cat among the pigeons," allowing Hull to push for this position he had always favored (Hilderbrand 1990: 189).

As Pasvolsky explained, the US was now willing to be "put on the same plane" as all the other states (Hilderbrand 1990: 194). Hull had endorsed qualitative multilateralism. The President approved this as well, noting privately that it would "make a statement that our people would understand the principle that a man should not sit in judgment on his own case" (FRUS 1944, vol. I: 73). Still, the Democrats worried about whether such a provision would past muster in the full Senate, and suspected the Republicans would introduce a reservation protecting the Monroe Doctrine to prevent exploitation in any instance that it became embroiled in a dispute with a Latin American country, as they had in 1919 (Hilderbrand 1990: 194–5).

Squaring the circle in Britain: Conservative preferences for a concert and Dominion objections

American proposals for a great-power concert resonated well with the inclinations of a Conservative-dominated government in Britain. Although the national unity government that shepherded Britain through the war included Labour and Liberal members in key posts, the Conservatives predominated, particularly in foreign affairs, where the key players were Prime Minister Winston Churchill and Foreign Secretary Anthony Eden. Overall Labour obtained only one third of ministerial slots (Jeffreys 1991: 38, 47, 55). Tory ideas were remarkably similar to those prevailing in conservative circles in both the

United States and the United Kingdom after WWI. Conservatives preferred to cooperate closely with a few allies in an informal arrangement based on consensus. Relying on a few trusted allies without any binding obligations was the expression of a lack of generalized trust and of a competitive social orientation natural for a party of the right. They resisted quantitative and qualitative multilateralism.

According to a diplomat central to the negotiations, the British government believed any postwar organization should be "regarded as a formal extension of the wartime alliance," which would take it upon itself to preserve the peace (Jebb 1990: 27). Eden wrote in a private memorandum: "It is impossible to say whether the League of Nations can ever be revived . . . But in the meantime, at any rate, we have the conception of the United Nations, a conception at once less ambitious and more practical than the conception of the League. And upon this idea of the United Nations we must build now the machinery of international co-operation" (WP [42] 516). Eden predicted that world opinion would demand a system for ensuring political cooperation and that the "foundations . . . already exist in the idea of the United Nations." The four powers were the "basis of any scheme for world organization" (WP [43] 300).

The great powers would act as "trustees for the peace of the world," as Prime Minister Winston Churchill described it privately to Stalin and publicly to the House of Commons (Hughes 1974: 187; *Hansard*, vol. 403: 497–8). Eden wrote that small powers need "firm and determined leadership by the Great Powers" (WP [42] 516). The latter would "have to take such dispositions for the restraint of aggression and for ensuring the peaceful settlement of disputes as the needs of a general security system may dictate. It may be hoped that the other nations . . . will, as a result of their recent experience, consent to the assumption by the World Powers of leadership for that purpose" (WP [43] 300). However, even if the smaller countries did not go along, "no opposition on their part should be allowed to prevent the World Powers from taking the necessary action for the restraint of aggression and for ensuring the peaceful settlement of disputes," Eden continued. "In other words, the final *decision* on such questions should rest with the World Powers acting unanimously" (WP [43] 300).[13]

---

[13] Although smaller powers could sit in on meetings in which they had special interests at stake, they would not even be allowed to vote (WP [43] 300;

Just as conservatives had stressed after WWI, the United Nations' main function would be to subjugate its enemies, in this case Japan and Germany, and hold them down permanently as the Concert of Europe had done with France (Jebb 1990: 24–6).[14] Similarly, conservative proponents understood the new concert as composed of righteous powers, which in Churchill's words would impose "complete disarmament upon the guilty" (E. J. Hughes 1974: 183–4). The latter would not be readmitted into the "society of nations" (WP [43] 300).

The United Nations would serve as an informal forum for states to discuss and work out their differences with no binding commitments (Goodwin 1957: 15–16; Reynolds and Hughes 1976: 20). Lacking generalized trust, the conservatives placed their faith in old-fashioned diplomacy. The memorandum presented to the Cabinet in July 1943, the "United Nations Plan for Organising Peace," stated: "In order that international peace and security shall be maintained there must be in the world some means by which States meet together to review and harmonise their political action. One of the objects of the Organisation, therefore, must be to create a meeting place where statesmen can come together for that purpose" (WP [44] 220, Memorandum A).[15] The Conservatives drew an explicit parallel with the Concert of Europe's diplomacy by conference and claimed the lineage of the legendary foreign secretary instrumental in its construction: "The establishment of a centre where the policies of the principal States of the world can be harmonized is in the great tradition of British policy, and

Hilderbrand 1990: 43). Small powers would be permitted to arm themselves to the degree that they contributed to the maintenance of international peace and security: "National independence should no longer be considered as a natural right, but as a privilege entailing for the independent State such corresponding obligations and contributions as may be necessary to ensure the maintenance of international well-being and peace" (WP [43] 300).

14 Eden's "United Nations Plan," the second memorandum on the subject considered by the Cabinet, identified two core principles – the continued cooperation of the great powers and restriction of German and Japanese power as long as possible so as to prevent their return into the ranks of the great powers (WP [43] 31).

15 "The main function of the World Council will be to ensure such intercourse between the statesmen of the countries represented on it as to enable them to secure solutions of international problems by discussion and co-operative action. For this purpose regular meetings with an appropriate procedure and secretariat are indispensable. No other single factor is likely to be so influential in producing harmony between the policies of States" (WP [44] 220, Appendix A).

we believe that the present proposals carry on a development which was supported by Castlereagh" (WP [44] 220). The only mention of voting in early documents was consistent with the understanding of the United Nations as a concert: "Naturally the decisions of the World Powers on all such subjects must be unanimous" (WP [43] 300). And maintaining comity among the great powers was the most important factor.[16]

The Conservative Cabinet explicitly opposed any type of positive guarantee of political independence or territorial guarantee that might threaten entrapment. Instead members would "promise to settle all disputes in such a manner as not to endanger the maintenance of international peace and security," a negative covenant. In the event of a breach of that commitment, the United Nations would deal with each issue on a case-by-case basis without any predetermined formula. The British government believed that "there should be no attempt to lay down in advance any rigid definition of the occasions on which ... action would be taken, but that the Members of the Organisation and the World Council should only be empowered to take action in accordance with the principles and objects of the Organisation" (WP [44] 220).

The Conservative-dominated British government also pushed for strong regional organizations. Churchill envisioned a "Council of the World" responsible for international peace and security composed entirely of the four great powers. Smaller powers would be represented only in a number of regional councils for the Pacific, the American and European spheres. The great powers would sit on more than one regional council depending on the stretch of their influence. The smaller councils would attempt to resolve disputes in their area, with the World Council serving as the ultimate arbiter and quasi-court of appeal. Churchill described it as a "three-legged stool" (WP [43] 331; WP [43] 233; Goodwin 1957: 6–7; Jebb 1990: 30; Reynolds and Hughes 1976: 31, 187–8; Campbell 1973: 11). Churchill's belief in the importance of regional councils was based on his expectations of abandonment. Countries would not make security commitments to

---

[16] The "primary and most important task would be to smooth out any frictions existing between [the great powers] so as to achieve that unity of purpose without which no ordered progress will be possible and the peace of the world is bound to be threatened. Where necessary, discussions on these subjects could be limited to the World Powers themselves" (WP [44] 220).

the peace and security of areas far away, something that the League experience had proven and the pessimist and conservative Cabinet member Leo Amery also stressed (WP [43] 339).[17] Again, collective security was a chimera for those with a more competitive social orientation. Diffuse reciprocity would not operate effectively.

Therefore, unlike the more idealistic and trusting American administration in the United States, the British Conservatives never countenanced anything like a revival of collective security. They preferred a less qualitatively and quantitatively multilateral institution. This rejection was partially a recognition of the failure of the League but also a general reflection of Conservative pessimism. Jebb wrote of his Foreign Office colleagues, "we were not utopians or even internationalists" and noted how Conservative politicians in the Cabinet "worked with the same underlying assumptions" as British diplomats (Jebb 1990: 25, 28). Strong conservatives such as Leo Amery objected even to the concert conception proposed by Eden as overly idealistic. In a memorandum presented to the Cabinet, he complained that the Foreign Secretary's plans rested on the same faulty premise as the League: "[N]othing contributed more to the grim reality of this universal war than the fiction of the 'indivisible peace' with no indivisible will to enforce peace behind it," he wrote. Amery's competitive social orientation was evident in his assessment of the League's failure, which was "the result, not of abnormal wickedness nor of abnormal feebleness on the part on statesmen, but of natural tendencies which are bound to reassert themselves." He cautioned that "ignoring all the stubborn realities in the varying outlook and behaviour of these intensely individualistic entities which we call nations" would "likely to lead to disaster, for ourselves and for the world" (WP [43] 39).

Domestic differences in the House of Commons

This lack of generalized trust was also evident in the contributions of rank-and-file Conservative members of parliament in the first debates

---

[17] "It was only the countries whose interests were directly affected by a dispute who could be expected to apply themselves with sufficient vigour to secure a settlement," he wrote. "If countries remote from a dispute were among those called upon in the first instance to achieve a settlement the result was likely to be merely vapid and academic discussion" (WP [43] 233; Goodwin 1957: 7; Jebb 1990: 31).

on postwar order. As there was never any formal vote in which members went on record about the United Nations, either in its planning stage or even after its signing, it is not possible to get a firm count on the distribution of opinion. And even if there had been a vote, such data would not be very revealing in light of the importance placed on party loyalty in a parliamentary system. However, in terms of their substantive contributions, only Conservative members of parliament, those most likely to lack generalized trust, criticized the premise of collective security during the few debates on the subject. And they grounded their objection in generally pessimistic notions of human nature and international relations.

Lord Dunglass proclaimed, "there is no foundation, in morals or in facts, upon which you can surely build a collective peace system on the model of the League of Nations at the present time...A study of the nature and history of man...would give very little ground for the assumption that he had either the ability or the wish to live at peace... [T]o ignore it would be a policy of folly" (*Hansard*, vol. 403, col. 805–7). Raikes made the same point about repeating the League experience, cautioning "that just the same weaknesses in human nature may materialize" (*Hansard*, vol. 403, col. 869). Beamish said his "plea is for realism," not a "childish faith in paper collective security" (*Hansard*, vol. 413, col. 873). Dunglass rejected the collective security premise that the British must relinquish some sovereignty to gain security as a "false dilemma." Britain's only responsibility was for its own security (*Hansard*, vol. 400, col. 805ff.). Pethick claimed that diffuse reciprocity could not serve as the basis for international cooperation: "Hon. Members may say that there must be give and take in all these matters, but the whole of history surely shows that there has been very little give, and it has always been a question of take. From the times of the earlier conquering tribes to the time of the great wars of the Middle Ages and down to this day we have had a succession of ruthless rulers who, backed by ruthless peoples, have cast their eyes covetously on other States and in fact have overrun them." He advocated simple great-power consultation and coordination after the war as the most appropriate strategy in a situation of great uncertainty (*Hansard*, vol. 403, col.835ff.).

Just as in the United States, there were ideological contrasts between left and right that indicate the central role played by generalized trust in defining preferences for international cooperation. Labour and

Liberal members recognized the failures of the League, but they were the only ones to argue that the League had merits. The only statements of support for qualitative multilateralism came from the two parties left of center (*Hansard*: Pethick-Lawrence [vol. 400, col. 813ff.], Mander [vol. 403, col. 970ff.] and Hynd [vol. 403, col. 579ff.]). The Liberal Mander declared that "absolute national sovereignty... is as much out of date as the divine right of Kings... [D]o not let us think for a moment that we can have safety in the world and maintain complete absolute national sovereignty" (*Hansard*, vol. 403, col. 970). Shinwell of Labour also argued that states could not have security and complete independence simultaneously (*Hansard*, vol. 403, col. 988ff.). Beveridge of the Liberals advocated for a firmer positive guarantee to assure smaller countries that help would be forthcoming, lest they fall back on destabilizing alliances for security (*Hansard*, vol. 410, col. 106). Only Liberals and Labour made explicit references to the negative influence of national sovereignty on world affairs (*Hansard*: Harris [vol. 403, col. 626ff.], Bevan [vol. 403, col. 633ff.], Petwhick-Lawrence [vol. 403, col. 688ff.; vol. 400, col. 813ff.] and Hore-Belisha [vol. 400, col. 1,002ff.]).

The influence of the Dominions

This clear partisan alignment, identical to that in the United States, indicates that British policy might have been different under a Labour or leftist-dominated government. However, while Labour had a few advocates of their point of view in the Cabinet such as Clement Attlee, its influence was relatively marginal (Jebb 1990: 28). The key force moderating British unilateralism and its preference for a concert was the position of the Dominions. As smaller powers, they were resistant to a great-power trusteeship. British officials recognized that the country's somewhat weak claim to great-power status equivalent to that of the United States and the Soviet Union depended on its ability to speak for the entire British Commonwealth, including the independent nation-states of South Africa, Canada, Australia and New Zealand. Officials responsible for Dominion affairs cautioned the government that if Britain "does not now champion wholeheartedly the reasonable claims of the smaller Powers, including the Dominions... she will forfeit the Dominions' confidence, and the British Commonwealth will lose its strength" (WP [43] 115). For this reason, securing

Dominion agreement on British plans was crucial (WP [43] 244; WP [44]; Goodwin 1957: 12). Jebb wrote that "Britain, at the head of the Commonwealth, could not ignore the middle and small powers" (1990: 35).

Dominion pressure was responsible for modifying the British position in a number of ways. The former colonies, particularly Canada, objected strongly to the notion that they would be excluded from the body ultimately responsible for world security and were incredulous of the British assurance that the United Kingdom would look after their interests in the new Council (WP [43] 244). In response, the government drew up a new "United Nations Plan for Organising Peace," which foresaw a "World Council" of five great powers, to which "might be added" representatives of six or seven smaller powers, potentially elected by the regional councils or by a United Nations assembly (WP [43] 300). This draft was considered and endorsed by a meeting of prime ministers of the Dominions and the United Kingdom in April 1944 (Goodwin 1957: 12; Jebb 1990: 35; Reynolds and Hughes 1976: 189). The inclusion of small powers became the concrete negotiating position of the British. Dominion influence was also seen in the British decision to push for a somewhat larger Council that would allow the inclusion of a Dominion member at all times, a preference for a two-thirds voting rule (as opposed to a simple majority) that would magnify the influence of the smaller countries, and an explicit mention that states whose interests were affected should have the right to lay their case before the Council even if they were not members (WP [44] 370; WP [44] 406; Goodwin 1957: 21–2; Hildebrand 1990: 192). Initial drafts had left these provisions open (WP [44] 220), but after consultation the Cabinet settled on the preference of the smaller countries (WP [44] 370), something reflected in the final Charter.

The Conservative government also came to oppose the absolute veto. Largely on the insistence of smaller powers, the British government agreed that parties to a dispute should be forced to abstain from voting, even the great powers (WP [44] 220, Appendix B). A British diplomat explained that the smaller powers could not accept the "drastic obligation" to have their disputes, when they threatened international security, settled by the United Nations unless the great powers also made such a commitment (Reynolds and Hughes 1976: 46–7). The absolute veto would leave the smaller countries powerless in a conflict against a great power. And the ability to obstruct the mere recommendation of ways to solve disputes would cut out the heart of the British conception of the UN as a forum for diplomatic discussion.

Of course all of these Dominion positions were strategic in nature, a product of their structural position, and had nothing to do with trust. However they had the effect of modifying the conservative preferences of the government, which were driven by a lack of generalized trust. This was pure politics, not an example of ideological persuasion. An opponent of great-power prerogatives in British planning, the diplomat Webster, described British policy as "a case of prejudgments, unmodi-fied by consideration of alternative possibilities, overridden because of the political necessity not to be split from the Dominions" (Reynolds and Hughes 1976: 86). However, there were limits. The Conservative government forcefully resisted efforts by the some of the Dominions to insert a positive security guarantee like Article X into the new United Nations Treaty (WP [45] 38; WP [45] 209).

Nevertheless, Dominion influence served to push the British posi-tion on the UN in the direction preferred by the Labour Party and Democrats in the United States. Whereas the more liberal State Depart-ment was forced to consider a less multilateral organization by the need to appease FDR and Republicans, the Conservative government in Britain moved in a more multilateral direction due to pressure from the Dominions. For this reason, the two countries, even though they were governed by parties with very different social orientations, were largely on the same page when it came time to convene a great-power meeting on the postwar institution.

Squaring the reciprocity circle: strategic distrust of the Soviet Union, qualitative multilateralism and the absolute veto controversy

In August 1944, negotiators from Britain, the Soviet Union and the United States met in Washington DC at the Dumbarton Oaks man-sion in Georgetown to agree on a preliminary institutional frame-work for the United Nations. Although the delegations had exchanged papers, the American plans were by far the most detailed and essen-tially served as the blueprint for discussions. They survived the meeting largely intact and were endorsed by the three powers as the basis for a larger international conference to create the international organization. However, one important question remained outstanding after the summit. Although there were other issues of contention, the most controversial issue at Dumbarton Oaks was the absolute veto. As mentioned above, the American delegation had split between those who prioritized the effectiveness of the new organization and those most concerned with what was actually ratifiable by the Senate, without any particular strategic consideration given to who was most likely to abuse the veto.

However, two factors, the Soviets' own position on the absolute veto and their actions in Eastern Europe, led the Americans to increasingly consider the issue more strategically. The Soviet delegation at Dumbarton Oaks vigorously opposed any restriction on the great-power veto. By taking such an intransigent position, the Soviet Union raised doubts about its own intentions. Its very position on institutional design created strategic distrust (Hilderbrand 1990: 212–13). The Dumbarton Oaks meeting adjourned with the absolute veto as the most important unsettled issue.

This suspicion of the Soviet Union was reinforced by its behavior in Eastern Europe as the war drew to a close. In early 1945, American officials became concerned that Soviet aims in Poland might be expansionist, including the installation of a communist government. The controversy over who would govern Poland, and most important whether the government in exile in London would be part of the coalition with the Soviet-installed Lublin government, was occurring at the same time as the Americans were attempting to resolve the absolute veto dispute through direct diplomacy with Stalin (Campbell 1973: 88; Gaddis 2000, Chapter 5; Schlesinger 2003: 10–14).

Unlike in earlier internal debates, Soviet motives and intentions become part of the deliberations within the administration. Soviet behavior, however, did not lead to an ideological reorientation. Soviet actions had the effect of reinforcing the determination of those American officials, the vast majority of the delegation, who had opposed the absolute veto from the beginning. Hull's position, along with Pasvolsky's, hardened (Hilderbrand 1990: 214; Stettinius 1975: 140). Those more idealistic and trusting Wilsonians who had argued against the absolute veto in principle now stressed that the Soviets had to be contained through this institutional means. Stettinius and

Pasvolsky believed that the Soviets might be stalling the talks on the UN because they did not want to have a peacekeeping body created before their armies marched into Eastern Europe (Hilderbrand 1990: 215). He stressed that it was better to have a United Nations without the Soviet Union than one without Britain and the Latin American states (Hilderbrand 1990: 220). Strategic distrust and generalized trust pushed in the same direction, towards restrictions on great-power prerogatives and a more qualitatively multilateral United Nations. It was in this period that one sees the first signs of the potent cocktail of idealism and anti-communism. The first Cold Warriors were liberal.

The proponents of the absolute veto, who were a small but vocal minority, did not necessarily lack generalized trust, and they did not trust the Soviets more than others did. Rather they saw continued good relations as more important than the ultimate mechanics of the international security organization. Their differences with the Pasvolsky group had bureaucratic, not ideological, origins. The military representatives to Dumbarton Oaks and in the working groups coordinating decisions on the United Nations were desperate not to alienate the Soviet Union and keep it from joining the front in the Far East. For this group, great-power unity trumped everything, even if the price was the absolute veto. They combined forces with those worried about Republican opposition to restrictions on the veto (Campbell 1973a: 53–4; Hilderbrand 1990: 187, 196, 219). However, there were no ideologically driven Democratic Party supporters of the absolute veto in the cooperatively oriented administration to my knowledge.

Soviet behavior had the effect of easing conservative anxiety about limiting the veto. As reviewed above, Hull had deliberately omitted the issue from his discussions in the Committee of Eight, anticipating objections on sovereignty grounds. They had now been informed of the controversy. In April, Vandenberg had approved the veto because it "would immunize all the major powers against military discipline" (Russell 1958: 498–9). In the context of possible Soviet obstructionism, however, Vandenberg began to think differently, writing in his diary that "such immunity ... would represent a new imperialism"(Vandenberg 1952: 120). Increasingly the senator began to criticize Soviet behavior, both publicly and privately (Vandenberg 1952: 136, 176–7, 182).

Nevertheless, Soviet actions were not enough to drive Vandenberg or Republicans in general to renounce the veto entirely. Even though Republicans were generally more critical of the Soviets than were Democrats, they were not more inclined to embrace multilateralism as a strategic solution. Conservatives' lack of generalized trust trumped their strategic distrust. While the veto was "immoral and indefensible . . . in any other application . . . it is fully justified in respect to the use of force because the Powers with the 'veto' will be the Powers which must largely furnish the force," Vandenberg wrote privately. Because of differences in social orientation, Soviet obstructionism, while it worked against Democratic preferences for the United Nations, actually served conservative ends by protecting the feature of the institution that could prevent entrapment and exploitation. The Senator wrote: "[T]he irony of the situation is that the greater the extent of the 'veto', the more impossible it becomes for the new League to involve America in anything against our own will." This was not all bad for the Democrats, however. Vandenberg wrote that "the greater the 'veto' the easier it becomes to fight off our critics in Congress, in the country and in the press when the new Treaty faces its ratification battle. Every cloud has a silver lining" (Russell 1958: 726; Vandenberg 1952: 200).

Given Soviet intransigence and the conservative position, the administration was compelled to offer some compromise if they wanted the United Nations to be created at all. The result was overdetermined. They arrived at a new formula that would remove the absolute veto over issues of peaceful settlement but reinstate it on questions of enforcing the peace. This squared the circle between generalized trust and strategic distrust on the one hand and generalized distrust on the other. Roosevelt's longtime aide, Harry Hopkins, traveled to Moscow to meet Stalin personally and plead for his consent to this solution (Campbell 1973a: 92). At the Yalta summit, the Soviet leader finally formally agreed to the formula. It remains today in the United Nations Charter. This was a grudging compromise on both sides. Hull called it the "absolute minimum of what we could accept" (Campbell 1973a: 50). Even on the way to Yalta, the longtime advocate of great power unity, FDR, was expressing his frustration that the absolute veto would prohibit the institution from acting (Campbell 1973a: 95). Some accounts argue that some restriction on the veto was important enough to the

Roosevelt administration to sacrifice Poland at the summit (Widenor 1992: 265).

Squaring the community circle: strategic distrust, quantitative multilateralism and the origins of Article 51

The Dumbarton Oaks proposals agreed to by the great powers, alongside the Yalta agreement, served as the basis for discussions of all the future members of the organization at an intergovernmental conference in San Francisco, convened in April 1945 to negotiate the final United Nations Charter. There a new veto issue emerged. As reviewed above, the Roosevelt administration strongly preferred a centralized global organization, reflected in the fact that any peace enforcement action by a regional organization was to be subject to the approval of the Security Council. Administration officials believed such an institution would better mobilize the collective weight of the international community and prevent a devolution into a system of smaller regional organizations, the proliferation of spheres of influence and an American return to isolationism. However, given the veto, any great power could prevent regional security organizations from taking action against aggression (Campbell 1973a: 176–7; Hoopes and Brinkley 1997: 192–6; Patrick 2009: 58–9).

In light of recent Soviet provocations, Latin American countries, concerned about communist infiltration and even overt aggression, began to lobby the United States for a restriction on the Security Council's authority over such matters so as to protect the recently negotiated Act of Chapultepec. This declaration, signed by the United States and other western hemisphere nations, stated that any act of aggression on signatories amounted to an act of aggression against them all. These central and southern American nations were expressing their strategic distrust of the Soviet Union. They were concerned that the Soviets would veto any effort on their part to come to the aid of a country under pressure from communists and wanted the institution designed in such a way as to avoid that possibility. This was the downside of the great-power veto. It could protect but also obstruct. There was another tension between generalized distrust and strategic distrust in terms of institutional design (Campbell 1973a: 176–7; Hoopes and Brinkley 1997: 192–6).

On behalf of the western hemisphere states, Nelson Rockefeller, Secretary of State for Latin American Affairs and a Republican, approached newly appointed Secretary of State Edward Stettinius about limiting Security Council jurisdiction over regional bodies or arrangements in these instances. However, Stettinius and Pasvolsky vehemently opposed any changes, arguing that it would allow great powers to establish their own regional groupings impervious to Security Council authority (Campbell 1973a: 176–7; Hoopes and Brinkley 1997: 192–6). It would lead to a de facto decrease in quantitative multilateralism by moving the management of international affairs to regional bodies. Stettinius complained that the Latin Americans "want to build a fence around the hemisphere . . . We have come to this conference to create an *international* organization" (S. C. Schlesinger 2003: 182 [emphasis added]).

At this point, Rockefeller engaged in some clever but sneaky politics, secretly alerting Vandenberg, a member of the American delegation in San Francisco, to the problem (Campbell 1973a: 166–7; S. C. Schlesinger 2003: 177–8). With the League debacle in mind, the American delegation had been carefully selected by the administration to reflect the range of ideological opinion in Congress, thereby easing the treaty's passage through the Senate. The Democrats had in mind Wilson's mistake of bringing only a single token Republican to Paris, and one who was out of step with his party (Campbell 1973a: 148; Notter 1949: 413). Vandenberg was particularly sympathetic to Rockefeller's argument, as the institution as it stood amounted to the extension of Security Council authority into the western hemisphere. He wrote, "[I]n the event of trouble in the Americas, we could not act ourselves; we would have to depend exclusively on the Security Council; and any one permanent member of the Council could veto the latter action (putting us at the mercy of Britain, Russia or China). Thus, little is left of the Monroe Doctrine" (Vandenberg 1952: 187). The issue of exploitation and interference that had contributed so much to the American decision not to join the League of Nations had reemerged.

Vandenberg saw the dilemma: "The Monroe Doctrine is protected only if we kick the daylights out of the world organization" (Vandenberg 1952: 188). Nevertheless, Vandenberg's solution, which he put in a formal letter to Stettinius at Rockefeller's request, was an explicit exception for the Act of Chapultepec in the United Nations

Charter, much like the exemption for the Monroe Doctrine in the League Covenant demanded by conservatives in 1919. Exploitation was more important than a more inclusive community circle. Vandenberg and Rockefeller gathered the support of several Latin American countries, who threatened not to join the future UN without such an exception. Vandenberg continually warned that the Senate would not ratify the Charter without the provision, and he threatened to insert a reservation in the instrument of ratification to protect the Monroe Doctrine, as Lodge had done twenty-six years before, if it were not in the final Charter. Stettinius, however, balked, leading to a standstill (Campbell 1973a: 165–7, 171; Hoopes and Brinkley 1997: 192–6; S. C. Schlesinger 2003: 178–9, 185; Vandenberg 1952: 189).

Another delegate, liberal Republican Harold Stassen, suggested the formula that would solve the dilemma, a general right to collective and self-defense to be enshrined in the Charter that would operate up until the point that the Security Council acted. If the Security Council was paralyzed by a Soviet veto, regional action against any communist aggression would be legal. However, the subordination of regional groups to the Security Council would remain as the latter could later supersede the former provided it could come an agreement. This pleased Pasvolsky and the other delegates. Article 51 was born, squaring the circle between unilateralism and quantitative multilateralism (Campbell 1973a: 172–5; Hoopes and Brinkley 1997: 194–5; Russell 1958: 693–6; S. C. Schlesinger 2003: 182).

The United States therefore had covered almost all of the bases of possible objection that had arisen after WWI. The veto in matters of enforcement prevented entrapment. Article 51 preserved the Monroe Doctrine and protected against exploitation. The only remaining issue was the right of withdrawal. Delegates Dulles and Vandenberg pressured the administration to mention such a right explicitly in the Charter. Those who trust less want more flexibility. Dulles cited uncertainty in his justification. The US "cannot foresee the future" (Vandenberg 1952: 195). Vandenberg predicted that the absence of the right of withdrawal would lead to great concern in the Senate (Vandenberg 1952: 194). The administration held out. However, it did not consent, either, to the British desire for an explicit statement forbidding withdrawal, conceived with the idea of keeping the United States in the UN. This would raise hackles in the Senate (Hilderbrand 1990: 103). The Roosevelt administration sought to play it down the middle. It argued to the Senate that such a right was understood even if it were not stated. But it preferred not mentioning it explicitly to avoid raising concerns internationally of a return to isolation that would undermine the assurance provided by American participation in the organization (US Senate 1945: 60). Vandenberg, isolated, concluded "it's not worth a row" (Vandenberg 1952: 194).

The circle squared in the United States: United States ratification of the UN Charter

On June 26, 1945, Secretary of State Stettinius submitted a formal report to the President on the San Francisco conference and the United Nations Charter. It mentioned many of the circles the Democratic administration had squared in the preceding years. The UN, he argued, was a compromise between idealism and realism: "The first function of the Charter is moral and idealistic: the second realistic and practical. Men and women who have lived through war are not ashamed, as other generations sometimes are, to declare the depth and the idealism of their attachment to the cause of peace. But neither are they ashamed to recognize the realities of force and power which war has forced them to see and to endure" (US Senate 1945: 36).

This mix was reflected in the UN's design: "[W]ithout precedent in international relations ... it differs from the traditional alliance and is unlike the Council of the League of Nations" (US Senate 1945: 73). The former "might have been justified on narrow strategic grounds, but it would have been repugnant to our traditional policy." The administration pushed instead for "the establishment of a general security system based upon the principle of sovereign equality of all peace-loving states and upon the recognition of the predominant responsibility of the great powers in matters relating to peace and security" (US Senate 1945: 72). The UN was a combination of a concert and a collective security arrangement which was "quasi-judicial in its conciliatory function" but "permitted for the play of political considerations" (US Senate 1945: 81).

There is a distinct sense of dissatisfaction in the document, of an opportunity lost. This is not surprising considering the more cooperative social orientation of the State Department. The UN protects sovereignty, Hull wrote, because the world is "not ready" for a world state (US Senate 1945: 40–41). The qualified majority voting procedure in the General Assembly was said to be "an *advance* over the procedure in the Security Council" (US Senate 1945: 75 [emphasis added]). However, the administration was not going to suffer the same fate as in 1919 by making perfection a necessity (Campbell 1973a: 63, 80).

Squaring the circle served its main purpose, of guaranteeing overwhelming support in the Senate. The administration was driven first and foremost to avoid a repetition of the League experience. With this in mind, Hull even took care to ensure that matters of domestic jurisdiction would be excluded (Russell 1958: 299, 406, 463). As Vandenberg wrote in his diary, "The things we did at Frisco to remove potential Senate opposition have paid rich dividends," something which could be said of the entire process of private bipartisan consultation (Vandenberg 1952: 218). The Senate Foreign Relations Committee stressed the protections of the veto and Article 51 when reporting the Treaty with only one dissenting vote – Hiram Johnson, one of the "irreconcilable" traditional isolationists who had voted against the League of Nations a quarter-century before (S. C. Schlesinger 2003: 272). When the Senate convened to consider the ratification of the United Nations Charter in July, Democratic Senator William Fulbright confessed, "I find myself somewhat suspicious of the unanimity with which the charter is apparently received by this body. Practically no measure of real importance has been accepted with such docility by the opposition." A few minutes into his speech, however, he offered an answer to his own question: "I cannot help but think that the principal reason for the unexpected approval in certain quarters of the Charter may have been induced by the assurance which some proponents have made that we sacrifice none of our American sovereignty" (US Congress,[18] 79:1: 7,962–3).

Even the issue of earmarking parts of the American armed forces for use by the Security Council proved uncontroversial. Vandenberg had predicted that this would become a major issue during ratification, ominously warning that almost all Republicans would support a reservation forbidding the use of American forces without specific congressional approval (Stettinius 1975: 141; Vandenberg 1952: 119). He wanted a guarantee that the Congress would be able to approve on a case-by-case basis the use of any national contingent committed for use to the United Nations since such a vote in the Security Council

---

[18] Hereafter CR, for *Congressional Record*.

amounted to a declaration of war. Entrusting that power to the executive was unconstitutional, according to Vandenberg, as it infringed on the Congress's prerogatives. Hull, however, insisted on this ability, as the point of earmarked forces was to allow the Security Council to act quickly. The President likened Vandenberg's position to calling a town meeting before arresting a criminal (Hoopes and Brinkley 1997: 164).

Vandenberg was correct that this provision would draw the ire of isolationists more sensitive to congressional powers and opposed to international cooperation of any type. However, he vastly overestimated their importance. Given the fact that the United States could use its great-power veto to prevent the dispatch of its forces against its will, American sovereignty was protected. Article 43, despite its implications for the institutional balance of power, was consequently completely uncontroversial during the ratification (Hilderbrand 1990: 149–51; Russell 1958: 264; Stettinius 1975: 299). The real issue with international cooperation was national sovereignty, not legislative sovereignty.[19]

Despite this bipartisan support, I dwell on the ratification process as it provides a window into whether the different ideological approaches of the select individuals representing their parties in the behind-the-scenes process can be gleaned in a setting in which many more individuals were called upon to express their opinions publicly. As the Charter was based on a compromise between unilateralists and multilateralists, the vote itself reveals very little information. Therefore, we must pay attention to the argumentation used by senators.

Vandenberg, the first Republican to speak in the debate, raised all the points that had led Lodge to push for reservations over twenty-five

---

[19] The Secretary had promised Vandenberg that Congress would be called upon later to approve the special agreement reached with the Security Council as to what forces it would make available in case of a crisis. When the administration submitted in December 1945 its agreement with the Security Council, which stated that the President would not require the authorization of Congress to vote for the use of troops provided the operation did not go beyond the limits set in the statute, it passed overwhelmingly by a vote of 65 to 7. The isolationist Wheeler offered an amendment requiring specific congressional approval in each instance of the use of American servicemen, but it failed 65 to 9. The great-power veto undercut all support for this kind of oversight (Campbell 1973a: 45; Russell 1958: 469–70; Vandenberg 1952: 116–9).

years earlier and noted how the UN protected against opportunism of all types:

Now, listen. The United States retains every basic attribute of its sovereignty. We cannot be called to participate in any sort of sanctions, military or otherwise, without our own free and untrammeled consent. We cannot be taken into the World Court except at our own free option ... Our domestic questions are eliminated from the new organization's jurisdiction. Our inter-American system and the Monroe Doctrine are unimpaired in their realities. Our right of withdrawal from the new organization is absolute, and is dependent solely upon our own discretion. (CR, 79:1: 7,956–7)

The main point was "though we cooperate wholeheartedly ... [W]e remain the captains of our own souls" (S. C. Schlesinger 2003: 266).

Others claimed the same factors allowed them to support the treaty. Brooks of Illinois had been worried about entrapment and exploitation, "about the ability of this organization to commit us to enforcement action without our consent" and concerned "with how much we were limiting the purposes and objectives of our historic Monroe Doctrine." He looked for flexibility, "any provision that might prevent our full determination as to the extent of our participation in the event that in the distant future ... we felt that we should withdraw." He felt reassured in all instances (CR 79:1: 8,104). Willis stressed that the Charter "protected the sovereignty of the United States of America" against entrapment by ensuring that only the United States could determine when its military forces would be used. Willis and Brooks were among the eight most conservative senators in the party. The only explicit praise of the veto came from Republican senators, all of whom were in the mainstream of their party (CR, 79:1, Revercomb [8,159ff.] and Cordon (8,173]). Less trusting individuals were not comfortable giving other countries control over American foreign policy.

Many contrasted the new institution favorably to the League. Capper of Kansas had voted against the League "with a clear conscience at the time" and had "no apologies to make now." He voted for the United Nations because "the retention of the national sovereignty of the United States is in the Charter itself this time" (CR 79:1: 8,087). Willis had the same opinion of the League and the UN (CR 79:1: 8,185).

As they had been in the League of Nations debate, Republicans were consistently more pessimistic than Democrats in their speeches, often grounding their unilateral preferences in general statements about the nature of social interactions and the trustworthiness of others. Cordon stressed that the "frailties of human nature...exist all over the world" in grounding his support for the veto (CR 79:1: 8,174). Capper stated, "No one makes the claim that this is a perfect instrument. Nor does anyone believe that a perfect instrument can be devised, making allowances for the vagaries of human nature" (CR 79:1: 8,087). Both senators were mainstream Republicans. Willis of Indiana made a colorful allusion to a Carl Sandburg children's poem, cautioning Americans not to be like Eeta Peeca Pie, "filled with wishes...unconcerned with the facts, disdainful of reality...[T]hese Americans go gaily along, agitating always for this or that reform...whether or not it will work at all." He cautioned Americans to be like Mincy Mo, "filled both with wishes and suspicions" (CR 79:1: 8,183).

Republicans believed that the merits of the United Nations were in its concert-like properties. Vandenberg declared, "My faith is in the Council table" (CR 79:1: 7,956). While recognition of the necessity of the preservation of great-power unity was bipartisan, the only positive references to the creation of a concert of the great powers came from Republicans (CR, 79:1, Capper [p. ,087], Revercomb [8159ff.] and Burton [8,017]). Lacking generalized trust, they fell back on the particularized variety. For Burton, "the entire world has been engaged in this struggle and through it the Allies have won the undisputed championship of the world. The best way to retain this or any other championship is to retain the championship team intact and in condition. Chapter VII of the Charter of the United Nations provides a means for doing this" (CR 79:1: 8,013).

Nevertheless, an international organization was no substitute for national, unilateral means. References to the necessity of military preparedness came only from Republicans, all mainstream or extreme conservatives (CR, 79:1, Brooks [8,104], Willis [8,183] and Revercomb [8,159]). Willis stressed that the "safety of America lies in our reliance on our own security and reliance on our own strength and virtue, rather than in charters and compacts and treaties" (CR 79:1: 8,184). Those who do not trust have to go it largely alone.

For Democrats, the lesson of WWII, as had been the case after the first, was that the international community could only create peace together. This was not altruism but rather a belief in the gains from reciprocity fostered by generalized trust. Interdependence cast the notion of sovereignty in a different light for Fulbright:

[O]ur Government . . . can no longer protect our people from the disastrous effects of war. Therefore, it is entirely essential, that our people consider the delegation of power to some other and higher organization which is reasonably designed to perform the function which this Government cannot perform . . . In creating a more effective instrumentality . . . how can it possibly be said to be the surrender of sovereignty or of anything else? It is not a surrender. It is the acquisition of a power previously nonexistent. (CR 79:1: 7,964)

With the exception of the liberal Republican Wiley, only Democrats made these kind of references to the need for cooperation (CR 79:1, Connally [7,953ff.] Chavez [7,958], Wiley [7,964], Hill [7,971], Pepper [8,069], Tunnell [8,100], Kilgore [8,129], Murray [8,130], Andrews [8,176] and McMahon [8,106]). Generalized trust served as anarchical social capital.

As a consequence, Democrats were much less enthusiastic about the emphasis on sovereignty in the United Nations design. Genuine multilateralism necessitates some loss of unilateral control. Fulbright declared such a focus "unfortunate because it reaffirms our allegiance to the concept of national sovereignty under which our civilization has so closely approached self-destruction. It is unfortunate because if the absolute sovereignty of the nation states is rigidly preserved, then it means a denial to begin with of the only evolutionary goal which might eventually give us a rule of law based on justice in place of capricious and ruthless rule of force" (CR 79:1: 7,963). Democrats expressed worries about the veto (CR, 79:1, Pepper [8,072] and Eastland [8,084]) but more often indicated a general unease with the institution's form in a way that Republicans did not, such as by frequently stating that the United Nations' design was less than perfect (CR, 79:1, Connally [7,953], Thomas [7,960], Fulbright [7,964], Johnson [8,003], McFarland [8,004], Lucas [8,019], Myers [8,105] and McMahon [8,106]).

Nevertheless, the Democrats, like the administration, were keenly aware of the League experience and determined not to repeat it. Democrats consistently invoked WWII as what would result from an American refusal to engage internationally (CR 79:1, O'Daniel [7,958], Guffey [7,959], Fulbright [7,962], Hill [7,973], Andrews [8,175], Lucas [8,019], Pepper [8,068], McClellan [8,083], Tunnell [8,018], Johnston [8,179], McMahon [8,106] and Chandler [8,112]).

Senator Ferguson of Wisconsin, one of the most liberal members of his party, was the only Republican to mention the League in these terms (CR 79:1: 8,000). Connally put it most dramatically: "[T]he League of Nations was slaughtered here on the floor. Can you not still see the blood on the floor? Can you not see upon the walls the marks of the conflict that raged here in the Chamber where the League of Nations was done to death" (CR 79:1: 7,954). Republicans barely mentioned the League, "possibly chagrined by their role in killing the League twenty-five years earlier," Schlesinger writes (2003: 273).

The exceptions to these clear partisan patterns of argumentation were almost exclusively liberal Republicans, who expressed more generalized trust. Wiley cautioned against letting fear prevent international collaboration to create peace as it had after the last war and stressed that representatives of fifty nations representing millions desired peace (CR 79: 1: 7,965). Senator Smith of New Jersey described his decision-making process: "[M]y fears and conservatism have given way to my faith and vision. We are able to pass another milestone and in passing it, we are saying to the other nations of the world: We all now know that none of us can live alone. We are all interdependent; We will trust you and you must trust us" (CR 79: 1: 8,036).[20] I can find only one exception to this general ideological pattern in the entire UN debate, the opposition of mainstream conservative Senator Bridges to the veto (CR 79:1: 8,165).

There were only a few traditional isolationists left in the Senate, as they had been badly hurt in congressional elections and were not a strong presence even before (Campbell 1973a: 67; Hoopes and Brinkley 1997: 165). Their arguments were identical to those used after WWI. The organization amounted to a great-power dictatorship that would embroil the United States in the power politics of the Old World and lead to war rather than peace. Participation in such a new Holy Alliance would destroy American democracy and make the United States into an imperialist power like Britain and now Russia. This directly contradicted the wishes of the founding fathers, particularly Washington, whose farewell address was again frequently cited (CR, 79:1, Langer [8,188ff.], Shipstead [8,116ff.] and Wheeler [7,973ff.]).

---

[20] Ferguson cautioned optimism based on the demonstrated ability over time for nations to "progressively cut down the area of anarchy in human relations" (CR 79: 1: 8,001). Austin made similar statements (CR 79: 1: 8,060ff.). Austin was the third most liberal Senator, Smith the sixth, Ferguson the thirteenth. Another exceptional Republican, Aiken ranked second.

However, given their limited numbers and the concessions granted to mainstream Republicans, the isolationists were left powerless. With the support of Democrats and liberal Republicans eager for American participation in some sort of international organization and mainstream Republicans assured by the protection of American sovereignty, the Charter passed overwhelmingly with 89 assenting and only 2 dissenting votes.

The circle squared in Britain: cross-party support for the UN

The British debate both before and after San Francisco was remarkably similar. Labour and Liberal members expressed support for the United Nations but noted that it was far from an ideal institution (*Hansard*, vol. 410, Attlee [col. 80], Jones [col. 98], Thomas [col. 122] and Levy [col. 730]; vol. 413, Warbey [col. 896] and Bevin [col. 948]). Their most frequent complaint was that great powers would encumber the United Nations, particularly when it might be called to act on behalf of small powers against the great either directly or through proxy (*Hansard*, vol. 410, Jones [col. 98], Beveridge [col. 104ff.], Nicolson [col. 118ff.], Thomas [col. 122], Hynd [col. 161ff], Levy [col. 730]; vol. 413, Warbey [col. 896]). The veto was especially egregious as it might prevent the use of the national contingents dedicated to an international force for the United Nations. The organization could not have true teeth with a veto, MPs argued (*Hansard*, vol. 410, Tinker [col. 142ff.]; vol. 413, see Durbin [col. 706ff.] and Martin [col. 922]).

As Fulbright had argued in the United States debate, the Liberal MP Clement Davies argued that states undermined their own interests by insisting on sovereignty:

It has taken man centuries to realize that if he wants to enjoy to the full measure his own individuality, he must surrender part of the sovereignty of his own individuality so that it conforms with that of other people, and in that way only has been established the rule of law within countries, so that there is greater freedom for the individual. It is not to be wondered at then that it is going to take probably still further time before States can realise that true freedom lies in their surrendering part of their sovereignty. (*Hansard*, vol. 413, col. 889)

Concerns about the veto were not altruistic.

Nevertheless, as was the case in the United States, even if a few denounced the organization as a revival of the Holy Alliance, leftist members of the legislature did not want to make the perfect the enemy of the good (*Hansard*, vol. 410, cols. 82, 118). Those who opposed the veto also recognized that it was necessary to bring in the United States and the Soviet Union, something which had cross-party support. In his opening statement to the House of Commons debate before the San Francisco conference, Labourite Clement Attlee, a member of the Cabinet and Lord President of the Council, said, "I think we must frankly recognize that if we insist on no power to veto we simply will not get the thing started. That is what we have to face" (*Hansard*, vol. 410, col. 88). Others in the party said the same (*Hansard*, vol. 410, Thomas [col. 122] and Levy [col. 73]).

Attlee's resignation to the veto, even if he was officially speaking for the government, stood in stark contrast to the contributions made by Conservative members of the Cabinet. Minister of State Richard Law, in ending the same debate, spoke somewhat mockingly of those who opposed the veto: "Listening to some of the speeches this afternoon, I had the feeling that the speakers regarded this world as a lump of clay which might quite easily be moulded to our heart's desire. But it is not that at all. It is a very hard and difficult world" (*Hansard*, vol. 410, col. 170). When the now former Foreign Secretary Eden spoke at the ratification debate, he made no apology for the veto and instead made the case for "diplomacy by conference" (*Hansard*, vol. 413, col. 674). As was the case in the United States, only Conservative members made positive references to the concert features of the UN (*Hansard*, vol. 413, Glyn [col. 713] and Digby [col. 720]). They alone expressed support for the veto (*Hansard*, vol. 410, col. 109).[21] And only the right stressed that the UN was no substitute for a strong national defense (*Hansard*, Wardlaw-Milne [vol. 410, col. 97], Viscount Hinchingbrooke [vol. 413, col. 145], Lord Dunglass [vol. 400, col. 808]).

As in the United States, the importance to the Liberals and Labour of having some sort of international organization, in combination with

---

[21] Those Tories who objected to this measure of unilateral control either had prior experience working with the League, hedged their support by stressing the continued importance of purely national armaments, were thinking in terms of a future conflict with the Soviets, couched their support as the only way to garner smaller-power consent, or had formerly been members of the Liberal Party. See comments by Salter, Hinchingbrook and Joynson-Hicks (*Hansard*, vol. 410, col. 109, 127ff.,132ff., 165).

Conservative support for a concert arrangement, guaranteed easy passage in the House. There was no division in the Commons, meaning
that there was such broad agreement that the matter was not put to a
vote. The treaty was passed with the equivalent of a voice vote in the US
Senate, although technically under British law consent of parliament
was never required.

From the United Nations to the North Atlantic Treaty

Generalized trust notwithstanding, the American administration knew
full well that the success of the United Nations depended on great-
power unity and in particular good relations with the Soviet Union.
In his report to the President before ratification, Hull noted that the
"cornerstone of world security is the unity of those nations which
formed the core of the grand alliance against the Axis" and that the
UN's "influence in world affairs . . . and its success in the maintenance
of peace and security will depend upon the degree to which unity is
achieved among the great powers" (US Senate 1945: 73). Of course it
was not to be.

The ferocity and vitriol with which the Cold War began had a sym-
bol. The Soviets used the veto 23 times in the first few years after the
United Nations came into being. Some 11 were applied to block the
admission of new members (US Senate 1973: 330). The Truman administration fretted that the great-power veto inhibited the United Nations
from functioning as a global security system. Politicians floated proposals to reform the United Nations in various ways, including the
removal of the great-power veto, but these were politically dead on
arrival in the Senate. It was in this context that the North Atlantic
Treaty was formed, as a kind of mini collective security arrangement
among America's most important allies, a more closed circle. As will
be seen, the alliance was formed "within the Charter but outside the
veto" as a way of pacifying both those with a competitive and those
with a cooperative social orientation. The Truman administration took
advantage of the fortuitous construction of Article 51 to justify a
regional defense arrangement that could take action in the case of
Security Council deadlock. Just three years after the San Francisco
conference, the United States again considered the creation of a new
multilateral security organization. That is the subject of Chapter 5.

5 | Closing the circle: the negotiation of the North Atlantic Treaty

Just as American interest and participation in the creation of the UN is often seen as inescapable, so too is the North Atlantic Treaty. In what could be called the conventional wisdom, the bipolar distribution of power, the reach of military technology, and ideological differences between the Soviet Union and the United States inevitably placed them at loggerheads, particularly over the fate of the European continent. The power of structure is said to be evident in the strong bipartisan support for the North Atlantic Treaty in the United States Senate.

The discussion leading up to the North Atlantic Treaty was indeed structurally compelled to a large degree. The precipitating factor in the creation of NATO was a series of Soviet provocations in 1948 that suggested malign Soviet intentions and eventually convinced even the more geographically insulated Americans, both Democrats and Republicans, of the need to act. This does not tell us much, however. As Lake points out, the existence of the Soviet threat does not explain in and of itself why the allies designed the alliance the way they did or why they aligned at all (1999: 128–9). Of more importance is that these countries chose to cooperate and the form that cooperation took.

American policy is particularly puzzling. The key question in the formation of NATO is not, as Ikenberry (2001) frames it, how the United States was able to convince Europeans of the safety of American leadership by embedding itself in a multilateral institution, but rather how the much more vulnerable and threatened Europeans were able to lure a wary United States into making a commitment to European security. As Weber (1992) points out, the United States' first inclination was to create a self-reliant Europe and return home. There is no evidence that Europeans feared "arbitrary" US behavior or that the United States was driven by making their "hegemony acceptable to the Europeans" through multilateralism (Ikenberry 2001: 200, 206).

Despite his critique of the realist account, Lake's (1999, Chapter 5) alternative is structural as well. He claims that the positive externalities of a division of labor made possible by the nature of military technology led the US towards cooperation in a way that was not true after WWI. The risks of opportunism were relatively low and more than outweighed by the potential economies of scale. In both Lake and Ikenberry, we find implied that the United States more or less formed a privileged group, willing to provide the public good of security with very little reciprocity due to its overwhelming interest in the security of Europe.

Lake's account, however, misses the fact that the perceived risks of opportunism were low because of the trusting premises of the Truman administration. The alliance was based on a particular idea about how to deal with the Soviet problem that was predicated on trust in America's European allies. The Democrats, marked by a cooperative social orientation consistent with their domestic ideological profile at home, argued that the Europeans had extremely low "morale." The implication was that the Europeans, after the difficulties of the war, had simply lost hope. But if the Americans made a gesture in the form of a security guarantee or material help, the Western Europeans could be expected to cooperate with the Americans. In other words, the Truman administration understood the situation in reassurance terms. Generalized trust served as a source of social capital for the Democratic administration to move first and led it to seek the gains of a multilateral security commitment. However, this was not altruism or a hegemon providing public goods. The Truman administration expected and anticipated European reciprocity.

The importance of generalized trust becomes more evident when we compare the position of Democrats and Republicans. Conservatives also recognized the potential threat of the Soviet Union, the rapidly decreasing value of geographic distance and isolation in providing security, and therefore the need for some kind of deterrent. However, facing the same structural incentives and presented with the same information, conservatives were systematically more concerned about European opportunism in the form of entrapment and free riding. They framed the same situation in prisoner's dilemma terms. The leader of this faction, Robert Taft, consequently proposed various unilateral alternatives that involved no qualitative and little quantitative multilateralism. These same issues were raised by "internationalist" Republicans, who, though more moderate, still favored a less binding arrangement with fewer members, and demanded that the Europeans first demonstrate their commitment and trustworthiness. Their preferences were captured in the "Vandenberg resolution" passed by the Senate. Rationalists cannot account for these differences, particularly in a setting in which structural circumstances should have overwhelmed ideological differences.

Since most accounts of NATO's formation neglect domestic politics, they draw faulty conclusions about the importance of structure. Kydd evaluates only the administration's point of view and is consequently led to believe that this was an objectively obvious reassurance situation (2005: 165–8). As observers looking back from the vantage point of today, this becomes clear. However, European preferences were uncertain to American decision-makers at the time, and more conservative politicians framed the situation differently. Lake reaches a substantively different but similarly erroneous conclusion. He notes and dismisses the Taft alternative as marginal, but because he devotes little attention to the behind-the-scenes domestic political consultations proceeding alongside the transatlantic negotiations, he misses that the Vandenberg faction had similar concerns (1999: 131, 170).

Recognizing that conservative Democrats and even the most ideologically like-minded Republicans had significant concerns about opportunism, the administration proceeded extremely cautiously. It incorporated conservative suggestions, such as a requirement of "self-help" and a somewhat weaker security guarantee. As was the case with the United Nations, the lack of controversy over the North Atlantic Treaty owed to smart politics, not the changed structural circumstances facing the US or any major realignment in ideological preferences. These protections undermined support for Taft's unilateral alternative, and the treaty's passage was relatively certain by the time it came before the Senate.

Differences between the two sides were pronounced enough that the position of the administration and its liberal congressional allies was often closer to the Europeans' preferences than to those of conservatives. Some correctly note that the Europeans, facing a potentially existential threat, wanted the strongest possible guarantees. But they neglect that the Truman administration's position was relatively similar (Kydd 2005: 165–8). The Democrats were forced to go slow primarily because of domestic political reservations, not because they felt less urgency given their more impregnable position. Not recognizing this two-track process leads these scholars to exaggerate the hesitance of American officials regarding what would become NATO (Lake 1999: 194–6; S. Weber 1992).

A number of constructivist scholars explain the formation of NATO and the form it took differently, by reference to a shared Western identity (K. W. Deutsch 1957; Hemmer and Katzenstein 2002; Jackson 2006; Patrick 2009; Risse-Kappen 1995). These types of arguments, generally the most prominent alternative in the literature to the rationalist or realist, can shade into altruism, implying that to protect the Western Europeans was almost to protect America itself. Identity implies a merging of selves. At other times, constructivists imply that common identity created the trust that made multilateralism possible. This would be particularized trust, based on a shared sense of self and common experiences.

I find that American decision-makers felt an affinity to and a common identity with the Europeans, but this was not sufficient to lead the United States into an alliance. American motives were narrower and more self-interested than constructivists acknowledge. A common faith in democracy and heritage in Western civilization were not central considerations in American decision-making and were used almost exclusively to muster support after the treaty had already been negotiated. The North Atlantic Treaty was based on a quid pro quo deal. And while almost all American decision-makers felt a shared identity with the Europeans based on a common heritage and shared values, support for the alliance and the form that it took was not universal.

The creation of NATO was no doubt easier than that of the League given the former's more limited membership and the presence of a common threat. A regional alliance required much less diffuse reciprocity than global collective security. NATO, in contrast to the League, was more of a closed than an open circle, in terms of both reciprocity and community. And of course it excluded from the circle the West's adversary, the Soviet Union. However, generalized trust was still a necessary condition for its creation. Had the Democrats not been in office, the North Atlantic Treaty might never even have come into being, or surely would have looked very different. Republicans initially favored non-institutionalized cooperation and likely would have at a minimum restricted the membership of the organization and diluted the security guarantee. They would have sought to close the circles of trust further, in terms both of quantitative and of qualitative multilateralism. NATO was a closing of the circle, but not a fully closed one. It still contained a multilateral security guarantee and included a large number of Western European states.

This chapter traces roughly chronologically the process of negotiation in 1948 and 1949 that culminated in the North Atlantic Treaty. I examine both the international negotiations and domestic discussion between the parties in the United States, weaving between them as in Chapter 4 since the two were so intertwined. Little attention is paid to the European side as the pronounced vulnerability of the prostrate continentals just three years after the devastating war drove their calculations, and to the extent that trust was involved it was particularized in nature: faith in the United States.

Events certainly mattered. The Europeans and North Americans did not form an alliance for its own sake. Fear of the Soviets was a prerequisite. Generalized trust allows multilateralism; it doesn't directly cause it absent a need. However, even as events propelled the Truman administration forward, there were large gaps between the Democratic administration and conservatives in the Senate. There is a consistent pattern of the Democratic administration contemplating a particular step before Soviet provocation, using the increased perception of threat to push an agenda already in its planning stages, only to find that the Republicans and conservative Democrats were still hesitant. The Democrats would then pull back, upsetting the more vulnerable Europeans. The notion of a constant ratcheting-up of American willingness to commit to an alliance in the face of Soviet provocation does not ring true. The process went in fits and starts. Arguably just as important as these exogenous shocks was the American electoral calendar. The Democrats were much more cautious before the 1948 election than after it. The empirical review again ends with a denouement, the ratification of the treaty in the United States Senate. Even though the outcome was relatively assured, the ratification debate provides another venue for testing the psychological argument by allowing us to judge whether dispositions to trust (or not to trust) on the part of a liberal administration and the select conservatives consulted behind the scenes are more widespread and representative of others with similar ideological profiles. I conclude by considering constructivist and political economy counterarguments.

Starting the reciprocity circle: reassurance and the beginning of transatlantic discussions

The Cold War came to a head in early 1948. The Soviet Union placed pressure on Norway for a non-aggression pact along the lines of the one forced on Finland. In February a communist government backed by the Soviet Union ousted the democratically elected Benes government in Czechoslovakia. The communist parties in France and Italy threatened to make large gains in upcoming elections, raising the specter of a loss of two more European countries to the Soviet orbit. The Berlin blockade, beginning in June 1948, indicated that the threat from the Soviet Union might not only be political and economic in nature. Military confrontation might accompany infiltration through fifth columns.

In this atmosphere of potential catastrophe, the idea for what would become NATO originated in Britain, not the United States. Foreign Secretary Ernest Bevin called for some sort of association of Western powers (Henderson 1983; Kaplan 2007). On the front lines of both indirect and potential direct aggression by the Soviet Union, the Western European nations, tremendously weakened by the war, were more eager than the United States for some kind of arrangement that would provide military aid and support in case of attack (Kydd 2005). The very idea of an association was constructed to solicit American involvement in Western European security. Bevin's language was carefully chosen, avoiding any insistence on a treaty or use of the politically sensitive term "alliance" so as not to provoke isolationist sentiment. The union was to be "of a formal or informal character backed by the Americas and the Dominions" (FRUS 1948: 5).

The intention of such an arrangement was to deter the Soviets, and this is the element of the North Atlantic Treaty that has received the most attention since it resonates with standard international relations theories about the balance of power. However, just as important was its role in promoting European morale (Achilles 1992: 11–12; FRUS 1948: 6; Henderson 1983: 4–6; Miscamble 1992: 115). Its goal was, in Bevin's private words, to "create confidence and energy on the one side and inspire respect and caution on the other" (FRUS 1948: 6). Bevin feared that individual West European countries would fall one by one to communism, each negotiating a separate peace with the Soviet Union. The World War II experience was fresh in European minds. The Western Europeans, undertaking the daunting task of economic reconstruction after the most devastating war in their history, under the looming threat of a vastly superior military threat, were facing a crisis of confidence. Bevin wrote to the Americans that it was "not enough to reinforce physical barriers." "Ethical," "spiritual" and "moral" forces were just as important (FRUS 1948: 5).

The weakened Europeans, however, could not act alone as this would attract the ire of the Soviet Union. They first needed the assurance that the United States would protect them (Henderson 1983: 4; Kaplan 2007: 30; Miscamble 1992: 15). Without this, the British stressed, there would be "piecemeal collapse of one Western bastion after another" (FRUS 1948: 6). "Potential victims" needed to "feel sufficiently reassured to refuse to embark on a fatal policy of appeasement" (FRUS 1948: 15). An American security commitment was necessary to boost European morale and give the Europeans the confidence necessary to stand up to the Soviet Union. As a British official noted in conversations with the Americans, "The plain truth is that Western Europe cannot yet stand on its own feet without assurance of support" (FRUS 1948: 14).

The Democratic Truman administration understood the situation in the same terms. In a memorandum for Secretary of State George C. Marshall, John Hickerson, Director of the State Department's Office of European Affairs, diagnosed the problem as an underestimation of American commitment not only by the Soviets but also on the part of the Europeans, "to the point of losing their will to resist" (FRUS 1948: 40). The Democrats framed the situation in reassurance terms, an indication of a cooperative social orientation and generalized trust. Administration officials expected that Europeans would cooperate in meeting the threat of communism provided that they were first assured of some kind of American support. Hickerson stressed that European "willingness to fight for liberty is closely related to the strength of the help available" and argued that "concrete evidence of American determination... would go far to reduce both dangers" (FRUS 1948: 40). The Secretary of State shared that view (Baylis 1993: 101). Because they trusted the Europeans, they were willing to move first. Hickerson argued this was a necessity: "A general stiffening of morale in free Europe is needed and it can come only from action by this country" (FRUS 1948: 40). Generalized trust served as a source of social capital leading them to take the first step to begin a reciprocity circle.

Although this framing of the situation occurred early on, the Czech crisis accelerated the American timetable. After the communist overthrow of the democratic government in Czechoslovakia, Marshall and President Truman approved ultra-secret tripartite exploratory talks with Britain and Canada on an "Atlantic security system" in March 1948 (Henderson 1983: 17; Kaplan 2007b: 68; Miscamble 1992: 123). The very first American position paper demonstrated the Democrats' more trusting disposition. Assembled by the Policy Planning Staff of the State Department and called PPS/27, it accepted as an "assumption" that the Europeans would cooperate if given assurance of support by the United States (FRUS 1948: 62).

This generalized trust led to support for a binding, qualitatively multilateral security commitment. This document contained the first suggestion of what would become the heart of the North Atlantic Treaty, that an attack on one would be an attack on all, justified legally under Article 51 of the United Nations Charter. Hickerson understood it in moral terms, as the Democrats had during the League debate: "[O]nly a moral commitment by the US to do whatever was necessary, including fight... would do the trick" (Achilles 1992: 12–13). It was also quantitatively multilateral. The plan was for a very inclusive arrangement open to all free nations in Europe and the Middle East "who may wish to adhere" (FRUS 1948: 63). Given the forthcoming nature of the Democratic administration's proposal, the three sides quickly reached agreement. The negotiations produced the Pentagon Paper, which accepted the notion of a mutual defense guarantee along the lines of PPS/27. The document also suggested a way forward for the conclusion of a pact that showed the American willingness to move first to reassure. The American administration would guarantee the security of those interested until a treaty was successfully completed (FRUS 1948: 71–2; Henderson 1983: 17; Kaplan 2007: 68; Miscamble 1992: 123).

The precise terms of the security guarantee were left outstanding. American representatives wanted members to pledge to "undertake to assist in meeting the attack" and to judge for themselves whether an armed attack had occurred. The more vulnerable British insisted that individual judgment as to whether an attack had occurred was implied and best not mentioned and favored a stronger commitment "to afford the party so attacked all the military, economic and other aid and assistance in their power" (Baylis 1993: 94–5). However, the

American insistence on members determining for themselves whether an attack had occurred was the result of concerns about the constitutionality of the guarantee, not entrapment (FRUS 1948: 69). And this should not distract from the extraordinary nature of the American position. The United States was actively considering a binding security commitment to a European alliance, something which it had never done, well before the Berlin blockade crisis of June 1948. Achilles recounts "by the time [the talks] were finished, it had been secretly agreed that there would be a treaty" (Achilles 1992: 19). The depth and sensitivity of the commitment made by the US in the talks was evident in the fact that Deputy Secretary of State Robert Lovett kept his copy of the Pentagon Paper in his safe (Achilles 1992: 15–16). The paper's name owes to the fact that discussions were held in the basement of the Pentagon where there would be more security, although ironically there was no representative of the Defense Department at the talks (Miscamble 1992: 124).

This was not international altruism, however, or the action of a hegemon willing to provide public goods despite free riding. The Truman administration expected the Europeans eventually to reciprocate in the common struggle against the Soviet Union. Hickerson stressed that the Europeans must themselves pool resources and resist "by every means at their disposal . . . any threat to the independence of any member whether from within or without" (FRUS 1948: 40). While planning documents stress that an American commitment would increase European confidence, the United States expected "reciprocal support" (FRUS 1948: 62). The Americans would provide assistance in case of attack "provided they defend themselves with every resource at their command" (FRUS 1948: 63). The more trusting Democrats insisted on, but also expected, reciprocity.

There was almost total support for a multilateral alliance in the State Department, with only two major exceptions. Charles Bohlen, legal counselor to the Secretary of State, was also the department's liaison to Congress. He based his opposition on a conviction that the Senate would never ratify a military alliance (Achilles 1992: 21; Kaplan 2007: 91).[1] George Kennan, the head of the Policy Planning staff, also objected to the pact. As a "realist," Kennan always fit

---

[1] Recall that the State Department liaison to Congress had drawn similar pessimistic conclusions about the absolute veto during planning for the UN.

somewhat uneasily in the Truman administration (Ireland 1981: Chapter 3). However, his role in the North Atlantic Treaty negotiations was virtually nonexistent, even by his own account (Kaplan 2007: 96). His own staff sneakily moved forward without him on planning for the alliance while he was away on a long trip to Asia (Miscamble 1992: 123).

A Monroe Doctrine for Europe: the conservative alternative

Rationalists might respond that the American position was the somewhat natural result of the objective security situation. The future allies shared, if not overlapping, certainly encapsulated interests in the security of Western Europe. This created a reassurance game in which cooperation is easier. The countries had a recent history of intense cooperation that facilitated strategic trust. And diffuse reciprocity demands much less trust in a regional security arrangement than in a global institution. Kydd reaches this conclusion using a rational, structural model (2005: 165–8).

Given all of these structural factors, it is very hard for rationalists to explain why there were pronounced domestic differences within the United States as to the virtues of security cooperation with the Europeans and the form it should take. Many conservative Republicans opposed a binding alliance with the Europeans. Their spokesperson was Robert Taft, Republican senator from Ohio and son of the former US President and chief justice of the Supreme Court. He possessed all the ideological elements of someone who lacked generalized trust.

Taft shared the same Puritan moral commitments as Lodge, stressing the necessity of traditional morality as a necessary restraint on human behavior (Wunderlin 2005: 12). "Before our system can claim success, it must not only create a people with a higher standard of living, but a people with a higher standard of character – character that must include religious faith, morality" and "self restraint" (Kirk and McClellan 1967: foreword). He gained the support of Prohibitionists early in his career (Wunderlin 2005: 20). As part of that moral code was the necessity of hard work rather than government handouts. He stressed initiative and enterprise (Kirk and McClellan 1967: 17; Wunderlin 2005: 26). In Taft's words, "Nothing can so quickly kill the incentive and the production of the people, as to encourage them to look to government as their benefactor and supporter . . . [N]o people as a whole can get something for nothing" (Taft 1997: 30–31). Without tough love, individuals could not be trusted not to abuse privileges. They would free-ride.

This is not enough evidence in and of itself to firmly capture Taft's level of generalized trust. However, in combination with other factors, a pattern becomes clear. During the treaty negotiations, Taft framed the situation completely differently than the Democratic administration, as a prisoner's dilemma situation in which the Europeans would take advantage of American cooperation. He and other conservatives were systematically more concerned with opportunism of all types. Taft feared that a binding treaty would induce moral hazard and lead to entrapment. Such an instrument required action "without any examination of the reasons for the aggression which may have occurred" (Taft 1951: 88–9). The United States could not judge whether a country "had given cause for the attack" (Taft 1997: 82–3). "If one of the members of the pact provides an attack, even by conduct which we disapprove, we would still apparently be bound to go to its defense. By executing a treaty of this kind, we put ourselves at the mercy of the foreign policies of 11 other nations," he cautioned (US Congress[2] 81:1: 9,206).

A binding alliance would also lead to free riding on the part of Europeans. "I believe that any obligation to use force in Europe should only be secondary, not to be effective until the peace-loving nations of Europe have exhausted their own resources... We cannot solve the problems of Europe unless the great majority of the European nations first agree on what that solution should be," he argued (Taft 1951: 38). Taft stressed self-reliance for the Europeans, just as he did for Americans. "Certainly it is unwise for any nation to become dependent upon the charity of another nation," he stressed (Taft 1951: 86). Taft cautioned: "Let's not promise a millennium which can only be reached by a people's own efforts and ability and character, and which we cannot deliver" (Taft 1997: 29).

This resonated with arguments the Republican were now making domestically, as the Republicans defined themselves in opposition to the New Deal (Gerring 1998, Chapter 4). Other conservatives in the Republican Party made the same connection between domestic and foreign affairs and drew the same conclusions about the

[2] Hereafter, CR for *Congressional Record*.

trustworthiness of the Europeans. Jenner, the third most conservative Senator according to NOMINATE scores, lamented: "What has
recently developed in America? We have now come to the point that
every time our people get a little stomach ache they run to Washington
for relief. That statement now applies to the whole world. Whenever
a country gets an ache or a pain its representatives run to Washington
for relief" (CR 81: 1: 9,556). These criticisms had a decidedly moralistic caste. Jenner accused the Europeans of "gorging themselves at the
expense of the American taxpayer" (CR 81: 1: 9,561).[3]

Taft and his supporters were no less anti-communist than the
Democrats. Taft later wrote that he knew by 1941 that the Soviet
Union was a "predatory totalitarian tyranny intent on establishing
communist dictatorship throughout the world" (Taft 1951: 6). He
was aware of the necessity of projecting force in a world shrunk by
military technology (Doenecke 1979; Lake 1999; J. L. Snyder 1991;
Taft 1951: 38; 1997: 59–63, 87–91). Sometimes characterized as an
isolationist, he was actually an American unilateralist. However, he
and other conservatives were led by their less trusting disposition and
competitive social orientation towards more unilateral solutions. If
the Europeans were unreliable, the United States needed a different
plan.

Taft, lacking generalized trust, rejected the idea of diffuse reciprocity. He opposed an agreement that "binds us for twenty years to
come to the defense of any country, no matter by whom it is attacked"
(Patrick 2009: 280). Rather than a multilateral security guarantee,
Taft imagined a "Monroe Doctrine for Europe," in which the United
States would declare its interest in the security of Western Europe,
thereby warning Russia not to contemplate any armed action in the
Western sphere of influence, much as the United States had done for
the western hemisphere. This proposal was virtually identical to that

---

[3] It is often maintained that the ultimate determinant of Midwestern Republican
opposition to multilateral security commitments was fiscal, driven by a concern
for balanced budgets rather than an alternative strategic conception. Alliances
meant defense aid for allies, anathema for a party that now marketed itself
electorally as the party of liberty defending individuals from the high taxes of
the New Deal welfare state (J. L. Snyder 1991). However, this neglects that
fiscal considerations about the expense of European rearmament were linked to
a belief that untrustworthy Europeans would leech resources from a generous
United States. And concerns about the budget cannot explain worries about
entrapment. This was a distrustful syndrome of attitudes.

offered by Knox in 1919. Taft made it clear that the virtues of uni-lateralism were in protecting against opportunism. Whereas a treaty pledged the US "in advance, to take any military action outside of our territory," a unilateral doctrine was non-binding. It "would leave us free to interfere or not interfere according to whether we consider the case of sufficiently vital interest to the liberty of this country." This would prevent entrapment. This was the "policy of the free hand" (Taft 1951: 12). The Monroe Doctrine also "imposed no obligation whatever to assist any American Nation by giving it arms or even economic aid" so as not to expose the United States to free riding (CR 81:1: 9,206). It also was more flexible. Taft lauded this aspect of the original: "We were free to modify it or withdraw from it at any moment" (CR 81:1: 9,206). Taft also advised a smaller commu-nity circle. His strategy included only a bilateral alliance with Britain so as to obtain bases around the world for strategic nuclear bombers (Doenecke 1979; Lake 1999; Patrick 2009; J. L. Snyder 1991: 268; Taft 1951: 38; 1997: 59–63, 87–91).

In sum there was a prominent unilateral alternative to the Truman administration's plan for a multilateral alliance. Rationalists cannot explain why these Taft Republicans differed in their institutional pref-erences. There was no difference in their views of geopolitical chal-lenges. Instead, as was the case in the United Nations and before that during the League of Nations battle, unilateralists had a more competitive social orientation, evident indirectly in their systemati-cally more pronounced expectations of opportunism and conservative political ideology. They trusted less in the same objective situation. By neglecting domestic politics and focusing only on the Democratic administration's views, Kydd falsely concludes that this was an objec-tive reassurance game (2005: 165–8).

The Truman administration, in its deliberations before the Pen-tagon talks, considered an alternative like that which Taft preferred. It rejected a suggestion made in the "Butler memorandum," named after a National Security staffer, that the US should simply issue a "unilat-eral assurance" that an attack by the Soviets on any of the countries concerned constituted an attack on the United States (FRUS 1948: 58–9). It was recognized that a declaration such as Taft's would be much more flexible, would leave less room for opportunism, and would avoid domestic political complications as it could be jettisoned after Tru-man left office. This was Kennan's preference (Achilles 1992: 15–16;

Henderson 1983: 16; Patrick 2009: 274). However, the Democrats went in a different direction. Generalized trust served as a form of social capital convincing them that there were greater gains to be had from cooperation.

The continuation of bipartisan consultation: the hidden domestic politics of the North Atlantic Treaty

For Lake, ideological differences over the likelihood of opportunism are largely moot, as although there was enough support for Taft's proposals to ensure a public debate on the question, structural features of the environment, such as the distribution of power among potential partners and the increasing reach of military weaponry, made the wisdom of the cooperative path clear to a vast majority (1999: 131, 170). The gains from cooperation trumped any concerns about opportunism, however much they varied. Only the Taft minority did not grasp this.

However, this misses the fact that concerns about opportunism were shared by all Republicans, both in the "isolationist" Taftite and "internationalist" wing of the party led by Senator Arthur Vandenberg. The latter were more "liberal" Republicans, based predominantly in the Northeast and supportive of a more progressive Republican electoral profile in domestic policy. Those identified by Kepley (1988) as "internationalist" Republicans had an average NOMINATE score of well over a standard deviation from the Republican mean.[4] Nevertheless, they were still more conservative than most Democrats, and therefore less trusting.

Lake overstates the degree of consensus on the cooperative solution and understates differences concerning the potential for opportunism because he does not devote much attention to the domestic political consultations proceeding alongside the transatlantic negotiations. This leads to the erroneous conclusion that structure compelled bipartisan consensus. Democratic and Republican preferences were very different, but this is only evident if we examine the private negotiations between the administration and congressional Republicans led by Vandenberg. The agreement that eventually emerged was the result of

---

[4] These were Vanenberg, Lodge, Saltonstall, Smith (NJ), Knowland, Morse, Aiken, Flanders, Tobey, Ives, Dulles and Smith (ME).

a behind-the-scenes compromise before the treaty reached the Senate floor.

The Truman administration was as careful as the Roosevelt administration to solicit Republican input and resolve differences privately before any treaty was presented to the Senate. As the Pentagon Paper had recommended, Lovett shared its contents, now known as NSC memorandum 9/1, with Vandenberg in a series of meetings to take the Republican's (and the Republicans') temperature. The Chairman of the Foreign Relations Committtee was not pleased with the draft, expressing the same concerns about potential opportunism and European trustworthiness as Taft and other unilateralists. Even in the wake of the Czech crisis, Vandenberg was more worried about both free riding and entrapment than the Democratic administration, asserting that the "majority of the countries [would] take one or two lines of action, either to fold their hands and let Uncle Sam carry them, or secondly, and in his opinion of equal and perhaps greater danger, to let them get a sense of false security which might result in their taking so firm an attitude as to become provocative and give the impression of having a chip on their shoulder" (FRUS 1948: 82). This fear of opportunism meant he had issues with the binding nature of the security guarantee. It was far too automatic, he complained: "[W]e must always have the right to determine for ourselves when we will act" (FRUS 1948: 82). When John Foster Dulles, the prominent Republican and presumptive next Secretary of State, was brought into the conversations, there was "unanimous agreement that the United States should not be in the position of taking any engagement for assistance of any sort which would be automatically brought into being by the act of someone else" (FRUS 1948: 107). Vandenberg thought that the Europeans would free-ride, coming to the US with their "shopping lists" (FRUS 1948: 105).

The Republicans had problems with both qualitative and quantitative multilateralism. Vandenberg also wanted to restrict any arrangement to fewer members, a smaller community circle. The senator complained that the administration was "trying to blanket too much of the world in a so-called regional pact" (FRUS 1948: 105). The proposal was "unlimited and open-ended to anyone who might reach for it" and Vandenberg predicted it would not garner the two-thirds majority necessary for Senate approval (FRUS 1948: 82).

NSC 9/1, like the Pentagon Paper, was based on a trusting premise and framed in assurance terms. It started with the assumption that the Europeans would cooperate "provided they are assured of military support by the United States" (FRUS 1948: 85–6). The less trusting Republicans wanted to reverse the order. Europeans must, in Dulles's words, first demonstrate "continuous and visible evidence of maximum efforts to take care of themselves" (FRUS 1948: 106). In other words, the US would require the Europeans to move first. But in any case there should be no automatic or formal security guarantee. Vandenberg and Dulles only imagined the standardization of equipment and pooling of military equipment. Europeans would "merely seek to become associated with sources of supply and assistance in the Western Hemisphere" (FRUS 1948: 106).

Recognizing the objections of less trusting and therefore more unilateralist conservatives, the administration proceeded cautiously so as to cultivate enough votes to pass the treaty. Policy-makers laid down two ground rules: involvement of the Senate Foreign Relations Committee and full bipartisan consensus given the fact that 1948 was an election year (Achilles 1992: 14; Kaplan 2007: 31). As the majority party, Republicans controlled the Senate and its committees, and any treaty would need two-thirds support. Because of concerns about Congress, top-ranking administration officials would not make the conclusions of the Pentagon Paper official American policy until they consulted with key congressional leaders. Marshall passed the Pentagon Paper along to the National Security Council without taking a position on it (Kaplan 2007: 69; Miscamble 1992: 123). And after the consultations with Vandenberg and Dulles, administration officials dramatically revised NSC 9/1, producing NSC 9/2, which stripped out any consideration of a security guarantee. The US would simply seek a coordinated military supply plan and in case of aggression only commit to military talks, as Vandenberg and Dulles had suggested (FRUS 1948: 116–19).

With domestic politics in mind, the Truman administration cautioned the Europeans to first demonstrate their cooperative intentions and commitment to their own collective defense through concrete action of their own (FRUS 1948: 8, 17).[5] Hickerson's aide, Theodore Achilles, complained about the policy, writing later that "this was our

---

[5] There was a precedent. In early 1948, Deputy Secretary of State Robert Lovett and Hickerson emphasized to the British that Congress was just at that moment considering approval of Marshall Plan funds and that mention of any further obligations would jeopardize the program by fostering the belief that the

theme song for the next few months: 'Show what you're prepared to do for yourselves and each other and then we'll think about what we might do" (Achilles 1992: 13). In response to this coaxing, the Europeans negotiated a collective defense agreement called the Brussels Pact, which contained an obligation to come to the military aid of any member in case of aggression. A new body, called the Western Union, would meet to integrate and coordinate European defense spending and doctrine, so as to make the most efficient use of scarce resources. For the British at least, the Brussels Pact was an attempt to demonstrate European resolve to the Americans so as to dampen predominantly Republican concerns about European free riding and elicit American support (Baylis 1993: 73: Kaplan 2007, Chapter 3).

At the same time, administration officials assured the Europeans that this was merely a necessity of domestic politics, and that they were committed to a multilateral alliance (Baylis 1993: 99; Henderson 1983: 17). The Deputy Secretary of State explained to them the "terrible difficulties in Congress" and how to convince even Senate internationalists like Vandenberg was the "most difficult challenge" (Baylis 1993: 98; Kaplan 2007: 69; Miscamble 1992: 127). Hickerson assured the British that there was no question of America's long-term relationship with whatever arrangement might emerge, but "every proof that the free states of Western Europe could give that they were resolved and able to stand on their own feet" would be helpful (Baylis 1993: 68; FRUS 1948: 10). He reminded them that bipartisanship was "essential in an election year with a Democratic administration, a Republican Congress, and the Chairman of the Foreign Relations Committee a potential candidate for the Presidency" (Truman Library Oral History Project, Interview with Theodore Achilles 1972, www.trumanlibrary.org/oralhist/achilles.htm). Lovett made similar assurances, but stressed that opponents "needed to be convinced that the five allies were working on arrangements of their own" (FRUS 1948: 132; Henderson 1983: 23). Marshall told the British they should have no doubt about the determination of the US, but warned, "It is vital . . . to the success of the aim we all have

relationship was one-sided rather than reciprocal. Prominent Republicans had argued for, and were successful in, whittling down the amount of aid (Achilles 1992: 12; FRUS 1948: 22; Henderson 1983: 8–10; Kaplan 2007: 31–3; Miscamble 1992: 119) in mind that any assurances from this country on this matter have maximum country-wide support and backing of the Congress" (FRUS 1948: 122–3; Henderson 1983: 24).[6]

All evidence indicates that this was the genuine position of the American government, and not a bargaining tool. Nor was it a sign of American hesitance due to its more favorable and geographically less exposed position. There is no document suggesting that this was a disingenuous attempt to play the domestic politics card so as to spur the Europeans on and lessen the defense burden of the United States. Rather the administration was coaching the Europeans on how best to solicit conservative support and help solve its domestic political problem. Achilles called pressure on Europeans to first demonstrate their trustworthiness "our official position... Yet, we had been pushing quietly ahead" (Achilles interview 1972). Recall that the administration had agreed already in March 1948 on the need for a treaty. The Americans were poised for action and sought to capitalize quickly on any European effort to mobilize conservative support. For instance, immediately after the conclusion of the Brussels Pact, Truman issued his now famous proclamation: "I am sure that the determination of the free countries of Europe to protect themselves will be matched by an equal determination on our part to help them to do so" (FRUS 1948: 55). Europeans understood this as signaling a commitment to some sort of transatlantic alliance. Belgian prime minister Paul-Henri Spaak believed that a "new page in the annals of history was thus turned on 17 March 1948... America's isolation was dead" (Baylis 1993: 62).

Not recognizing the domestic political game the administration was playing leads Weber consistently to overstate the differences between the Truman administration and the Europeans over the nature of the

---

[6] Nevertheless, the British were frustrated. In a letter to Lovett, Baron Inverchapel, the British ambassador to the United States, wrote, "Mr. Bevin does not feel that, in the political field, he enjoys quite the same measure of outspoken support from the United States, and he holds it to be essential to the success of his plan that something of this kind should be forthcoming." In response to American references to domestic constraints, the letter stated that Bevin "appreciates your difficulties," but was also "conscious of a risk of getting into a vicious circle. Without assurance of security, which can only be given with some degree of American participation, the British government are unlikely to be successful in making the Western Union a going concern. But it appears from your letter that, until this is done, the United States Government for their part does not feel able to discuss participation" (FRUS 1948: 19). See also Baylis 1993: 68; Henderson 1983: 10; Kaplan 2007: 42).

treaty and to understate the commitment of the Democrats (1992: 647–9). He erroneously concludes that American diplomats were constantly holding more eager Europeans at bay and only got behind the idea of a binding multilateral security guarantee after the Berlin blockade. In fact, Democratic preferences were often closer to those of Europeans than to those of Republicans, something that poses a further puzzle for rationalist, structural accounts.

Tightening the circle: the Vandenberg resolution

During Lovett's consultations with Republicans, Vandenberg suggested, as an alternative to a security pact, a resolution expressing the Senate's vague advice to the President to pursue "association" with "regional arrangements as affect its national security" dedicated to the maintenance of international peace and security (FRUS 1948: 93). It would serve as a Senate endorsement of negotiations with the Europeans. The administration embraced the idea not because of its content but because, sponsored and guided through the Foreign Relations Committee by its Republican chairman, it would make the Senate co-owners of the process. Dean Acheson, who would soon become Secretary of State, later wrote: "All too often the executive sweated through difficult negotiations then laid the treaty before a detached and uninformed Senate in which a minority could reject it; by getting the Senate to give advice in advance of negotiation, Vandenberg got the Senate to accept responsibility in advance of giving consent to ratification" (Acheson 1969: 266).

Vandenberg had his own reasons for supporting the resolution. As relations between the superpowers broke down, most evident in the repeated use of the veto by the Soviet Union in the United Nations, senators had introduced a multitude of resolutions to his Foreign Relations Committee advocating radical overhaul of the UN, including reform of the veto or its transformation into some type of world government.[7]

---

[7] S. 56 called for the development of the United Nations into a world state. S. 133 and concurrent resolution 50 implicitly called for the use of a reformed United Nations as an alliance against the Soviet Union. Texts can be found in CR 81:1: 8,084–5, 9,781–2, 10,143). The latter two resolutions both called for reform of the veto and expressed the will of the Senate to move ahead without any countries that would prohibit any such changes, a clear allusion to the Soviets. Vandenberg did not like that concurrent resolution 50 restricted the use

Vandenberg wanted to avoid any creation of international hierarchy and even any UN reform that would infringe on American sovereignty. He still feared entrapment and opposed changes to the UN that "would allow others to tell us when we must go to war" (Kaplan 2007: 95). "I do not believe that Americans are ready to give up their sovereignty in respect to decisions which would take us into war," he wrote in his diary. "But I am very sure we are prepared to waive any 'veto' upon the pacific settlement of international disputes and I shall continue to work toward this end." He was also "unable to believe that it is in any degree feasible to seek unitary *world Government*," dismissing it as hopelessly idealistic (Vandenberg 1952: 402, 415). Vandenberg even opposed any expansion of international law as "falling straight into the lap of the world government boys" (Vandenberg 1952: 66). A Senate resolution would forestall precipitous action by the Congress by acting as a substitute for other more radical resolutions supported by "One Worlders" and the "Wallace fringe,"[8] and help to steer the debate away from the "hysterical conversation" predominating at the time (US Senate 1973: 57, 59; Vandenberg 1952: 44). It would simultaneously promise a solution to the European problem (Vandenberg 1952: 408).

Foreign Relations Committee chairman Vandenberg advocated justifying any new arrangements within the existing United Nations institution by reference to Chapter VIII, which foresaw the creation of regional security arrangements, and Article 51, which allowed for collective self-defense in the instance that the Security Council was incapacitated (Kaplan 2007: 96). Article 51 "permits congenial nations with common interests in peace and security to defend *themselves . . . 'until the Security Council has taken the measures necessary to maintain international peace and security.'* That single world 'until' is the key to everything," he wrote in his diary (Vandenberg 1952: 419). This allowed for "the basis for a complete reorganization of the United Nations inside the Charter and outside the veto" (Vandenberg 1952: 403), which became Vandenberg's mantra (Vandenberg 1952: 416, 410; 480). The senator was again looking for a way to prevent

of the veto in enforcement but not on issues of peaceful settlement, believing that it completely reversed the problem (Vandenberg 1952: 404).

[8] This was an allusion to former Vice President Henry Wallace, who advocated rapprochement with the Soviet Union and a "New Deal for the World" (Wallace 1948).

Soviet obstructionism without significantly reforming the veto and surrendering American sovereignty. The advantage of his solution was that it could "be *made to work without* Charter amendments" (Vandenberg 1952: 419).[9] He was trying to square strategic and generalized distrust.

The resolution was also to be on Vandenberg's terms. The Senate would proclaim that it would "take particular notice of countries" which showed their determination to resist aggression and would be "prepared to consider," but not promise, only "association." The Europeans, although they would not be specifically mentioned, would have to demonstrate prior trustworthy intentions and begin the reciprocity circle. Such association would be based on "mutual aid and self-help," a key principle to prevent any free riding (FRUS 1948: 84, 93).

While the usual narrative of the Vandenberg resolution's passage is one in which both sides had the same conception of what needed to be done, coordinating efforts to bring the more reluctant Republicans slowly along, this was not the case. Vandenberg saw a Senate resolution as slowing down and diluting rather than accelerating conclusion of a pact (Ireland 1981: 93; Williams 1985: 11–12). He wanted the resolution to go no further than the position he and Dulles endorsed in their conversations with Lovett. Years later, when asked about whether the resolution was consistent with the administration's concept, Hickerson recalled: "I'm sure all my colleagues were influenced by the axiom that politics is the art of the possible. Our suggestions were not so much substantive as stylistic changes to make it a little smoother here and there, but the ideas were his" (Truman Library Oral History Project, Interview with John Hickerson 1972–73, www.trumanlibrary.org/oralhist/hickerson.htm.).

During the closed-door Foreign Relations Committee hearings on the resolution, Republicans and ideologically conservative Southern Democrats expressed the same concerns about opportunism that Dulles and Vandenberg had. The Democratic senator from Texas and

---

[9] The connection between the problem of the United Nations and what would become NATO was evident in the infelicitous title of the Senate Foreign Relations Committee report on the Vandenberg resolution – "Reaffirming the Policy of the United States to Achieve International Peace and Security through the United Nations and Indicating Certain Objectives to Be Pursued" (US Senate 1973).

ranking member of the committee, Tom Connally, insisted on a weak arrangement to avoid entrapment: "A lot of little weak countries might, if we did not have these [more unilateral] provisions, vote 'Yes; we are going to war,' and if we were to be drawn in as a result of that action we would have the bag to hold" (US Senate 1973: 8). Connally was among the most conservative quartile of the party as measured by the NOMINATE scores. Senator Lodge stated that in his understanding, the resolution "emphatically does not mean that we will be the protectors and guardians of these countries who will yell for 'uncle' every time they get into trouble" (US Senate 1973: 20). Hickenlooper wanted to ensure that the US would get something in return for any help (US Senate 1973: 46). Vandenberg was keen to avoid the "old Lend-Lease method," moving away from a "giveaway atmosphere" (US Senate 1973: 54).

As a consequence, there was a need for the demonstration of good intentions before the US would take any further steps. Vandenberg wanted to establish a "basis which does not involve us until we see the actual creation in Western Europe of a new evolution which is a definite and specific advantage to the national security of the United States" (US Senate 1973: 54). He emphasized that the US would only consider association if the Europeans "can succeed in proving to us that [they] mean business in connection with it" (US Senate 1973: 29). Any American action would be "at our option as a result of the activities of these . . . countries who might integrate their own security efforts in a fashion which would invite some sort of cooperation on our part in our own interest" (US Senate 1973: 1). Even the moderate Lodge stated that unless Europeans set up proper integrated staff and standardized equipment, the US "shouldn't have anything to do with them." He wanted to strengthen the language so as to require "evidence" of self-help and mutual aid (US Senate 1973: 20).[10]

In testifying before the committee, senior officials clearly played along with less trusting senators to ensure bipartisan support. Lovett

---

[10] More liberal democratic senators had different concerns, mainly that the resolution was a first step in undermining the United Nations by creating a parallel and rival political–military institution. They were supportive, but feared the emphasis on military means might lead to objections on the part of those who placed more weight on international law. Thomas would claim that they could not combine collective security and the balance of power (US Senate 1973: 58–63)

stressed that the administration was not offering any kind of automatic security guarantee like the Europeans wanted, even though this was clearly in the minds of American officials. And the Europeans must take the first step. He stressed the "fundamental necessity for these people to be helping themselves and helping each other long before they come to us. They must not take the attitude, 'I'm tired, Daddy. Carry me,' right at the start" (US Senate 1973: 20). As seen above, however, in private documents Democratic officials did not frame the situation in this way. And when Republican Senator Smith suggested removing any reference to "mutual aid," Lovett reacted strongly that this would take from Europe "this small help and encouragement" (US Senate 1973: 54). Lovett was concerned with European morale: To "keep those people firm in their desire to pull together and to act as a unit is something that we must not let slip by" (US Senate 1973: 40).

In Lovett's estimation, the formula of "self help and mutual aid" amounted to a "common denominator," both between Europeans and Americans and also Republicans and Democrats (US Senate 1973: 4). So it proved. After emerging from the Foreign Relations Committee, the Vandenberg resolution passed easily by 64 to 4 in the Senate on June 11, 1948. It recommended on behalf of the Senate "association of the United States, by constitutional process, with such regional and other collective arrangements as are based on continuous and effective self-help and mutual aid, and as affect its national security."

Broadening the circle: the Washington exploratory talks and the 1948 elections

Even if Vandenberg's preferences were different than those of the administration, the Democrats used the resolution as a justification for convening top-secret multilateral talks just twelve days after the passage of the Vandenberg resolution. Marshall was waiting for the Vandenberg resolution to give him the authority to negotiate and make the Senate owners of the process. Marshall mentioned the resolution explicitly in his order to proceed (FRUS 1948: 139; Miscamble 1992: 131). While the Secretary of State's decision coincided with the beginning of the Berlin blockade, coming one day before, the blockade was not the impetus for the Democratic administration's action. It certainly helped consolidate support for moving forward. Hickerson had frequently remarked to the Europeans that the path would be significantly more difficult in the Senate if the Soviets stopped acting provocatively (Henderson 1983: 15). "Much would depend on whether some fresh Soviet action maintained the present tense atmosphere. If complete calm prevailed it would be so much more difficult to sell the idea of a pact to Senatorial leaders," he told them (Baylis 1993: 98). However, the quote indicates the very fact that the administration was in favor of a pact and was simply waiting for the right time to push the agenda. Hickerson recalled the beginning of the talks: "*In the meantime*, the Berlin Blockade had come along and given a *further* boost to the urgency of this idea" (Truman Library Oral History Project [emphasis added]).

The ambassadors to the summit tasked a working group to develop specific proposals, where American officials proved much more flexible when not under constant domestic political pressure. A consensus document from the working group called the Washington Paper recommended a treaty with "unmistakably clear provisions binding parties to come to each other's defense" that would "hearten the peoples" of Western Europe and deter the Soviet Union (FRUS 1948: 243). Morale and deterrence were still the signposts and would be best provided for with a collective security guarantee. What would constitute "unmistakably clear provisions," however, was the subject of debate. There were differences on the language of the guarantee. The same divisions that had emerged during the tripartite Pentagon talks between the United States and the United Kingdom reemerged, only now it exposed a transatlantic difference. The more vulnerable and weak Europeans favored as binding an obligation as possible. The negotiators came to no consensus, simply specifying in the Washington Paper the preference of both sides (FRUS 1948: 247). The Europeans also wanted a treaty that would last longer. The French in particular made much of this provision, at one point asking for a 99-year commitment (Kaplan 2007: 188). For their part, the Americans were skeptical of Senate approval of any treaty with a duration of more than ten years (Achilles 1992: 20).[11]

---

[11] During the exploratory talks, the French delegate at one point threatened that the French would not sign unless it ran for fifty years, at which point the relative vulnerability of the Americans and Europeans became obvious. Achilles wrote later: "We told him bluntly that we didn't give a damn whether

Again, despite the different structural positions of the two sides, the greatest inhibitions in American policy were domestically based, not international. Even the pact's greatest advocates in the US agreed that no treaty could contain an automatic security guarantee as this would amount to a declaration of war, a congressional prerogative. A firm guarantee, like that of the Brussels Treaty, would not work (FRUS 1948: 173, 211; Kaplan 2007: 123). Recognizing that the requirement of constitutionality served to weaken the guarantee, Hickerson suggested, as language that might prove both legal and automatic, that each member would "in accordance with its constitutional processes, assist in repelling the attack by all military, economic and other means in its power" (FRUS 1948: 247). This was also listed as a possibility in the final document.

Equally important was Senate consent. In his opening statement at the conference, Lovett stressed that bipartisanship was a must in an election year and indicated that nothing concrete could be done until after the presidential election and the return of Congress in 1949. Should the US make a commitment, he emphasized the need for Europe to be able to support the administration's recommendation to Congress through carefully documented statements about what Europe was doing to help itself. They would need to show that the Europeans had done everything possible on their own (FRUS 1948: 149, 187; Henderson 1983: 36–7). The deal would have to be reciprocal as Congress would not support a "naked arrangement" in which the US gave military supplies to Western Europe without anything in return (FRUS 1948: 216). Any "one-way street" such as Lend-Lease would not muster enough support (FRUS 1948: 220).

The importance of domestic politics becomes even clearer when we note the transformation in American preferences following the 1948 elections. After the talks concluded, ambassadors submitted the Washington Paper to their capitals for study, waiting for the results of American presidential and congressional elections. All were anticipating what was perceived to be the inevitable electoral defeat of President Truman. The difference in the Truman administration's negotiating

or not France signed, that we couldn't go beyond ten, that everybody else would sign, and that he knew damn well the French government was wetting its collective pants at least once a day for fear the US wouldn't sign, or ratify" (Achilles 1992: 20).

position before and after its re-election gives an indication of just how much the Democrats felt constrained by their domestic political circumstances. After Truman's surprise victory over the Republican candidate, Governor Thomas Dewey, the administration proceeded with a vigor and energy that surprised the Europeans. Lovett stressed his desire to have the final treaty drafted quickly and to strike while the iron was still hot, pushing it through the Senate for ratification (Kaplan 2007: 165, 186; Miscamble 1992: 133). Given the need for two-thirds support, the text would still have to be based on bipartisan agreement, but with control of the Foreign Relations Committee returned to the Democrats, a gain of nine seats in the Senate, and without the fear of making the pact into an electoral issue, the administration was now in a position to better leave its ideological stamp on the treaty. Negotiators quickly reached consensus on a final draft on December 24, 1948 (FRUS 1948: 333ff.).

With the Democrats under fewer political constraints, the language of the guarantee was much tighter. The security commitment now stressed that the allies would make maximum efforts and specifically mentioned and frontloaded military action. The US dropped its insistence that each party could judge whether an armed attack had occurred and that military force not be mentioned. They even agreed to omit reference to "constitutional processes" in the security guarantee itself, something that the Europeans argued would weaken the pact (Baylis 1993: 108; Henderson 1983: 70; Kaplan 2007: 188). In the draft treaty's language, an attack on one was an attack on all, with the pledge "to assist the party or parties so attacked by taking forthwith such military or other action, individually and in concert with the other parties, as may be necessary to restore and assure the security of the North Atlantic area" (Achilles 1992: 22; Baylis 1993: 108). The Democrats were now more forthcoming about the term of the treaty as well. Negotiators could not come to a compromise on the duration of the pact, with Europeans insisting on at least fifty years. However, the Americans were now contemplating forty years, well over their initial idea of ten (Henderson 1983: 71). American negotiators did not concede to the Europeans out of a lack of bargaining leverage, of course. Nothing had changed in that regard. Nor had there been an increase in Cold War hostility. It was the change in domestic political circumstances that allowed the Democrats' more trusting instincts to emerge.

Nevertheless, the administration had to contend with potential congressional opposition, and it had not been keeping key figures appraised as it had earlier in the process (Williams 1985: 14–16). Upon replacing Marshall as Secretary of State, Dean Acheson began in haste to bring Vandenberg and Connally, now chairman of the Foreign Relations Committee, up to speed. In private both were concerned. The draft treaty "gave an impression of crescendo and haste which perhaps overstated the problem. It implied that the United States was rushing into some kind of automatic commitment" (FRUS 1949: 74). And after the isolationist Forrest Donnell made an attack on the treaty in the Senate based on a newspaper report that it would include a "moral commitment" to come to the aid of Western Europe if attacked, Vandenberg and Connally made a full-blown effort to amend elements of the draft treaty's Article V (Acheson 1969: 281; Kaplan 2007: 197). Connally was concerned about entrapment and free riding. His response to Donnell was to guarantee that he would not be "letting European nations declare war and letting us fight" (Henderson 1983: 90). "We cannot be Sir Galahads, and every time we hear a gun fired plunge into war and take sides without knowing what we are doing and without knowing the issues involved," he said (Kaplan 2007: 201).

In a second meeting with Acheson, the two senators insisted that it must be made clear that there was "no obligation, moral or otherwise, to go to war" in case of armed aggression (FRUS 1949: 109). Connally went to so far as to propose removing the phrase that an attack on members amounted to an attack on all of them, to be replaced by an "attack on one would be regarded as a threat to the peace of all" (FRUS 1949: 109; Henderson 1983: 91; Kaplan 2007: 201). Vandenberg was more circumspect, believing that Article V was the great contribution of the pact, serving to warn the Soviets of American determination. However, he also wanted it "made plain" that individual countries would determine for themselves what action they might take, removing a degree of the automaticity in the draft treaty and retaining a greater degree of sovereignty (FRUS 1949: 109). The two attempted to restore more state discretion into the treaty by suggesting that rather than a member pledging itself to take action "that may be necessary" to restore security, it would take the action "it may deem necessary" (FRUS 1949: 109). The administration consented to this suggestion.

The two senators also pushed to remove any reference to military action, complaining that, as phrased, the document implied that military action was necessary but not necessarily sufficient (FRUS 1949: 109). Connally even wanted to remove "forthwith" from the guarantee (Henderson 1983: 89; Kaplan 2007: 199; Vandenberg 1952: 476). However, the President prevailed upon Connally to agree to the phrase "including the use of armed force" as a potential action in case of aggression. Truman stressed that this was essential to the success of the pact as a military deterrent (FRUS 1949: 117).[12] In consultations with the Foreign Relations Committee, the administration also instituted more flexibility, bringing down the binding term of the treaty to twenty years, after which parties would have the right to withdraw with one year's notice. However, the treaty could continue indefinitely if no state renounced its obligations (Truman Library Oral Hickerson interview 1972–73).

Another circle squared: the ratification of the North Atlantic Treaty

After winning over Connally and Vandenberg, Acheson took the draft treaty to the Foreign Relations Committee to ensure its support. There, the more conservative members expressed reservations consistent with a competitive social orientation and less generalized trust. The formerly classified transcripts are now public. Lodge wanted assurances that Article III, the direct heir to Vandenberg's formula of "self-help and mutual aid," was sufficient to protect against European free riding. He wanted to be certain that the US could revoke military aid if the Europeans were "lying down on the job." "I just wondered whether

---

[12] The British were demonstrably vexed by US hesitation. Bevin sent a telegram to Acheson saying he was "seriously disturbed" by the developments in the United States. The British had "been basing our policy on the confident expectation that the US was willing to join in the creation of a solid Atlantic Community," he wrote. "We were willing to take the risks which such a pact involved for us on the assumption that the obligations were equal all around" (Baylis 1993: 110). The more vulnerable British were worried that aid would take too long to arrive and that the more flexible language would weaken the deterrent effect of the treaty (Achilles 1992: 22). Acheson tried to argue to Europeans that the mention of "military or other action" was an "unnecessary embellishment" and that it was crucial for senators that any response would be determined individually rather than in concert (Kaplan 2007: 200).

they feel they have us lashed to the mast for 20 years," he said, and "could sit back and let us do it" (US Senate 1973: 153). Connally complained about the number of signatories and questioned whether the Europeans might not abandon the United States in case of war or wait to be protected by the United States (US Senate 1973: 231, 248). Republican senator Hickenlooper suggested a further dilution of Article V by changing the language from "action, including the use of armed force" to "action, which may include the use of armed force" (US Senate 1973: 138). Vandenberg was also dissatisfied with the number of signatories: "[O]ne of our troubles is to keep them out instead of keep them in" (US Senate 1973: 138). He wanted a more restricted community circle.

Democrats, greater generalized trusters, had different concerns. As the Foreign Relations Committee considered the treaty, Claude Pepper, one of the three most liberal senators, questioned whether the pact was legally consistent with the United Nations and whether the treaty might not exacerbate tensions with the Soviet Union and thereby undermine the institution (US Senate 1973: 96, 119). His solution, however, reflected his more trusting disposition as one of the most liberal members of the Senate. Pepper wanted an even more inclusive pact to include other "peace loving nations" as "part of this thing which is the sole defender of the democracies and the freedom of the peoples of this world" (US Senate 1973: 246). Pepper imagined an arrangement more akin to the League of Nations: "We should protect the security of everybody by collective security and not by these groups getting together in various parts of the world to protect themselves by their own efforts" (US Senate 1973: 318). And the senator from Florida was even less concerned with equivalence in reciprocity. The pact should include others "if they don't contribute but one small boy and one air rifle" (US Senate 1973: 248).

Given Acheson's legwork with Connally and Vandenberg during the international negotiations, the treaty proved uncontroversial. A committee report unanimously recommended its ratification. Acheson gave explicit credit to Vandenberg for the formula of Article III, that "no party can rely on others for its defense unless it does its utmost to defend itself and contribute toward the defense of the others" (US Senate 1973: 348). As the treaty was submitted for full consideration and a vote by the Senate, conservative supporters of the treaty stressed these protections. In his opening remarks presenting the treaty, this was Connally's main theme (CR 81:1: 8,812ff., 9,459). Article V provided enough discretion to allay sovereignty concerns about entrapment while still serving as a warning to the Soviet Union, for which support was truly bipartisan (CR 81:1, Gurney [9,426], Morse [9,575], Vandenberg [8,891]; Smith [9,911], Knowland [9,374], Lodge [9,114], Connally [8,817], Humphrey [9,778] and Graham [9,798]).

The Republican rump

This left Taft isolated, supported only by a small coalition of extreme conservatives and traditional isolationists. Nevertheless, it is useful for the purposes of the argument to review their concerns. They were similar to those mentioned in the League and United Nations debates. As the Senate began, its deliberations reminded the pact supporter Henry Cabot Lodge Jr. of the arguments made by supporters of his father. They gave "the impression that the last two world wars had never taken place. Some of the statements I have heard made . . . take one back to the days 25 years ago," he said (CR 81:1: 9,902).

Opponents were concerned with opportunism of all kinds. By committing the United States in advance, the security guarantee of Article V placed constraints on American freedom to choose appropriate action and threatened entrapment. Donnell stated:

The instant before the treaty shall be ratified no contract exists by which attack requires that the United States of America will assist any one of the 11 signatories against which shall have occurred an armed attack. Full freedom exists in the United States to determine, what, if anything, it shall do . . . The instant however that the North Atlantic Treaty shall have been ratified, the moment the clock before us arrives at the point at which ratification occurs, the condition will have been vastly changed. Article 5 . . . becomes a binding obligation. (CR 81:1: 9,639)

Malone agreed that "for the first time [the treaty] removes our prerogative to be the sole judge when our peace and safety is threatened" (CR 81:1: 9,888). This meant for him the danger of moral hazard because "an attack may result from a war of which one of our own signatories is actually the provoking cause" (CR 81:1: 9648). Others expressed identical objections (CR 81:1, Mundt [9,455] and Donnell [9,803]). In this way, Article V of the North Atlantic Treaty had the same faults as the League's Article X and did not compare favorably to the United

Nations according to opponents like Watkins (CR 81: 9,094, 9,898). "They are in large part new obligations," said Donnell. "They are not those in which we are involved under the United Nations Charter. We are not today under obligations of this magnitude" (CR 81: 9,648).

While opponents claimed that Europeans would ensnare the United States in foreign wars, they simultaneously argued that the Europeans would timidly abandon the United States in the event of war (CR 81:1, Donnell [9,565], Watkins [9,105], Jenner [9,565]). Donnell predicted that if there were a difference of opinion on the circumstances of an attack, "alleged unanimity of action on the part of all the signatories to repel an attack would fall about as fast as ice would melt beneath the sun" (CR 81:1: 9,565). Watkins predicted that the "allies will stick together when the necessity is present, when the emergency is on, but they will rapidly forget their pledges the moment pressure is removed." The League had also suffered from this problem: "Thus, the League of Nations failed – not because the League was not a proper instrument for peace, but because the member nations, individually and collectively, failed to enforce that pathway to peace" (CR 81:1: 9,092).

Opponents also believed that the Europeans would take advantage of American largesse, pointing as evidence to the fact that the Europeans had prepared their wish lists for military aid even before the ink was dry on the treaty (CR 81:1, Watkins [9,097, 9,458] and Malone [9,103]). Donnell stated that some Europeans "considered the pact and the contract to be entered into as a sort of a bank account on which they could begin to write checks" (CR 81:1: 9,892). Kem foresaw a "sinkhole for billions of American dollars" (CR 81:1: 9,627). The Europeans could not be trusted to keep up their end of the bargain, and would free-ride on American defense spending. Opponents also took issue with other limitations on American sovereignty, such as the term of the treaty (CR 81:1, Mundt [9,461], Jenner [9,553], Malone [9,889], Donnell [9,890, 9,773, 9,033], Watkins [9,906, 9,811], Taft [9,206] and Kem [9,627]) and the pact's size (CR 81:1, Donnell [9,639] and Watkins [9,906]).[13]

---

[13] Donnell asserted, "I hold that our Nation should have the right, as the circumstances arise, to determine its course of action, rather than to tie ourselves up for 20 long years so that we cannot get out of what we tie ourselves during that lengthy period" (CR 81:1: 9,033). They wanted

For some, the issue was particularized distrust of Europe, evident in the familiar argumentation about how the pact would amount to a new Holy Alliance with the imperialist Old World. The alliance would only serve to prop up the colonial empires of France and Britain, who they were convinced were playing both sides in their own dealings with the Soviets. Participation in such an alliance would make the United States itself into a tyranny as it embraced European habits of power politics and secret diplomacy and militarized American society. History showed that alliances only led to wars, and opponents instead stressed staying true to Washington's farewell warning (CR 81:1, Langer [9,374ff., 9,428ff.], Mundt [9,455ff.], Jenner [9,553ff.], Malone [9,888ff., 9,098ff.], Donnell [9,890ff.], Watkins [9,898ff.] and Kem [9,769]). They even objected to any obligation to consult in the case of attack, an echo of Borah's objections even to participation in a concert arrangement after WWI (CR 81:1: 9,641). Simple contact with the Europeans would draw the United States into European intrigue.

However, just as was the case with the Borah isolationists thirty years before, it does not seem possible to extricate these feelings about Europe from a deeper generalized distrust, based on a pessimistic view of human nature. Treaty opponents drew connections between their general views of the trustworthiness of others and particular types of opportunism. Donnell warned of moral hazard and entrapment:

> It is not at all impossible, it is a matter of human nature, that such an official would, in his attitude toward other nations, be influenced by his realization that back of him, in the event of an attack by any one of such other nations, would be the united force of 11 other signatories. It is easily possible, while we are speculating on this matter, that his attitude might become overbearing and characterized by reckless disregard and misconduct toward other nations. Such an attitude on his part might provoke an attack by some other nation, and thereby bring immediately into operation, article 5 of the North Atlantic Treaty. (CR 81:1: 9,033)

Watkins made the connection with free riding on American defense spending: "I think it would be a strong temptation to them if they had someone who was willing to take care of defense and furnish

flexibility. Taft said, "This treaty, adopted to deal with a particular emergency today, is binding upon us for 20 years to cover all kinds of circumstances which cannot possibly be foreseen" (CR 81:1: 9,206).

them with arms, to use their own money for some other purpose and let the good friend carry the load as long as he was willing to do it. That would be the human-nature side of it" (CR 81:1: 9,103). While the United States might be an exception, American allies were untrustworthy: "The signing of the treaty will probably bind us, but it probably will not bind our so-called allies" (CR 81:1: 9,105). He declared summarily, "I do not believe *any* group of nations, selfish as the nations are today, can be brought into an organization to provide peace" (CR 81:1: 9,107).[14]

Those conservatives and isolationists opposed to the treaty endorsed Taft's plan of a Monroe Doctrine for Europe, a unilateral option that would preserve American sovereignty (CR 81:1, Wherry [9,882] and Jenner [9,018, 9,559]). Vandenberg had tried to make the connection between the treaty and the Monroe Doctrine, arguing that the former's key virtue was a clear demonstration of resolve and a warning to "keep off the grass," a phrase that stuck in the debate (CR 81:1: 8,894). Taft and the isolationists retorted that the pact was not unilateral since it was not under the complete control of the United States: "The Monroe Doctrine left us free to determine the merits of each dispute which might arise and to judge the justice and the wisdom of war in the light of the circumstances at the time. The present treaty obligates us to go to war if certain factors occur" (CR 81:1: 9,206).[15] Connally and Lodge skillfully pointed out the contradiction in Taft's arguments. A unilateral option would impose no obligations on Europe, leaving their defense completely up to the United States, a much more expensive proposition (CR 81:1: 9,894, 9,902). However, such a paradox makes

---

[14] This was the reason the League failed: not because the United States declined to join, but because its members "all had their own selfish interests and the moment the pressure of national interests outweighed the general good each nation went its own way in pursuit of selfish policies" (CR 81:1: 9,094). He made the same connection between human nature and abandonment: "It should be kept in mind that each of our proposed allies in the new alliance have their own selfish interest to serve, and when the pressure becomes strong enough, alliance or no alliance, pact or no pact, they will follow the line of their own selfish interests" (CR 81:1: 9,092).

[15] Malone emphasized that "we are the sole judges, under the Monroe Doctrine, when such peace and safety are threatened. While under the North Atlantic Pact, we would divide that responsibility with 12 European nations" (CR 81: 9,889). Donnell stressed the difference between multilateralism and unilateralism: "We are entering into a contract under which the other fellow has some rights against us" (CR 81: 9,644). See also Donnell (CR 81: 9,648).

perfect sense if we understand Taft's objections as an expression of generalized distrust. Conservatives did not expect that the treaty would actually bind the Europeans.

There were strikingly different emphases in the debate that indicate again that the North Atlantic Treaty was more a deal than a consensus. References to the importance of reassurance and making the first move to restore European morale came exclusively from Democrats (CR 81:1, Magnuson [9,456ff.], Lucas [9,804], McMahon [9,826], Long [9,204], Kefauver [9,212], Pepper [9,810] and Wiley [9,023]). The same was true of the need for cooperation to reach mutually beneficial gains and the feeling of a moral obligation under Article V (CR 81:1, Morse [9,575], Baldwin [9,769], and Humphrey [9,778]). Earnest support from Republicans in this vein was confined to the party's most liberal members (CR 81:1, Morse [9,577ff.] and Flanders [9,361]).[16] The only exception I found in my review of the treaty debate was Ferguson, a mainstream Republican who thought more like a mainstream Democrat (CR 81:1: 9,365).

The Democratic difference

Democrats were more comfortable with uncertainty and potential opportunism than Republicans, which allowed them to take more of a chance on cooperation. In rebutting critics, Baldwin argued: "Because sometimes men break their agreements it does not mean that it is not desirable to have a contract in writing...I do not think we can give up the whole thing, because in the past some treaties have been broken, and say they are a futile thing" (CR 81:1: 9,775). When asked about the risk of entrapment, Graham responded, "That is stated as a possibility. Of course, if you were to talk about possibilities, we could never get together about anything" (CR 81:1: 9,803).

Where Democrats took issue with the treaty, it was on very different grounds than Republicans. A common concern was not to undermine the United Nations by developing an exclusionary organization (CR 81:1, Humphrey [9,777-8] and Gillette [9,197ff.]). Many wanted a broader community circle and were often willing to support a significant degree of international hierarchy. The liberal Democrat Kefauver wanted to develop the North Atlantic Treaty into a federal union

---

[16] Flanders and Morse were among the top six most liberal Republicans.

within the United Nations (CR 81:1: 9,212). Senator Taylor, the only Democrat to eventually vote against the pact, preferred an effort to make the United Nations into a world government with exclusive control over armaments in the hands of an international force (CR 81:1: 9,780ff.). He was, not coincidentally, the most liberal member of the Senate, with a ideology score that was almost 3.5 standard deviations from the party mean!

Democrats justified these schemes through reference to generalized trust. Sparkman, although favoring ratification of the North Atlantic Treaty, proposed an international police force as well, dismissing those who claimed it could not be done: "There are those who say that it is ideal and even Utopian to see the establishment of a strong international organization to control wars of aggression. 'War of aggression,' they say, 'is part of human nature; it is inherent in human society. War has always existed and always will exist. No greater error could be made than to accept this moral defeatism as truth" (CR 81:1: 9,118ff.). Gillette also believed in the possibility of a world state because of his faith in the trustworthiness of others: "What possible objection, then, can there be to spending a fraction of that sum for the development of a creative peace, a peace that maintains itself because the basic war-making causes of insecurity and fear will have been eliminated and because human difference – always present and to be welcomed – will then be dealt with in a parliament of man in a civilized and Christian spirit" (CR 81:1: 9204). Although liberal Democrats might have differed as to the solution, they were united as to the source of the problem – veto power in the United Nations (CR 81:1, Thomas [8,900] and Graham [9,800]). This was something that mainstream Republicans were not willing to part with.

Wilson's ghost: moral obligations and the North Atlantic Treaty

Despite conservative and isolationist objections, passage of the treaty was relatively assured given the protections insisted upon in private negotiations. The only concern that emerged was the treaty's association with another initiative of the administration, the Military Assistance Program to provide aid to Europe and others. While the administration had dutifully consulted Vandenberg and Connally on the treaty, it had not done the same in regard to the arms project, and clumsily unveiled the latter at the same time as the United States signed the former (Kepley 1988: Chapter 2; Williams 1985: 31–2). This undermined the argument made by the administration that the pact was not a military alliance, an argument made so as not raise the hackles of isolationists, who, if only a small minority, were still vocal.[17] Vandenberg was greatly concerned about the appearance of the pact when introduced alongside a military assistance program (Vandenberg 1952: 479, 498). In the committee deliberations he stressed that "if the North Atlantic Pact is going to take on the overriding character of a permanent military alliance instead of the overriding character of an arrangement which is going to make a military alliance shortly unnecessary, there just ain't going to be any North Atlantic Pact, because you won't get the votes for it" (US Senate 1973: 242).

The Secretary of State poured fuel on this fire by implying a moral obligation under Article III to provide the Europeans with military aid. The Democratic administration approached the North Atlantic Treaty moralistically, much as Wilson had done with the League. Mindful of the latter's failures, Acheson was careful never to make such a claim explicitly. Nevertheless, he approached the line. He later remembered that he "would oppose attempting to win votes for the treaty by denigrating its commitments, to the annoyance of the Senators" (Acheson 1969: 283). Acheson stated: "[T]here is something in the treaty which requires each Member of the Senate, if you ratify this treaty, when he comes to vote on the military assistance program, to exercise his judgment less freely than he would have exercised it if it had not been for this treaty. No Member of the Senate, after the treaty is ratified, in exercising his judgment, can properly say to himself, 'I do not believe

---

[17] The Foreign Relations Committee report on the treaty assured that the pact was not an "old fashioned military alliance" of the type Washington had warned against. The North Atlantic Treaty was purely defensive, completely transparent, consistent with the United Nations Charter, and comprised almost solely of peace-loving democracies. "If it can be called an alliance," read the report, "it is an alliance only against war itself" (US Senate 1973: 381–2). Even the committee report on the Vandenberg resolution stressed that the regional organizations in mind "are not to be confused with military alliances. They are directed against no one" (US Senate 1973: 331). For this reason, Vandenberg also wanted the pact justified under Chapter VIII of the UN Charter as a regional arrangement rather than under Article 51. Otherwise it would come across as a "naked, bare, military alliance, and nothing else" (US Senate 1973: 289, 291).

in the principle of mutual assistance'" (CR 81:1: 9,095). Every country had to make an "honest judgment" about how it could help others, but "if the pact is ratified, then it cannot be said that there is no obligation to help" (US Senate 1973: 214). Congress could legally refuse an arms bill, Acheson said, but that would essentially amount to a repudiation of its moral obligations: "I could not get up, after ratifying the treaty, and make a case for the fact that the United States cannot help these countries" (US Senate 1973: 234). Acheson stressed there was no "*definite* obligation," but that only served to imply that there was an obligation of a moral nature (CR 81:1: 9,097). State Department reports walked the same line, claiming that the arms program and the treaty were separate matters but that the former was a "vital corollary" of the latter (CR 81:1: 9,097).[18]

Acheson did the same with the security guarantee. When asked about the meaning of Article V, he implied that honesty and integrity required action. Declining to refuse an obligation, he said: "Decent people... kept their contract obligations... We were decent people, we could keep our promises, and our promises were written out and clear enough" (Acheson 1969: 283). "[E]verybody in the world knows that the United States will not do something which it knows is not adequate," the Secretary said privately, and "there can be no doubt about what is necessary" (US Senate 1973: 114–15). Article V did not mean that the United States would go to war automatically in case of armed aggression, but it also did not mean that legislators could act "contrary to [the treaty's] provisions... No power but their own sense of right could force them to do their part in enabling the nation to keep its lawful promise, but that did not affect either the lawfulness or the meaning of the promise" (Acheson 1969: 283).

With very little in the treaty to object to, opponents were forced to seize on these intimations from the administration about moral if not legal obligations to arm the Europeans and to come to their aid

---

[18] For their part, more conservative legislators such as Connally and Vandenberg bluntly objected to such an inference (see in CR 81:1 comments by Connally [9,459, 8,814], Vandenberg [9,580, 8,894], Lodge [9,116] and Smith [9,191]) or explicitly disavowed such an obligation in their support for the treaty (see in CR 81:1 comments by Mundt [9,461], Knowland [9,373], Cain [9,623] and Martin [9,628]). Only Democrats and liberal Republicans believed in a moral obligation and promised their support for the arms program on this basis (see in CR 81:1 comments by Morse [9,577ff.], Gillette [9,883], George [9,898] and Graham [9,798]).

with armed force if attacked. As a consequence, Watkins introduced a reservation to the North Atlantic Treaty that would nullify any obligation to act under Article V so as to prevent entrapment.

The language was remarkably similar to the reservation made to the League Covenant's Article X, adopting a policy of default non-compliance with the security guarantee unless Congress decided otherwise.[19] However, only 11 senators voted for the measure, while 84 voted against (CR 81:1: 9,915). Their average NOMINATE score, even if we include the traditional isolationists (and domestically liberal) Donnell and Langer, was well to the right of the party as a whole.

Next a coalition of those concerned about free riding supported a reservation sponsored by senators Wherry, Watkins and Taft.[20] It read, "The United States of America ratifies this treaty with the understanding that article 3 commits none of the parties thereto, *morally or legally*, to furnish or supply arms, armaments, military, naval or air equipment or military, naval, or air supplies to any other party or parties to this treaty" (CR 81:1: 9,880 [emphasis added]). However, the assurance of the Vandenberg formula was enough to ensure that the reservation failed by a vote of 21 to 74. Shortly afterwards the treaty passed unchanged 82 to 13 (CR 81:1: 9,916). Again those voting for the amendment and against the treaty were considerably more conservative than their parties as a whole with the exception of a number of a 'one world' Democrats.[21]

---

[19] "The United States understands and construes article V of the treaty as follows: That the United States assumes no obligation to restore and maintain the security of the North Atlantic area or to assist any other party or parties in said area, by armed force, or to employ the military, air, or naval forces of the United States under article V or any article of the treaty for any purpose, unless in any particular case the Congress, which under the Constitution, has the sole power to declare war or authorize the employment of the military, air or naval forces of the United States, shall by act or joint resolution so provide" (CR 81:1: 9,898).

[20] Wherry was the most conservative member of his party and the Senate as a whole.

[21] The only Democrats to vote against their administration at any point were Taylor, Byrd and Johnson (Colo.). As already noted, Taylor was the most liberal senator by far in the party, and he preferred a world state. Byrd was the most conservative Democrat, with a voting record more like a mainstream Republican. Johnson was the eighth most conservative Democrat according to NOMINATE scores.

Alternative arguments: constructivism and political economy

Up to this point, I have focused almost exclusively on rationalist explanations of cooperation and institutional creation, neglecting a number of other counterarguments. For constructivist theorists, the essential ingredient for explaining the creation and design of NATO, as well as its subsequent operation, is identity. Hemmer and Katzenstein make the strongest and most convincing case, arguing that NATO would never have come about, at least in the form that it did, without a feeling of "mutual identification" among the allies (2002: 576). The North Atlantic states were a "shared community," and democracy "established a basis for identification that transcended military-strategic considerations" (Hemmer and Katzenstein 2002: 575, 589). They write, "One of the most striking aspects of the discussion surrounding the formation of NATO is the pervasive identification of the United States with Europe" with "constant references to a 'common civilization,' a 'community, a shared 'spirit,' 'like-minded peoples' and 'common ideals'" (2002: 593). They cite quotations of American justification for the alliance, "that the North Atlantic already existed as a political community and that the treaty merely formalized this preexisting community of shared ideals and interests" and find these to be credible evidence of the importance of identity (2002: 593). Patrick Thaddeus Jackson (2006) offers a related but somewhat different account that stresses the key role of the concept of shared "Western civilization" in American justification for the alliance.[22] He writes of a "natural community that shared, broadly speaking, similar political and cultural values with Europeans" (2006: 270).

In constructivist estimation, identity drove not only the creation of NATO but also the institutional form. The multilateral form of NATO "requires a strong sense of collective identity," Hemmer and Katzenstein write (2002: 576). "Once the North Atlantic was constructed as a

---

[22] Jackson refuses to speculate on whether this shared identity was the true motivation for American decision-makers, arguing only that it was critical for allowing alliance proponents to outmaneuver opponents rhetorically and successfully argue for the pact. Nevertheless the empirical evidence Jackson offers is similar if not identical to that used in Hemmer and Katzenstein's account. Advocates of the alliance won the argument based on their pleas for the protection of democratic government and Western civilization as a whole, which were one in the same.

region that put the United States in a grouping of roughly equal states with whom it identified, multilateral organizing principles followed closely" (2002: 588). Jackson similarly claims that the "indivisible notion of security was a logical consequence of thinking of the alliance members as belonging to a common 'Western Civilization'" (2006: 219). Common identity necessarily led to NATO and its multilateral form.

In proposing what would become the Atlantic alliance, British Foreign Secretary Bevin did indeed describe it as a "spiritual union," an alliance of countries sharing a common identity based on democratic values and a common heritage in "Western civilization." He stressed the "common ideals for which the Western Powers have twice in one generation shed their blood." Bevin wrote in correspondence with the Americans: "Almost all the countries I have listed have been nurtured on civil liberties and on the fundamental human rights." The "federation of the West" needed to "contain all the elements of freedom for which we all stand" (FRUS 1948: 1–5). In Bevin's eyes, this was not to be an alliance based merely on interests, but the "common way of life of the Western democracies" (FRUS 1948: 14). "It is not enough to reinforce the physical barriers which still guard our Western civilization," he argued. "We must also organise and consolidate the ethical and spiritual forces inherent in this Western civilisation of which [the United States and Great Britain] are the chief protagonists" (FRUS 1948: 5).

Even though there is evidence that clearly indicates that Bevin was less than genuine in his convictions,[23] according to constructivists this feeling of common identity was shared by decision-makers in the United States and motivated their efforts to create a transatlantic alliance. This overstates the case. Shared identity was certainly used by the advocates of the alliance to convince those who were more

---

[23] At the same time as he was soliciting an American security commitment, Bevin wrote in a Cabinet memo that the British "despise the spiritual values of America" and should in the long term "develop our own power and influence to equal that of the United States of America and the USSR," so as to "show clearly that we are not subservient to the United States or the Soviet Union" (Baylis 1993: 66). Bevin seems to have been motivated first and foremost by short-term security. When the Americans did not respond favorably to Bevin's ideas immediately, he quickly switched gears and asked for a bilateral alliance, only to be rebuffed (FRUS 1948: 12).

skeptical but *after* the former had settled on its merits. The "constant" references referred to by Hemmer and Katzenstein actually amount to a relatively small number of quotations from officials after they began mobilizing domestic support for the treaty. In particular, constructivist accounts recycle the same speech by Secretary of State Acheson on how the Soviets threatened "the civilization in which we live," "the ideas on which the United States was founded," which went back "more than 2,000 years, to the very beginning of Western civilization" (Hemmer and Katzenstein 2002: 585; Jackson 2006: 219; Patrick 2009: 289).

However, in private correspondence and deliberations, a common civilization and shared democratic values come up very infrequently, and generally in a perfunctory way, such as in remarks to open up negotiating sessions. The Europeans were much more likely to make reference to a common identity than the Americans, likely due to the fact that they were more threatened and somewhat desperate for an alliance commitment (FRUS 1948: 152). When the administration referred in private documents to the "free nations of Europe," it was as a moniker to distinguish the Western democracies from the Eastern bloc already under the boot of Stalin (FRUS 1948: 10, 40–41, 55, 62–3, 73). Even those few opponents of a multilateral treaty in the administration, most notably George Kennan, used the term in the same way (FRUS 1948: 116–17). Keeping Europe free was the object of the alliance, but not solely for freedom's sake. Freedom was to be the effect of the treaty; it was not the primary cause.

Implicit in Hemmer and Katzenstein's story is a kind of selflessness on the part of the United States consistent with a focus on identity. By helping the Europeans, the Americans were helping themselves as they were part of the same group. The very notion of identity implies at least a partial merging of the self and other based on shared membership in a group. Quoting Finnemore, the authors note that identification "emphasizes the affective relationships between actors…" (2002: 587). This is evident in the fact that even though the European countries had been destroyed by the war and were no longer deserving of great-power status, the United States treated them as equals. The Americans did not press their power advantage over the Europeans. They pulled back based on a shared sense of self (2002: 588). Jackson similarly argues that recourse to the concept of Western civilization engendered "American responsibility for preserving Europe," which

implies magnanimity and paternalism on the part of the Americans
(2006: 222).[24]

However, as we have seen, the United States based its decisions on
an expectation of reciprocity. While Acheson and Truman, in their
respective formal statements after the signature of the treaty on April
4, 1949, did make reference to the "common democratic way of life"
of its signatories, they also emphasized the need for reciprocal cooperation to reach mutual gains in an environment of security interdependence (US Senate 1973: 345). "The security and welfare of each
member of this community depend upon the security and welfare of
all. None of us alone can achieve economic prosperity or military
security," proclaimed the President (US Senate 1973: 344).

Nor was American support based on far-sighted strategic restraint.
Ikenberry (2001) sees the form NATO took as emblematic of American self-binding, a signal to the Europeans of the benign nature of
its leadership. But the latter was never an issue. For the Europeans,
multilateralism served to cement US participation, not to constrain the
exercise of its power. For the Americans the concern was not how to
allay European fears of oppression, but how to ensure the US would
get something in return for its help.

Constructivists might reply that their account of NATO's origins
is perfectly consistent with the theoretical account identified above.
American self-restraint and its magnanimous overprovision of certain public goods was simply the first part of a long-term reciprocal
exchange. Perhaps I am overstating their reliance on identification.
However, constructivists still differ in that they argue implicitly that
common identity is the foundation of moralistic trust. Hemmer and
Katzenstein briefly note the presence and role of trust, but imply that

---

[24] This same tendency to emphasize the role of identity in NATO, and to imply a
certain selflessness on the part of the United States as a result, is also present in
Risse-Kappen's (1995) study of the operation of NATO following its creation.
Risse-Kappen also refers to the "democratic community affecting collective
identity," the "we-feeling" and "at least partial identification" among the
Americans and Europeans (1995: 31–2). Identity's effect is manifest in how
NATO operates, on the basis of consultation, persuasion and accommodation
given the shared democratic norms of its members. Because it is a democracy
like the others, the United States allows weaker members a disproportionate
role and gives them much more consideration than we might otherwise think
given the asymmetric distribution of power. The implication is that the United
States does not act on the basis of pure self-interest but restrains itself for the
good of the larger group.

belonging in a common group comes first. "Perceived affinities of various types *reinforced the political trust rooted in common democratic political institutions*, 'we-feeling, and 'mutual responsiveness' that Karl Deutsch and his associates have described as central ingredients of the emergence of the North Atlantic community" (2002: 588 [emphasis added]). This is particularized trust, driven by a shared sense of self.

An argument predicated on particularized trust, however, cannot explain the division between proponents and opponents over the treaty. Taft Republicans did not have a different conception of American identity and America's relationship to Europe. They were the ideological heirs of the conservative internationalists discussed above. Indeed Taft's own father, the former President, was one of that group's primary strategists during the League fight, endorsing Lodge's formula for a League. As Democrats did, Taft argued that the "special problems of Europe and its importance to the cause of freedom throughout the world force us to act there more vigorously and make some exceptions to the general rules of policy. Our cultural background springs from Europe, and many of our basic principles of liberty and justice were derived from European nations" (Taft 1951: 80). Nevertheless, he and other conservatives opposed the alliance. The civilizational justification of the alliance as a community of democracies was barely present in the debates, amounting to only a few scattered references that did not distinguish proponents and opponents of the treaty (CR 81:1: 8,900, 9,769).

Fordham makes a political economy argument, claiming that domestic differences over the North Atlantic Treaty and other foreign policy issues are partially determined by patterns of trade and investment by firms in the home states of senators. Those whose constituents had a greater stake in European security wanted a firmer commitment to the Continent. Given the regional nature of American trade ties, we therefore observe bipartisan overlap in foreign policy preferences among legislators in the postwar period at least, particularly among those representing Eastern states with stronger financial and trade ties with Europe. Political economy creates a cleavage between Midwestern isolationist Republicans and Eastern internationalist Republicans. The latter were "Europe-firsters," the former "Asia-firsters" (Fordham 1998a 1998b; J. L. Snyder 1991).

The political economy argument has great weaknesses in accounting for the origins of NATO. In an exhaustive study of congressional rollcall voting, Rieselbach (1966: 107) concluded that Midwestern "isolationism," what I have been calling unilateralism, was a function not of geography or region but rather of the more entrenched presence in the area of more conservative Republicans, those who should be the least trusting. Even if we were to concede that coastal Republicans had a greater material stake in European security, this argument cannot account for the significant differences between Democratic and Republican internationalists, the two groups that drove the American policy process. The more unilateralist position of moderate, mostly northeastern, Republicans was particularly surprising as their constituents shared the economic profile of Democrats from the same region. Political economy arguments would expect them to embrace the most binding alliance possible. Their leader, Vandenberg, consistently worked against this and to reduce defense spending (Kepley 1988: Chapter 2; Williams 1985: 31–2). Another reason to be skeptical of the political economy argument is that, as seen above, the same cleavages arose during negotiations over the design of the United Nations even though it involved a more general security arrangement to govern global security in which there were no clear differences in economic stakes between or among parties. And the ideological alignments after the war were also virtually identical to the interwar period, when the sectoral profile of American firms and industry was much different (Narizny 2007). This suggests ideology was more important.

As was the case with the League, objections to NATO are sometimes interpreted as concerns not over national but rather over congressional sovereignty, as an infringement on the congressional right to declare war. There are strong indications, however, that constitutionality was a pretext for concerns about opportunism. Vandenberg and Connally had made sure that the treaty made specific reference to "constitutional processes," and Democratic officials weakened the automaticity preferred by the Europeans to ensure that a state of war could not be brought about simply by aggression against the parties (Vandenberg 1952: 476). Congress would have to declare war for the United States to use significant force, even if the executive branch might take other, non-military action without legislative consent. The Foreign Relations Committee report stressed that the pact did not affect the balance of executive and legislative powers in the foreign policy arena (US Senate 1973: 373–4). One might interpret the Watkins reservation as merely a defense of legislative powers under the constitution. However, such a proposal would not have needed to make non-action the default in the case of an attack. A reservation devoted solely to the protection of constitutional prerogatives could have simply tasked Congress with deciding the appropriate action in any instance of aggression. Indeed Watkins introduced such a resolution but only after the first failed (CR 81:1: 9,898).

Where genuine, concerns about congressional prerogatives were primarily an isolationist anxiety based on a unique conception of American identity. Legislative prerogatives were what separated the New World from the Old World. Under the treaty, Watkins feared, "Our freedom of action would be gone, and that is the heart of our Constitution. That is why our people came here, so that no monarch, no one man could send them into a battle which they did not want to fight, and make them take up the wars of other peoples" (CR 81:1: 9,900).

More important, differences over executive prerogatives cannot explain the broader complex of concerns about the treaty that a focus on generalized trust can, since fears about abandonment, free riding, the number of signatories and the duration of the treaty had nothing to do with congressional prerogatives. While there were periodic references to the treaty's effect on the constitution (CR 81:1: 9,807, 9,899), opponents focused overwhelmingly on European trustworthiness. Nor can such an argument explain the ideological and partisan nature of much of the debate since separation of powers issues should have united legislators across parties.

To claim that identity did not drive the creation of NATO is not to claim that a common identity among NATO members has not arisen from the shared experiences of the past sixty years. It likely sustains the alliance now that its original *raison d'etre* has largely disappeared. Support for NATO is now truly bipartisan. And to argue that NATO began with the expectation of reciprocity rather than a presumption of free riding based on hegemonic interest does not mean that the United States did not do the lion's share of the lifting in the alliance. Both, I believe, reflect how the Cold War evolved. The United States began the postwar period as a reluctant hegemon, but this changed as it increasingly defined its own identity in opposition to the Russians. I would surmise that as divisions between the Soviet Union and the United States hardened and the perceived threat increased, even conservatives increasingly felt solidarity with the Europeans. And by the 1970s, Europeans felt more risk from entrapment than abandonment.

The United States seemed to be more willing to fight than the Europeans.

Nevertheless, it is mistaken to argue that the identity and the interest in cooperation absent burden-sharing was there from the beginning. NATO nurtured a sense of common identity but the alliance did not arise from it. I argue that trust made this possible, more specifically generalized trust that the Democrats largely had and the Republicans generally did not. Even moderate "internationalist" Republicans preferred an arrangement well short of an alliance. Without the Democratic lead, the North Atlantic Treaty might never have come into existence. A Republican administration under Eisenhower might have been inclined towards such an arrangement had it not already been created, although his Secretary of State John Foster Dulles was not a strong proponent of the way Democrats designed NATO. However, they would have had to pay more attention to the Taft wing of the party. The internationalist Eisenhower administration with its "pactomania" never came close to committing to anything as binding as NATO. By the time a true bipartisan consensus in favor of NATO formed in the 1960s, as part of the growing rivalry of the Cold War, the strategic rationale for NATO as it had been constructed was significantly weaker. When the Soviets achieved strategic nuclear parity with the United States, the extended deterrence of the United States came into question, a problem that the alliance never was able to truly solve. It is possible that in that new strategic context, a collective security arrangement would have proved impossible to negotiate, trust or no trust.

6 | *Coming full circle: fear, terrorism and the future of American multilateralism*

Generalized trust served as a crucial ingredient in the United States' postwar program of multilateralism. It is necessary to explain many of the features of international security institutions, and the very creation of the organizations themselves. What does the social psychological argument offered in previous chapters have to tell us about American foreign policy today, particularly in light of the frequent declaration that the bipartisan pillar of multilateralism is now crumbling? In this chapter, I come full circle to consider the contemporary issues raised in this book's opening pages.

Just as many claimed that the lessons of WWII led to a fundamental shift in American foreign policy, some today argue that the terrorist attacks on New York and Washington led to a striking reorientation in America's approach to international relations. Most deftly, Hemmer (2007) argues that the "lessons of 9/11" are to remain hyper-vigilant to the possibility of terrorism and to disrupt and preempt attacks before they come to fruition. Crudely stated, 9/11 is the new Pearl Harbor. And just like that surprise attack, 9/11 is said to have led to a lasting structural shift in the political spectrum as a whole. Democrats and Republicans alike have committed to restrictions on civil liberties at home and to the war on terror abroad. Hemmer's claims bear a striking resemblance to those offered by Legro (2005) on how external events affected American grand strategy after Pearl Harbor and fostered the creation of a bipartisan consensus.

In this narrative, the casualty is ironically the approach that resulted as a consequence of the lessons ostensibly learned by both parties at that last formative moment – multilateralism. In this view, unilateralism is the natural result of a new structural realignment in international relations, the advent of the war on terror. The United States cannot afford to eschew any freedom of action on an issue of life and death. At most the United States might assemble coalitions of the willing composed of those it trusts the most, but it will not submit to any multilateral restrictions. The war in Iraq is of course the most obvious example.

I have shown in previous chapters that the claim that WWII changed everything in American foreign policy in regards to multilateral engagement is incorrect. The same is true of 9/11. The terrorist attacks did lead to a temporary shift in the American public and even among its political elites, one that cannot be understood without the companion to generalized trust – fear. The nature of the terrorist attacks and terrorism in general – highly surprising, coming from a heretofore unknown or underestimated threat, difficult to locate and impossible to predict – creates a climate of generalized distrust that other types of international threat do not. The September 2001 assaults led to a structural decline in generalized trust in the American population as a whole.

As fear is a generalized form of distrust, it creates an environment in which previously unconnected dangers can be joined. Fear was the crucial element that allowed the Bush administration to link 9/11 to Iraq and was also decisive for promoting cross-party support for the latter's invasion. It is responsible for the failure of the "marketplace of ideas," the fact that the lack of specific information linking Saddam Hussein's regime to terrorism did not seem to inhibit the United States' decision or the public's assent to use force (Kaufmann 2004). Fear is not the same as strategic distrust, just as generalized trust is different than strategic trust – it is not based on information. And it was pronounced enough after 9/11 that even the absence of a UN authorization did not significantly dampen public and bipartisan support. Fear promoted a bipartisan acceptance of unilateral practice. This was not so much because multilateralism threatened opportunism, although that likely influenced American policy, but because fear created an overwhelming imperative to act that multilateralism would have restrained.

To argue, however, that fear helped link 9/11 to Iraq is not to say that the Bush administration's endorsement of an invasion was structurally determined or that a Democratic administration would have reacted similarly. Consistent with the expectations of previous findings in political psychology, while there was an overall shift in foreign policy views in the American public as a whole after 9/11, there was also an interactive effect. Conservatives reacted particularly strongly to the new and uncertain security environment. This cocktail of fear and conservatism is necessary to explain why the Bush administration responded in the way it did. Conservatives were predisposed towards the adoption of the "possibilistic" mindset that justified the opening of a new front in the "war on terror." This interaction proved potent, and it exacerbated the unilateralism already present in the administration's early days. Of course, garnering public support required the Republicans to make a connection between these two threats, but the strategic manipulation of fear does not mean that they were acting purely instrumentally for other, ulterior motives.

Democrats, as they are more trusting dispositionally, would have behaved differently in office, I believe. While they reacted fearfully to 9/11, that day's effect was not nearly as powerful for them. And while 9/11 remains a vivid reminder to conservatives of the dangerous world around us, its effect on liberals seems to have waned. Psychological research indicates that generalized trust serves as a kind of shock absorber that blunts the impact of threatening events. The immediate period after 9/11 was therefore a crucial window of opportunity, outside of which there would have not been bipartisan support for the war in Iraq. And as more and more time separates Americans from those terrible days, the domestic politics of foreign policy have reverted to a more familiar pattern in which Democrats are significantly more multilateralist than Republicans. After a brief departure, the Democrats have come full circle to their core ideological roots.

While Democratic presidential candidates in 2004 and 2008 made many criticisms of the Bush administration's foreign policy, the most persistent and trenchant has been of its unilateralism. A return to engagement and the use and reform of multilateral institutions is arguably the most prominent theme in the Obama administration's foreign policy. Just as Wilson argued, Democratic officials claim that cooperation is in the United States' interest given the interdependent nature of global challenges. It is still too early to assess whether this rhetoric will match reality, but there are certainly indications that the Democrats will follow through on this pledge.

The Republican Party, however, seems to remain committed to unilateralism. This is not surprising considering the seemingly ever-widening ideological gulf between the two parties. There is unanimous agreement among scholars of American politics that both Democrats and Republicans are becoming more ideologically cohesive and polarized. Given that liberalism and conservatism are, according to the argument of this book, largely a reflection of dispositions to and levels of trust, it is natural that divisions between multilateralists and unilateralists will worsen as parties drift apart. By any number of quantitative indicators, congressional Republicans and Democrats are as polarized now as they were in the early twentieth century, which marked the previous high point. Of course, it is not coincidental that this is when the parties engaged in the most bitter ideological struggle over foreign policy of the age, the League of Nations fight. American parties have come full circle in this way as well, although this is hardly welcome news for the United States or the world.

In the pages that follow I consider the effect of 9/11 on American foreign policy and the Bush administration's connection of terrorism to Iraq. I do not painstakingly review the history of recent and all-too-familiar events, and of course this account must remain speculative as it is not possible to engage in a thorough qualitative case reconstruction in so recent a case. Instead I focus on how the literature in social and political psychology would have led us to expect these dynamics, and argue that the interaction of terrorism and political ideology are necessary to account for the parties' responses to 9/11. I then briefly examine the alternative offered by the Democrats following their election in 2008. I connect increasingly vitriolic debates over multilateralism and unilateralism to the growing ideological polarization of American political parties and end with some words of hope for multilateralism.

The "gathering storm": fear, 9/11, and the road to Iraq

The very term "terrorism" captures the fact that this method of political violence is meant to stoke fear, a general sense of danger. While all threats to physical safety increase fear, terrorism is unique. It differs from a hostile nation-state on one's borders or another ethnic group fomenting civil war. The exceptional attributes of terrorist-induced fear lie in its uncertain nature. Terrorism, according to Crenshaw, appears as "anonymous, sudden and random." It shocks "because its milieu and its specific victims are unpredictable." The uncertainty associated with terrorism means that it creates not just fear of a specific adversary but a generalized fear. It "arouses awe, anxiety and a mystical dread," a sense of "existential insecurity" (Crenshaw 1986: 401–2). We can think of fear as the opposite of generalized trust, a feeling that the world is a dangerous place in which many are out to harm us.

There is a large literature, based on both archival data and experimental research, showing that collective events indicating that the world is a dangerous place lead populations as a whole in politically more conservative directions (Sales 1973). Support for strong authoritative institutions and traditional morality is the natural solution to societal threats. It is the logical response to fear. McCann (1997) for instance finds that in situations of threat, conservative candidates win by greater margins in American elections than in calmer, more peaceful times.

Terrorism is no exception. In keeping with Jost's premise that conservatism serves as a means by which individuals cope with fear and threat, Bonanno and Jost (2006) find exposure to terrorist threat increases the level of political conservatism of individuals, in terms both of their self-identification and also their positions on other unrelated domestic positions such as affirmative action, taxation and same-sex marriage. This result has been replicated by Nail and McGregor (2009), and the same has been found in other countries as well (Echebarria-Echabe and Fernandez-Guede 2006). It is not surprising that in situations of heightened terrorist threats, individuals endorse restrictions on civil liberties or the use of coercive and violent means to combat terrorism. In this way, terrorism is no different than other threats. That threats and uncertainty induce changes in attitudes in substantively unrelated areas, however, indicates that the fear created is generalized rather than specific in nature. It leads to a fundamental ideological change in worldview, with predictable manifestations in political positions as a whole.

Another strand of research, "terror management theory," demonstrates that subtle reminders of mortality lead individuals towards a defense of their cultural worldviews (Cohen, Ogilvie, Solomon, Greenberg and Pyszczynski 2005; Cohen, Solomon, Maxfield, Pyszczynski and Greenberg 2004; Greenberg et al. 1990; Greenberg, Simon, Pyszczynski, Solomon and Chatel 1992; Landau et al. 2004). Psychologists working in this tradition typically find that when mortality is made salient for subjects in experiments, individuals rate more favorably those with similar religious or political beliefs and have more negative feelings towards those who are different when compared to those for whom death was not primed. Worldview defense following the priming of mortality amounts to, in the parlance of this book, a bolstering of particularized trust in the face of fear. It is an insider–outsider distinction, a characterization of the world as marked by a battle of good versus evil induced by external threat. National solidarity is a product of generalized distrust. Studies indicate that the causal arrow runs from threat to identity and not from identity to threat, not only generally but in the specific case of Iraq (Cohrs, Moschner, Maes and Kielmann 2005; McFarland 2005; Sahar 2008).

Conservatism leads to greater support for aggressive measures to counter terrorism, just as it affects support for military force to deal with traditional threats. Researchers have found consistent links between levels of right-wing authoritarianism and support for restrictions on civil liberties, stereotypical views of Islam as a denigrated out-group, and the expansion of the war on terror to include an invasion of Iraq (Crowson, DeBacker and Thoma 2005; Davis and Silver 2004; Kam and Kinder 2007). Crowson (2009) shows that the causal pathway begins with the belief that the world is a dangerous place, then to rightist political views, and finally to these specific foreign policy positions. Therefore it is not surprising that an increase in conservatism as a whole, induced by the fear generated by terrorism, helps create a broad societal consensus to use coercive means to eradicate the threat.

The insights of political psychology seem essential for explaining how the terrorist attacks of 9/11 propelled the United States towards the invasion of Iraq in 2003. Kaufmann (2004) laments the failure of the American "marketplace of ideas," seeking to explain the puzzle of how the administration could convince the public of the need to use force to deal with the threat of Iraqi weapons of mass destruction given that there was no convincing evidence of Saddam Hussein's link to terrorism or 9/11 or that his weapon's program was developed enough to be dangerous. A properly functioning democracy, he argues, should have rejected the dubious nature of the administration's claims. However, Kaufmann misses the uniquely psychological impact of 9/11. The fear induced by terrorism was, like generalized trust, not epistemological in nature. Generalized distrust is not based on specific information about a particular threat but rather a sense that the world is dangerous.

Only by reference to the nature of fear can we begin to comprehend the administration's desire to link Iraq to the broader war on terrorism and its success in doing so, a process that began in earnest in the summer of 2002. Fear leads individuals to act on the basis of possibilities, however unlikely, rather than on the basis of probability, as strategic distrust does (Brooks 1997; Rathbun 2007b). Possibilistic reasoning is not based on a careful parsing of information and intelligence to calibrate the proper response. Fear leads individuals towards worst-case analysis; it creates a sense of foreboding about what might happen.

In the Iraq case, it was not so much that Saddam Hussein *would* transfer WMD to terrorists or even use them against the United States, but that he *could* (Flibbert 2006: 338; Kaufmann 2004: 8–9). The standard of proof was far lower for the invasion of Iraq in the wake of 9/11 than Kaufmann understands. This was an emotional and psychological process, not a rationalist one. As Bush himself characterized it, "[O]ur greatest fear is that terrorists will find a shortcut to their mad ambitions when an outlaw regime supplies them with the technologies to kill on a massive scale" (2002).

Administration officials made no secret of their new frame of mind. As Secretary of Defense Donald Rumsfeld declared after the invasion, the administration "did not act in Iraq because of dramatic new evidence of Iraq's pursuit of weapons of mass murder. We acted because we saw the existing evidence in a new light, through the prism of our experience on September 11" (Jervis 2003: 372). When Rumsfeld was asked why it was suddenly necessary to disarm Iraq and why containment was no longer sufficient, he answered: "What's different is 3,000 people were killed." There was a new epistemological standard for action. "I suggest that any who insist on perfect evidence are back in the 20th Century and still thinking in pre-9/11 terms," he continued (Hemmer 2007: 215). Even the more dovish Secretary of State Colin Powell used possibilistic logic: "Should we take the risk that [Saddam Hussein] will not someday use [WMD] at a time and a place in a manner of his choosing? The United States will not and cannot run that risk for the American people." Powell did not assert that Iraq would, but rather that it "*could* one day kill hundreds of thousands of people in our country or any other" (Kaufmann 2004: 10 [emphasis added]).

The power of fear was also evident in how the administration characterized this new security challenge as a "war on terror" between the forces of good and evil. These were attacks not only on American citizens and their material assets but also on their values. Al Qaeda "reject basic human values and hate the United States and everything for which it stands," said the President (Krebs and Lobasz 2007: 430; McCartney 2004: 417). Already on September 12, the administration was defining the situation in Manichean terms (McCartney 2004: 408–9). The war on terror is "as simple as that," said Bush. "It's good versus evil, and freedom is under attack" (McCartney 2004: 422). Bush promised to "rid the world of evildoers" (Flibbert 2006: 337). Krebs and Lobasz report that 381 of the President's addresses from 2001 to 2006 employed the language of good and evil (2007: 426). From this characterization, it was a simple and logical step to his warning in his emergency address before Congress, in which he proclaimed, "Either you are with us or you are with the terrorists" (McCartney 2004: 413).

The Bush administration's response is consistent with terror management theory. Reminders of mortality induce individuals to invoke worldview defense as a way of psychologically coping with threat. Fear is implicit but unmistakable in the administration's framing – the world is a dangerous place with many out to harm the United States. Just as generalized trust is based on an attribution about others' trustworthy character rather than their interests, fear is premised on a belief that others are dispositionally evil and intent on destruction and violence.

Fear led the Republicans somewhat naturally to the embrace of a strategy of preemption. Evil implies something that cannot be reasoned with; terrorists are fanatics who will stop at nothing (Jervis 2003: 369; Krebs and Lobasz 2007: 426; McCartney 2004: 417). Consequently, the traditional strategy of defense and deterrence did not apply. Bush asserted, "The best way to secure America is to get the enemy before they get us . . . I will not forget the lessons of September the 11th" (Hemmer 2007: 212). Rice drew the conclusion: "Take care of threats early" (Hemmer 2007: 215). This doctrine was formalized in the administration's National Security Strategy, which maintained that "traditional concepts of deterrence will not work against a terrorist enemy whose avowed tactics are wanton destruction and the targeting of innocents" (Schmidt and Williams 2008: 197). Evil had to be dealt with decisively before, as Bush would frequently maintain metaphorically, storm clouds could gather (Krebs and Lobasz 2007: 439; McCartney 2004: 418). Bush declared in his West Point address in June 2002: "We cannot defend America by hoping for the best . . . If we wait for threats to fully materialize, we will have waited too long . . . We must take the battle to the enemy, disrupt his plans, and confront the worst threats before they emerge" (McCartney 2004:

419). This is why Iraq had to be disarmed. Powell declared, "Leaving Saddam Hussein in possession of weapons of mass destruction for a few more months or years is not an option, not in a post-September 11th world" (Kaufmann 2004: 10).

Preemption could not wait for specific intelligence either. Indeed the very notion of preemption was to eradicate potential threats before they became actual threats. Preemption is war on the very possibility of what can happen. Rice famously declared, "The problem here is that there will always be some uncertainty about how quickly [Saddam Hussein] can acquire nuclear weapons, but we don't want the smoking gun to be a mushroom cloud" (Flibbert 2006: 317). Similarly, said Bush, "The first time we may be completely certain he has nuclear weapons is when, God forbid, he uses one" (Kaufmann 2004: 10). Bush explained, in justifying the campaign against Iraq, that before 9/11 the "President could stand back and say, well, maybe this gathering threat is an issue, maybe it's not. After September the 11th that complacency is no longer relevant" (Hemmer 2007: 132). Under the threat of terrorism, "the doctrine of containment just doesn't hold any water" (Jervis 2003: 372).

Kaufmann notes the worst-case nature of American decision making but attributes it to a cynical ploy to mobilize public opinion for a war that the Bush administration wanted for some other, ulterior motive that is never specified (2004: 9). In order to build public support for a potential war against Iraq, the administration certainly played on public apprehension about 9/11. Krebs and Lobasz note how officials "slyly" mentioned Iraq in the same breath as 9/11, and how placing Iraq into an "axis of evil" put Hussein on the same moral plane as Al Qaeda (2007: 442). As Bush argued, "You can't distinguish between Al Qaida and Saddam when you talk about the war on terror. Because they're both equally as bad and equally as evil and equally as destructive" (Krebs and Lobasz 2007: 444). In a content analysis of Presidential speeches, Gershkoff and Kushner (2005) find that 9/11 and Iraq were frequently juxtaposed if not explicitly linked, and that as the administration built the case for war in fall 2002, references to terrorism hit levels not seen since the immediate aftermath of the attacks in November 2001. In his State of the Union address in January 2003, President Bush raised a frightening possibility: "Imagine those 19 hijackers with other weapons and other planes – this time armed by Saddam Hussein. It would take one vial, one canister, one crate slipped into this country to bring a day of horror like none we have ever known" (Hemmer 2007: 213).

The administration was indeed drawn to interpret intelligence that was ambiguous at best in the worst possible light, and it certainly manipulated fear in order to gain support for its agenda. But that does not imply in and of itself that their concerns were not genuine. In fact, this is exactly what we would expect from a fearful administration in a democratic country that needs public support to go to war. Many analysts note how there is little if any evidence that the administration was disingenuous, only that they were overly fearful (and that only in retrospect) (Flibbert 2006: 313; Hemmer 2007: 223; Jervis 2003: 373). As Jervis pithily puts it, the administration "privately overestimated and publicly exaggerated" the extent of Iraq's WMD program (2003: 371).

In carrying the public, the administration was remarkably successful. Two thirds of the public supported the invasion of Iraq at its onset in March 2003. This is not surprising considering the academic findings on the psychology of terrorism reviewed above. Research suggests that society as a whole will become more fearful and therefore supportive of aggressive action after a terrorist strike. Just after 9/11, even before any public campaign, 74 percent of respondents supported invading Iraq. This generalized sense of threat allowed the Bush administration to link Iraq to the prospect, if not the certainty, of another attack on the United States. Gershkoff and Kushner (2005) find a link between invocations of terrorism and public support for the war in Iraq. While support for an invasion dipped to 50 percent in the summer of 2002, it increased again as the administration began to mobilize opinion. The framing was therefore important. By late 2002, different polls showed that 70–90 percent of respondents believed that Saddam Hussein would eventually attack the United States with WMD (Kaufmann 2004). This broad support was evident in Congress as well. Krebs and Lobasz (2007) note that the administration's framing of the conflict as one between good and evil was hegemonic, with nary a peep from the other side of the aisle. Democrats voted in large numbers to authorize the use of force against Iraq. Fear enabled the administration to lead both mass and elite opinion (Flibbert 2006: 313).

Fear encouraged unilateralism, although not in the same way as documented in previous chapters of this book. Fear raised the perceived stakes for the United States of not taking action, which convinced the administration that Iraq must be disarmed regardless of whether the United Nations sanctioned a military operation. It was not so much that the Bush administration distrusted members of the Security Council (although many in the government certainly did), but that fear led to a sense of vulnerability that trumped the downside of taking action without the approval of the international community. Even at his most multilateralist, when the President made the case for putting pressure on Iraq before the UN General Assembly in the fall of 2002, he stressed that the United States would take matters into its own hands if the United Nations refused to enforce its previous resolutions:

My nation will work with the U.N. Security Council to meet our common challenge. If Iraq's regime defies us again, the world must move deliberately, decisively to hold Iraq to account. We will work with the U.N. Security Council for the necessary resolutions. But the purposes of the United States should not be doubted. The Security Council resolutions will be enforced, the just demands of peace and security will be met or action will be unavoidable and a regime that has lost its legitimacy will also lose its power... We must choose between a world of fear and a world of progress. We cannot stand by and do nothing while dangers gather. (Bush 2002)

Bush's own words betray that fear was his motivating force.

Return to multilateralism: the Democratic Party and the Obama administration

Claiming that there was a broad societal shift in generalized fear after 9/11 is not the same as claiming that an invasion of Iraq and America's aggressive response to terrorism in general were inevitable. In fact, based on the psychological findings about the interaction of threat and political ideology, I would argue that only a less trusting conservative administration would have linked Iraq and Al Qaeda and invaded the Middle East. Even while threat increases fear and therefore conservatism in the population as whole, there is also evidence of a significant interaction effect between threat and preexisting political ideology. Research shows that an increase in societal threat in any number of forms – economic, political or security – increases support for conservative political views primarily, sometimes exclusively, among more fearful individuals predisposed towards conservatism in the first place. Feldman and Stenner, both together and separately, argue that authoritarian views are "activated" by external threat, but only for those individuals with a proclivity towards a more pessimistic outlook in the first place (Feldman 2003; Feldman and Stenner 1997; Stenner 2009b). McCann (2008) finds that only conservative states respond to increased homicide and violent crime rates with greater numbers of death sentences and executions. And in time of threat, only states that lean conservative already tend to elect more Republican officials (McCann 2009). Liberal states show no change in either case. Greenberg et al. (1990; 1992) discover that subtle cues to provoke fear of death lead only conservatives towards more favorable evaluations of in-groups and unfavorable evaluations of out-groups. There is no effect on liberals. Generalized trust provides a reservoir buffering liberals from the effects of a threatening environment (Weise et al. 2008). As a consequence, they draw very different policy conclusions.

Therefore, while terrorism leads both liberals and conservatives towards the endorsement of coercive means to deal with the threat both home and abroad, it is not surprising that others have found that it has a disproportionate effect on the right (Canetti-Nisim, Halperin, Sharvit and Hobfoll 2009; Davis and Silver 2004; Kam and Kinder 2007). This would indicate that a Democratic administration would have responded very differently. Even if it had been inclined to draw possibilistic links between Iraq and terrorism, it likely would have been more inclined to seek multilateral endorsement of any American military action. Even Hemmer, who argues that 9/11 has served as a salient historical experience that has led to an "ideational shift in American foreign policy" as a whole, believes that a Gore administration would have handled things very differently (2007: 226).

This conclusion of course rests on a counterfactual that is impossible to prove. What it is possible to say is that the unilateral way in which the Bush administration proceeded in Iraq and its broader denigration of the utility of international organizations have been the elements of Republican foreign policy most criticized by Democrats. After their flirtation with unilateralism, the Democrats came full circle back to their roots. While Democratic presidential candidates differed over whether the war in Iraq had been a mistake and whether to withdraw American forces, all lamented that the Bush administration had acted largely alone in such a way as to alienate American allies and the world at large. The 2004 Democratic platform stated: "[T]he Bush Administration has walked away from more than a hundred years of American leadership in the world to embrace a new – and dangerously ineffective – disregard for the world... They act alone when they could assemble a team... Time and again, this Administration confuses leadership with going it alone and engagement with compromise of principle" (Democratic Party 2004: 3). As regarded Iraq, it "did not build a true international coalition" and "disdained the United Nations weapons inspection process" (Democratic Party 2004: 8). In his speech accepting the Democratic nomination for President in 2004, John Kerry promised to be a president "who restores America's respect and leadership so we don't have to go it alone in the world" (Kerry 2004). Contender for the nomination John Edwards wrote of policies that "drove away our friends and allies," Hillary Clinton of "an unprecedented course of unilateralism" (Clinton 2008; Edwards 2007: 20). Barack Obama complained that the Republicans "disdained diplomacy and bullied allies" (2007b). In his first speech before the United Nations as President, Obama lamented that "America has acted unilaterally, without regard for the interests of others" (2009).

The most consistent foreign policy theme of Obama and Clinton, both as dueling candidates for the 2008 presidential nomination and in their respective roles as President and Secretary of State since 2009, is that the world is highly interdependent and that meeting global challenges requires international cooperation. As a candidate, Obama wrote that "America cannot meet the threats of this century alone, and the world cannot meet them without America ... [T]he security and well-being of each and every American depend on the security and well-being of those who live beyond our borders" (2007c).[1] In her confirmation hearing, Clinton testified, "[T]he clear lesson of the last twenty years is that we must both combat the threats and seize the opportunities of our interdependence. And to be effective in doing so we must build a world with more partners and fewer adversaries (2009b).[2] Upon entering office, in the address that most explicitly laid out the administration's general approach to international affairs, the Secretary spoke of "building the architecture of global cooperation," and of using the "ability to convene and connect." She promised a

---

[1] See also Obama (2007b).
[2] She mimicked Obama's campaign rhetoric: "America cannot solve the most pressing problems on our own, and the world cannot solve them without America."

"new era of engagement based on common interest, shared values, and mutual respect," to "solve problems in concert with others," and "to build partnerships and solve problems that no nation can solve on its own" (Clinton 2009a). This was the same message offered by Woodrow Wilson, and Democratic politicians explicitly invoke his legacy and that of other multilateralists from the party's past (Democratic Party 2004: 3).[3]

This policy is based not on some sense of international altruism but rather on American self-interest. President Obama said to the world's leaders at the UN: "Now, like all of you, my responsibility is to act in the interest of my nation and my people, and I will never apologize for defending those interests. But it is my deeply held belief that in the year 2009 – more than at any point in human history – the interests of nations and peoples are shared . . . No longer do we have the luxury of indulging our differences to the exclusion of the work we must do together" (2009). Obama and Clinton even evoked concepts from the international relations literature on cooperation. The Secretary of State referred to solving "collective action problems" (Clinton 2009a).

Multilateral institutions are a key means of achieving these ends, which marks a clear contrast with the prior Republican administration. As a candidate, Clinton wrote: "Contrary to what many in the current administration appear to believe, international institutions are tools rather than traps. The United States must be prepared to act on its own to defend its vital interests, but effective international institutions make it much less likely that we will have to do so" (2008). The party's 2008 platform promised to "revitalize global institutions" and to "rededicate" the United States to the UN (Democratic Party 2008: 39). As a candidate, Obama pledged to "rebuild the alliances, partnerships and institutions necessary to confront common threats and enhance common security" (2007c). Where international institutions are not functioning well, Democrats have called for reforming rather than abandoning them. This was a plank in the party platform and a theme of Obama as a candidate (Obama 2007c; Democratic Party 2008). Clinton has written: "[I]instead of disparaging these institutions for their failures, we should bring them in line with the power

---

[3] The 2004 platform described the party's "tough-minded tradition of engagement and leadership – a tradition forged by Wilson and Roosevelt in two world wars, then championed by Truman and Kennedy during the Cold War."

realities of the twenty-first century" (2008). She expressed this same sentiment as Secretary of State (Clinton 2009a 2009b).

The Democrats have also embraced the qualitative multilateralism that generalized trust makes possible. Obama said, "In the 21st century we cannot stand up before the world and say that there's one set of rules for America and another for everyone else" (2007b). However, Democrats also argue that by committing to multilateral practice, the United States nevertheless gains by achieving outcomes otherwise impossible to obtain. "In the wake of the Second World War, it was America that largely built a system of international institutions that carried us through the Cold War," said Obama during the presidential campaign. "Leaders like Harry Truman and George Marshall knew that instead of constraining our power, these institutions magnified it" (Obama 2007b). He has said the same of the UN. "We helped create the United Nations – not to constrain America's influence, but to amplify it" (Obama 2008).

The Democrats frequently speak of quantitative multilateralism as well, of cooperating not only with allies with whom they share an identity but also with those outside a closed community circle. The 2004 party platform lauded the historical "exercise of American leadership to forge powerful alliances based on mutual respect with longtime allies and reluctant friends; with nations already living in the light of democracy and with peoples struggling to join them." The 2008 platform stated: "[W]hen we do use force in situations other than self-defense, we should make every effort to garner the clear support and participation of others. The consequences of forgetting that lesson in the context of the current conflict in Iraq have been grave" (Democratic Party 2008: 33). Clinton speaks of "uniting diverse partners around common concerns" and offering "a place at the table to any nation, group, or citizen willing to shoulder a fair share of the burden. In short, we will lead by inducing greater cooperation among a greater number of actors . . . tilting the balance away from a multi-polar world and toward a multi-partner world" (2009a).

The Democrats have a default inclination to engage first in formal international cooperation to solve problems. Clinton wrote as a candidate that "US foreign policy must be guided by a preference for multilateralism, with unilateralism as an option when absolutely necessary to protect our security or avert an avoidable tragedy." The US should "make international institutions work, and work through them when possible" (2008). As Secretary of State, she has written the same.[4]

The more trusting and multilateralist instincts of the Obama administration are best seen in relief when compared to the past practice of the Bush administration and to what might have occurred had Republicans won the 2008 election. The foreign policy thinking of John McCain and Mitt Romney strongly suggest that the right would have governed differently. During the campaign, McCain explicitly called for the formation of an institution of trusted allies to rival the United Nations. Rather than reform the global institution, McCain (2007) promised to convene a conference for the creation of a "League of Democracies" composed of "like-minded nations working together for peace and liberty." This recalls the conservative internationalist vision of a concert of great powers, and McCain explicitly gave credit for his vision to Theodore Roosevelt. As a less trusting conservative, McCain fell back on particularized trust. Romney (2007) indicated the same inclination towards cooperation with smaller groups sharing American interests. This recalls the Bush administration's reliance on "coalitions of the willing," something that rationalists understand as the functional inclination of administrations of all ideological types but one that is likely much more pronounced in conservative governments lacking generalized trust (Kreps 2008).

It is still too early to judge whether the Obama administration's return to multilateralism will bear fruit. Generalized trust is but one factor in both the creation and the use of multilateral institutions. There must also be some common interest in cooperation that trust promotes. It cannot resolve distributional conflicts over tough zero-sum issues, such as the burden different states will bear in reducing greenhouse gases in any climate change treaty. And multilateral institution-building is different than choosing to operate within the framework of an existing multilateral institution at any given time. If an issue is important enough, even those with multilateralist instincts might prefer to act unilaterally. And on any single issue, the strategic calculation foreseen by rationalism in which states judge the likely alignment of votes and act appropriately, is much easier. Finally, the United States, as a global superpower, has unique interests that

---

[4] "We should use the United Nations and other international institutions whenever appropriate and possible" (Clinton 2009b).

predispose it towards unilateralism in a way not true of other states. We expect more unilateralism on the part of countries whose interests are different than everyone else's and who have the ability to take action into their own hands in a way that smaller, less powerful countries, do not.

A recent example of many of these ideas was the decision by NATO members to sidestep the United Nations and proceed to bomb Yugoslavia without Security Council authorization. Russia and China made no secret that they would block any UN endorsement of force on behalf of the Kosovar Albanians, so a strategic calculation about whether to pursue a multilateral path was clear. And in this instance, the humanitarian considerations for the Western allies simply overwhelmed the desire to preserve international comity. Even still, the Democratic Clinton administration did pursue the operation within NATO, adding a great degree of quantitative and qualitative multilateralism that the Bush administration never countenanced in Afghanistan or Iraq, and which increased the costs for the US.

Party polarization and the future of American multilateralism

Even if we witness a multilateralist turn in American foreign policy, there is no guarantee of any kind of long-term consistency given the intense ideological polarization between the parties. When the electoral pendulum swings back towards the right, the shift will likely be dramatic in foreign policy. Those who study Congress agree that beginning in the 1970s Republicans and Democrats have drifted farther apart ideologically. Politicians in the United States have "sorted," meaning that each party is increasingly homogenous. There are fewer and fewer liberal Republicans or conservative Democrats. Parties are philosophically purer. Much of this process has been driven by the realignment of the South in which conservative Democrats found a more hospitable ideological home in the Republican Party. As we saw in chapters 3 and 4, the foreign affairs positions of those Democrats fit uneasily with their northeastern colleagues; the same was true of domestic politics on issues well beyond race. However, significant sorting is also present in the Northeast at well. It is a national phenomenon (Poole and Rosenthal 2007; Sinclair 2006; Theriault 2008).

Poole and Rosenthal find that in the immediate postwar period, when parties were more pluralist, the proportion of senators whose

NOMINATE scores were closer to the mean of the opposing party than their own was between 5 and 7 percent. It has sunk to between 1 and 2 percent in recent years (Poole and Rosenthal 2007: 105). That is akin to the levels seen in previous periods of intense partisanship in Washington. Theriault notes that in the 2003–4 Congress, no Republican House member had a more liberal NOMINATE score than the most conservative Democratic House member. And the divide between the most conservative Democrat and the most liberal Republican was more than 7 percent of the entire scale (2008: 17).

Not only have liberals and conservatives increasingly sorted themselves into the appropriate party, but American politicians have become increasingly polarized. Democrats as a whole are more liberal, Republicans more conservative than in the past (Poole and Rosenthal 2007; Sinclair 2006; Theriault 2008). The previous high point of party polarization was in the late nineteenth and early twentieth century (Poole and Rosenthal 2007: 85). This was, not coincidentally, the time at which the United States witnessed the most ideologically contested debate on foreign affairs in its history – the League of Nations fight documented in Chapter 2. Party divergence indicates more variation in generalized trust, which has a profound effect on preferences for multilateralism and unilateralism. The low point in party polarization was, not surprisingly, the early post-WWII period. Even though differences between liberals and conservatives were still pronounced, it is likely that some degree of ideological compression was necessary even to initiate a process of private consultations over foreign policy. With the recent rise in polarization, the United States has come full circle.

Given that political ideology is largely an expression of generalized trust, we can therefore expect increasing contestation over the degree to which the United States should embrace multilateral institutions as a means for realizing American foreign policy goals. Bipartisan consultation will be difficult, bipartisan agreement even more so. We can also anticipate for some time forward decisive shifts in the level of multilateralism of the American government as it changes hands from one party to another, a vicious circle of another type.

This might invite gloom on the part of those who yearn for a more consistently multilateral policy. There is, however, a silver lining in the findings of this book. The processes of international cooperation are not the product of structural forces compelling states to collaborate or go it alone. We have seen that even when these incentives were claimed to be the strongest, after WWII, the United States had a clear choice. International organizations are the manifestations of the dispositional tendencies of those who create them. They are but reflections of us. Multilateralism and unilateralism are "isms" in our own minds. And in a democracy, where we have the power to elect those who lead us, we are able to choose our leaders, and therefore affect the course of world affairs. We fashion the circles of trust.

Trusting in international cooperation

What can we say about the legacy of generalized trust? This book shows that it promotes qualitative multilateralism and quantitative multilateralism as a means towards the end of greater international peace. But does multilateralism deliver on its promise? Pinpointing the effects of international organizations on conflict resolution is a tricky business, but some recent quantitatively based studies indicate that they do have a pacifying effect, both by intervening in conflicts among states but also by facilitating information transfer and a socialization process in which interests gradually converge over time. Boehmer, Gartzke and Nordstrom (2004) find that joint membership in security IOs is associated with a lower probability of military conflict, provided that those organizations are "structured" or "interventionist" in character. Their categorical schemes are different than mine, but qualitatively multilateral organizations would fall under these two rubrics. Mere talk shops, the concert-like arrangements favored by conservatives in this book, did not have a statistically significant ameliorative effect in international relations. Qualitative multilateralism pays off.

Similarly, Bearce and Bondanella (2007) report that interests converge in the same sort of organizations, indicating a socialization effect that would favor peace in the long-term. The same is not true of "unstructured" or "minimal" IOs. International institutions might be built on trust but they also build it further. Uslaner, on whose (2002) work I rely so heavily in this book, argues that generalized trust among individuals does not increase by interacting with those like us, only with those whom we do not know or identify with. The same might be true in international affairs, an argument for quantitative multilateralism and a broader community circle.

Skeptics might caution us that an overreliance on international institutions is delusional. They are no substitute for a strong national

defense and unilateral action. This is the familiar realist line in international relations, unsurprisingly since realists of all stripes are bound
together by the motivating force of fear, the opposite of generalized
trust (Rathbun 2007b). However, realists miss that generalized trust
can yield greater material payoffs for cooperators that make them
stronger and better able to take the risk of trusting again in the future.
Obviously the risks of cooperation in international politics are higher
relative to other arenas but so might be the rewards. That is the very
essence of anarchical social capital and the basis on which ever more
complex and prosperous human societies are built, what evolutionary biologists call "reciprocal altruism." The democratic peace, at its
heart the generalized trust that prevails among liberal societies, has
certainly facilitated the security and prosperity that prevails in the
Western world (Cederman 2001b). I am not suggesting a teleological
progression towards a world state, only the obvious potential gains
from intergovernmental collaboration.

Realists would counter that the stakes are simply too high in international politics, and that such trust leaves states vulnerable to opportunism. Generalized trusters are simply too naïve to prosper in anarchy.
Research in social psychology suggests otherwise. Because of their general fearfulness, competitors have been found to be the worst judges
of actual intentions in experimental settings (Maki and McClintock
1983). They presume a lack of trustworthiness even where it is not
the case. Empirically, competitors find it more difficult to use communication to build trust (Cook and Cooper 2003: 212). And overly
fearful decision-makers can lead us into conflict just as easily as overly
trusting ones, of course. Jervis (1976) long ago cautioned that we are
more likely to overestimate hostility than underestimate it.

Generalized trusters, in contrast, are more open to different signals
of the intentions of others (Rotter 1980). In experiments, cooperators
are the best predictors of the intentions of others (Maki and McClintock 1983; Yamagishi 2001). This suggests that they are best suited to
finding the necessary and proper balance between trust and skepticism.
As we have seen, generalized trust is never total. It is not pacifism or
gullibility. Overall it seems best to trust in international cooperation.

Works cited

Abbott, Kenneth W., and Duncan Snidal. 1998. "Why States Act through Formal International Organizations." *Journal of Conflict Resolution* 42(1): 3–32.

2000. "Hard and Soft Law in International Governance." *International Organization* 54(3): 421–56.

Acheson, Dean. 1969. *Present at the Creation: My Years in the State Department.* New York: Norton.

Achilles, Theodore. 1992. *Fingerprints on History: The NATO Memoirs of Theodore C. Achilles.* Kent, OH: Lyman L. Lemnitzer Center for NATO and European Community Studies.

Adorno, Theodor W. 1950. *The Authoritarian Personality.* New York: Harper.

Alcock, James E., and Diana Mansell. 1977. "Predisposition and Behaviour in a Collective Dilemma." *Journal of Conflict Resolution* 21(3): 443–57.

Altemeyer, Robert A. 1988. *Enemies of Freedom: Understanding Right-Wing Authoritarianism.* San Francisco: Jossey-Bass.

1998. "The Other 'Authoritarian Personality.'" *Advances in Experimental Social Psychology* 30: 47–92.

Ambrosius, Lloyd E. 1987. *Woodrow Wilson and the American Diplomatic Tradition: The Treaty Fight in Perspective.* Cambridge University Press.

Axelrod, Robert M. 1984. *The Evolution of Cooperation.* New York: Basic Books.

Axelrod, Robert M., and William D. Hamilton. 1981. "The Evolution of Cooperation." *Science* 211(4,489): 1,390–6.

Barber, Bernard. 1983. *The Logic and Limits of Trust.* New Brunswick, NJ: Rutgers University Press.

Baylis, John. 1993. *The Diplomacy of Pragmatism: Britain and the Formation of NATO, 1942–1949.* Kent, Ohio: Kent State University Press.

Bearce, David H. and Stacy Bondanella. 2007. "Intergovernmental Organizations, Socialization, and Member-State Interest Convergence." *International Organization* 61: 703–33.

Berg, Joyce, John Dickhaut and Kevin McCabe. 1995. "Trust, Reciprocity, and Social History." *Games and Economic Behavior* 10(1): 122–42.

Binning, Kevin R. 2007. "'It's Us Against the World': How Distrust in Americans versus People-In-General Shapes Competitive Foreign Policy Preferences." *Political Psychology* 28(6): 777–99.

Blyth, Mark. 2002. *Great Transformations: Economic Ideas and Institutional Change in the Twentieth Century*. Cambridge University Press.

Boehmer, Charles, Erik Gartzke and Timothy Nordstrom. 2004. "Do Intergovernmental Organizations Promote Peace?" *World Politics* 57(1): 1–38.

Bonanno, George A., and John T. Jost. 2006. "Conservative Shift among High-Exposure Survivors of the September 11th Terrorist Attacks." *Basic and Applied Social Psychology* 28(4): 311–23.

Brady, David, and Joseph Stewart, Jr. 1982. "Congressional Party Realignment and Transformations of Public Policy in Three Realignment Eras." *American Journal of Political Science* 26(2): 333–60.

Brann, Peter, and Margaret Foddy. 1987. "Trust and the Consumption of a Deteriorating Common Resource." *Journal of Conflict Resolution* 31(4): 615–30.

Brewer, Marilynn B. 1981. "Ethnocentrism and Its Role in Interpersonal Trust." In *Scientific Inquiry and the Social Sciences*, eds. D. Campbell, B. Collins and M. Brewer, pp. 214–31. San Francisco: Josey-Bass.

Brewer, Marilynn B., and Roderick M. Kramer. 1986. "Choice Behavior in Social Dilemmas: Effects of Social Identity, Group Size, and Decision Framing." *Journal of Personality and Social Psychology* 50(3): 543–9.

Brooks, Stephen G. 1997. "Dueling Realisms." *International Organization* 51(3): 445–77.

Bueno de Mesquita, Bruce. 1988. "The Contribution of Expected Utility Theory to the Study of International Conflict." *Journal of Interdisciplinary History* 18(4): 629–52.

Bull, Hedley. 1977. *The Anarchical Society: A Study of Order in World Politics*. New York: Columbia University Press.

Busby, Joshua W., and Jonathan Monten. 2008. "Without Heirs?: Assessing the Decline of Establishment Internationalism in U.S. Foreign Policy." *Perspectives on Politics* 6(3): 451–72.

Bush, George W. 2002. "President Bush's Address to the United Nations." http://archives.cnn.com/2002/US/09/12/bush.transcript/.

Campbell, Thomas M. 1973a. *Masquerade Peace: America's UN Policy, 1944–1945*. Tallahassee: Florida State University Press.

    1973b. "Nationalism in America's UN Policy, 1944–1945." *International Organization* 27(1): 25–44.

Canetti-Nisim, Daphna, Eran Halperin, Keren Sharvit and Stevan E. Hobfoll. 2009. "A New Stress-Based Model of Political Extremism: Personal Exposure to Terrorism, Psychological Distress, and Exclusionist Political Attitudes." *Journal of Conflict Resolution* 53: 363–89.

Cederman, Lars-Erik. 2001a. "Back to Kant: Reinterpreting the Democratic Peace as a Macrohistorical Learning Process." *American Political Science Review* 95(1): 15–31.

2001b. "Modeling the Democratic Peace as a Kantian Selection Process." *Journal of Conflict Resolution* 45(4): 470–502.

Clinton, Hillary. 2008. "Security and Opportunity for the Twenty-First Century." *Foreign Affairs* 86 (November/December): 2–18.

2009a. "Foreign Policy Address at the Council on Foreign Relations."

2009b. "Nomination Hearing to be Secretary of State." www.state.gov/secretary/rm/2009a/01/115196.htm.

Cohen, Florette, Daniel M. Ogilvie, Sheldon Solomon, Jeff Greenberg and Tom Pyszczynski. 2005. "American Roulette: The Effect of Reminders of Death on Support for George W. Bush in the 2004 Presidential Election." *Analyses of Social Issues and Public Policy* 5(1): 177–87.

Cohen, Florette, Sheldon Solomon, Molly Maxfield, Tom Pyszczynski and Jeff Greenberg. 2004. "Fatal Attraction: The Effects of Mortality Salience on Evaluations of Charismatic, Task-oriented, and Relationship-oriented Leaders." *Psychological Science* 15(12): 846–51.

Cohrs, J. Christopher, Barbara Moschner and Jurgen Maes. 2005. "Personal Values and Attitudes Toward War." *Peace and Conflict* 11(3): 293–312.

Cohrs, J. Christopher, Barbara Moschner, Jurgen Maes and Sven Kielmann. 2005. "The Motivational Bases of Right-Wing Authoritarianism and Social Dominance Orientation: Relations to Values and Attitudes in the Aftermath of September 11, 2001." *Personality and Social Psychology Bulletin* 31(10): 1,425–34.

Conover, Pamela Johnston, and Stanley Feldman. 1981. "The Origins and Meaning of Liberal/Conservative Self-Identifications." *American Journal of Political Science* 25(4): 617–45.

Cook, Karen S., and Robin M. Cooper. 2003. "Experimental Studies of Cooperation, Trust and Social Exchange." In *Trust and Reciprocity: Interdisciplinary Lessons from Experimental Research*, ed. E. Ostrom and J. Walker, pp. 209–44. New York: Russell Sage Foundation.

Cook, Karen S., Russell Hardin and Margaret Levi. 2005. *Cooperation without Trust?* New York: Russell Sage Foundation.

Cooper, John Milton. 2001. *Breaking the Heart of the World: Woodrow Wilson and the Fight for the League of Nations.* Cambridge University Press.

Cozzarelli, Catherine, Anna V. Wilkinson and Michael J. Tagler. 2001. "Attitudes toward the Poor and Attributions for Poverty." *Journal of Social Issues* 57(2): 207–27.

Crenshaw, Martha. 1986. "The Psychology of Political Terrorism." In *Political Psychology*, ed. M. G. Hermann. San Francisco: Jossey-Bass.

Cronin, Bruce. 1999. *Community under Anarchy: Transnational Identity and the Evolution of Cooperation.* New York: Columbia University Press.

Crowson, H. Michael. 2009. "Right-Wing Authoritarianism and Social Dominance Orientation as Mediators of Worldview Beliefs on Attitudes Related to the War on Terror." *Social Psychology* 40(2): 93–103.

Crowson, H. Michael, Teresa K. DeBacker and Stephen J. Thoma. 2005. "Does Authoritarianism Predict Post-9/11 Attitudes?" *Personality and Individual Differences* 39(7): 1,273–83.

Curti, Merle. 1957. "Woodrow Wilson's Concept of Human Nature." *Midwest Journal of Political Science* 1(1): 1–19.

Czernin, Ferdinand. 1964. *Versailles, 1919: The Forces, Events, and Personalities that Shaped the Treaty.* New York: Putnam.

David, Edward. 1970. "The Liberal Party Divided 1916–1918." *The Historical Journal* 13(3): 509–32.

Davis, Darren W., and Brian D. Silver. 2004. "Civil Liberties vs. Security: Public Opinion in the Context of Terrorist Attacks on America." *American Journal of Political Science* 48(1): 28–46.

Dawes, Robyn M. 1980. "Social Dilemmas." *Annual Review of Psychology* 31: 169–98.

Dawes, Robyn M., Jeanne McTavish and Harriet Shaklee. 1977. "Behavior, Communication, and Assumptions about Other People's Behavior in a Commons Dilemma Situation." *Journal of Personality and Social Psychology* 35(1): 1–11.

De Cremer, David, and Mark Van Vugt. 1999. "Social Identification Effects in Social Dilemmas: a Transformation of Motives." *European Journal of Social Psychology* 29(7): 871–93.

Democratic Party. 2004. *Strong at Home, Respected in the World*, 2004 Democratic Party platform. www.presidency.ucsb.edu/platforms.php.

 2008. *Renewing America's Promise*, 2008 Democratic Party platform. www.presidency.ucsb.edu/papers_pdf/78283.pdf.

Deutsch, Karl Wolfgang. 1957. *Political Community and the North Atlantic Area: International Organization in the Light of Historical Experience*. Princeton University Press.

Deutsch, Morton. 1960a. "The Effect of Motivation Orientation upon Threat and Suspicion." *Human Relations* 13(2): 123–39.

1960b. "Trust, trustworthiness and the F-Scale." *Journal of Abnormal Social Psychology* 61: 138–40.

Divine, Robert A. 1967. *Second Chance: The Triumph of Internationalism in America during World War II*. New York: Atheneum.

Doenecke, Justus D. 1979. *Not to the Swift: The Old Isolationists in the Cold War Era*. Lewisburg, Pa.: Bucknell University Press.

Donnelly, Jack. 1982. "Human Rights and Human Dignity: An Analytic Critique of Non-Western Conceptions of Human Rights." *American Political Science Review* 76(2): 303–16.

Downs, George W., David M. Rocke and Peter N. Barsoom. 1998. "Managing the Evolution of Multilateralism." *International Organization* 52(2): 397–419.

Duckitt, John. 1989. "Authoritarianism and Group Identification: A New View of an Old Construct." *Political Psychology* 10(1): 63–84.

2001. "A Dual-process Cognitive-motivational Theory of Ideology and Prejudice." *Advances in Experimental Social Psychology* 33: 41–113.

2006. "Differential Effects of Right Wing Authoritarianism and Social Dominance Orientation on Outgroup Attitudes and Their Mediation by Threat from and Competitiveness to Outgroups." *Personality and Social Psychology Bulletin* 32(5): 684–96.

Duckitt, John, and Kirstin Fisher. 2003. "The Impact of Social Threat on Worldview and Ideological Attitudes." *Political Psychology* 24(1): 199–222.

Duckitt, John, and Chris G. Sibley. 2009. "A Dual-Process Motivational Model of Ideology, Politics, and Prejudice." *Psychological Inquiry* 20(2–3): 98–109.

Duckitt, John, Claire Wagner, Ilouize du Plessis, and Ingrid Birum. 2002. "The Psychological Bases of Ideology and Prejudice: Testing a Dual Process Model." *Journal of Personality and Social Psychology* 83(1): 75–93.

Dueck, Colin. 2006. *Reluctant Crusaders: Power, Culture, and Change in American Grand Strategy*. Princeton University Press.

Dworkin, Ronald. 1978. *Taking Rights Seriously*. Cambridge, Mass.: Harvard University Press.

1985. *A Matter of Principle*. Cambridge, Mass.: Harvard University Press.

Echebarria-Echabe, Agustin, and Emilia Fernandez-Guede. 2006. "Effects of Terrorism on Attitudes and Ideological Orientation." *European Journal of Social Psychology* 36(2): 259–65.

Edwards, John. 2007. "Reengaging with the World: A Return to Moral Leadership." *Foreign Affairs* 86 (September/October): 19–36.

Egerton, George W. 1978. *Great Britain and the Creation of the League of Nations: Strategy, Politics and International Organization, 1914–1919*. Chapel Hill: University of North Carolina Press.

Farris, Charles D. 1960. "Selected Attitudes on Foreign Affairs as Correlates of Authoritarianism and Political Anomie." *Journal of Politics* 22(1): 50–67.

Feather, Norman. 1985. "Attitudes, Values, and Attributions: Explanations of Unemployment." *Journal of Personality and Social Psychology* 48(4): 876–89.

Feldman, Stanley. 2003. "Enforcing Social Conformity: A Theory of Authoritarianism." *Political Psychology* 24(1): 41–74.

Feldman, Stanley, and Karen Stenner. 1997. "Perceived Threat and Authoritarianism." *Political Psychology* 18(4): 741–70.

Flibbert, Andrew. 2006. "The Road to Baghdad: Ideas and Intellectuals in Explanations of the Iraq War." *Security Studies* 15(2): 310–52.

Fordham, Benjamin O. 1998a. *Building the Cold War Consensus: The Political Economy of U.S. National Security Policy, 1949–51*. Ann Arbor: University of Michigan Press.

——— 1998b. "Economic Interests, Party, and Ideology in Early Cold War Era U.S. Foreign Policy." *International Organization* 52(2): 359–96.

Fortna, Virginia Page. 2003. "Scraps of Paper? Agreements and the Durability of Peace." *International Organization* 57(2): 337–72.

Fox, John, and Melvin Guyer. 1977. "Group Size and Others' Strategy in an N-Person Game." *Journal of Conflict Resolution* 21(2): 323–38.

FRUS (Foreign Relations of the United States diplomatic papers). 1942. Vol. III: Europe. United States Department of State. US GPO.

——— 1944. Vol. I: General. Washington, DC. US Department of State. US GPO.

——— 1948. vol. III: Western Europe. Washington, DC: US Department of State.

——— 1949. vol. IV: Western Europe. Washington, DC: US Department of State.

Furnham, Adrian. 1982. "Why Are the Poor Always with Us?: Explanations for Poverty in Great Britain." *British Journal of Social Psychology* 21: 311–22.

Campbell 1973: 88; Gaddis, John Lewis. 2000. *The United States and the Origins of the Cold War, 1941–1947*. New York: Columbia University Press.

Garraty, John A. 1943. *Henry Cabot Lodge: A Biography*. New York: Knopf.

Garrett, Geoffrey. 1992. "International Cooperation and Institutional Choice: The European Community's Internal Market." *International Organization* 46(2): 533–60.

Gerring, John. 1998. *Party Ideologies in America, 1828–1996*. Cambridge University Press.

2001. *Party Ideologies in America, 1828–1996*. Cambridge University Press.

Gershkoff, Amy, and Shana Kushner. 2005. "Shaping Public Opinion: The 9/11–Iraq Connection in the Bush Administration's Rhetoric." *Perspectives on Politics* 3(3): 525–37.

Goldgeier, James M., and Philip E. Tetlock. 2001. "Psychology and International Relations Theory." *Annual Review of Political Science* 4: 67–92.

Goodwin, Geoffrey L. 1957. *Britain and the United Nations*. New York: Manhattan Publishing Company.

Greenberg, Jeff, Tom Pyszczynski, Sheldon Solomon, Abram Rosenblatt, Mitchell Veeder, Shari Kirkland and Deborah Lyon. 1990. "Evidence for Terror Management Theory II: The Effects of Mortality Salience on Reactions to Those who Threaten or Bolster the Cultural Worldview." *Journal of Personality and Social Psychology* 58(2): 308–18.

Greenberg, Jeff, Linda Simon, Tom Pyszczynski, Sheldon Solomon and Dan Chatel. 1992. "Terror Management and Tolerance: Does Mortality Salience Always Intensify Negative Reactions to Others Who Threaten One's Worldview?" *Journal of Personality and Social Psychology* 63(2): 212–20.

Grieco, Joseph M. 1988. "Anarchy and the Limits of Cooperation: A Realist Critique of the Newest Liberal Institutionalism." *International Organization* 42(3): 485–507.

Haas, Ernst B. 1980. "Why Collaborate?: Issue-Linkage and International Regimes." *World Politics* 32(3): 357–405.

Halevy, Nir, Lilach Sagiv, Sonica Roccas and Gary Bornstein. 2006. "Perceiving Intergroup Conflict: From Game Models to Mental Templates." *Personality and Social Psychology Bulletin* 32(12): 1,674–89.

Hardin, Russell. 2001. "Conceptions and Explanations of Trust." In *Trust in Society*, ed. K. S. Cook, pp. 3–39. New York: Russell Sage Foundation.

2006. *Trust*. Cambridge: Polity.

Hawkins, Darren G., David A. Lake, Daniel Nielson and Michael J. Tierney, eds. 2006. *Delegation and Agency in International Organizations*. Cambridge University Press.

Hayashi, Nahoko, Elinor Ostrom, James Walker and Toshio Yamagishi. 1999. "Reciprocity, Trust and the Sense of Control: A Cross-Societal Study." *Rationality and Society* 11(1): 27–46.

Hemmer, Christopher. 2007. "The Lessons of September 11, Iraq and the American Pendulum." *Political Science Quarterly* 122(2): 207–38.

Hemmer, Christopher, and Peter J. Katzenstein. 2002. "Why Is There No NATO in Asia? Collective Identity, Regionalism, and the Origins of Multilateralism." *International Organization* 56(3): 575–607.

Henderson, Nicholas. 1983. *The Birth of NATO*. Boulder, Colo.: Westview Press.

Hilderbrand, Robert C. 1990. *Dumbarton Oaks: The Origins of the United Nations and the Search for Postwar Security*. Chapel Hill: University of North Carolina Press.

Hoffman, Aaron M. 2002. "A Conceptualization of Trust in International Relations." *European Journal of International Relations* 8(3): 375–401.

2006. *Building Trust: Overcoming Suspicion in International Conflict*. Albany: State University of New York Press.

Holsti, Ole R., and James N. Rosenau. 1988. "The Domestic and Foreign Policy Beliefs of American Leaders." *Journal of Conflict Resolution* 32(2): 248–94.

1996. "Liberals, Populists, Libertarians, and Conservatives: The Link between Domestic and International Affairs." *International Political Science Review* 17(1): 29–54.

Hoopes, Townsend, and Douglas Brinkley. 1997. *FDR and the Creation of the U.N.* New Haven: Yale University Press.

Howard, Rhoda E., and Jack Donnelly. 1986. "Human Dignity, Human Rights, and Political Regimes." *American Political Science Review* 80(3): 801–17.

Hughes, Charles Evan. 1916. *Speeches of Hon. Charles Evan Hughes and Hon. Nathan L. Miller and Platform*. Saratoga Springs: Republican State Convention.

Hughes, E. J. 1974. "Winston Churchill and the Formation of the United Nations Organization." *Journal of Contemporary History* 9(4): 177–94.

Hull, Cordell. 1948. *The Memoirs of Cordell Hull*. New York: Macmillan Co.

Ikenberry, G. John. 2001. *After Victory: Institutions, Strategic Restraint, and the Rebuilding of Order after Major Wars*. Princeton University Press.

Inglehart, Ronald. 1977. *The Silent Revolution: Changing Values and Political Styles among Western Publics*. Princeton University Press.

Inglehart, Ronald, and Scott C. Flanagan. 1987. "Value Change in Industrial Societies." *American Political Science Review* 81(4): 1,289–319.

Ireland, Timothy. 1981. *Creating the Entangling Alliance: The Origins of the North Atlantic Treaty Organization*. Westport, Conn.: Greenwood Press.

Jackson, Patrick Thaddeus. 2006. *Civilizing the Enemy: German Reconstruction and the Invention of the West*. Ann Arbor: University of Michigan Press.

Janoff-Bulman, Ronnie. 2009a. "Political Attitudes and Complexity: Responses From a Motivational Perspective." *Psychological Inquiry* 20(2–3): 177–82.

　　2009b. "To Provide or Protect: Motivational Bases of Political Liberalism and Conservatism." *Psychological Inquiry* 20(2–3): 120–8.

Jebb, Gladwyn. 1990. "Founding the United Nations: Principles and Objects." In *The United Kingdom – The United Nations*, ed. E. Jensen and T. Fisher, pp. 21–47. Houndmills: Macmillan.

Jeffreys, Kevin. 1991. *The Churchill Coalition and Wartime Politics, 1940–1945*. Manchester University Press.

Jervis, Robert. 1976. *Perception and Misperception in International Politics*. Princeton University Press.

　　1978. "Cooperation under the Security Dilemma." *World Politics* 30(2): 167–214.

　　2003. "Understanding the Bush Doctrine." *Political Science Quarterly* 118(3): 365–88.

Johnson, Donald Bruce. 1978. *National Party Platforms*, vol. I, *1840–1956*. Urbana: University of Illinois Press.

Jost, John T., Jack Glaser, Arie W. Kruglanski and Frank J. Sulloway. 2003. "Political Conservatism as Motivated Social Cognition." *Psychological Bulletin* 129(3): 339–75.

Jost, John T., Jaime L. Napier, Hulda Thorisdottir, Samuel D. Gosling, Tibor P. Palfai and Brian Ostafin. 2007. "Are Needs to Manage Uncertainty and Threat Associated With Political Conservatism or Ideological Extremity?" *Personality and Social Psychological Bulletin* 33(7): 989–1,007.

Jugert, Philipp, and John Duckitt. 2009. "A Motivational Model of Authoritarianism: Integrating Personal and Situational Determinants." *Political Psychology* 30(5): 693–719.

Kahler, Miles. 1992. "Multilateralism with Small and Large Numbers." *International Organization* 46(3): 681–708.

Kam, Cindy D., and Donald R. Kinder. 2007. "Terror and Ethnocentrism: Foundations of American Support for the War on Terrorism." *Journal of Politics* 69(2): 320–38.

Kanagaretnam, Kiridaran, Stuart Mestelman, Khalid Nainar and Mohamed
    Shehata. 2009. "The Impact of Social Value Orientation and Risk
    Attitudes on Trust and Reciprocity." *Journal of Economic Psychology*
    30(3): 368–80.
Kaplan, Lawrence S. 2007. *NATO 1948: The Birth of the Transatlantic
    Alliance*. Lanham, Md.: Rowman & Littlefield.
Kaufmann, Chaim. 2004. "Threat Inflation and the Failure of the Market-
    place of Ideas: The Selling of the Iraq War." *International Security*
    29(1): 5–48.
Kelley, Harold H., and Anthony J. Stahelski. 1970. "Social Interaction Basis
    of Cooperators' and Competitors' Beliefs about Others." *Journal of
    Personality and Social Psychology* 16(1): 66–91.
Kelley, Harold H., and John W. Thibaut. 1978. *Interpersonal Relations: A
    Theory of Interdependence*. New York: Wiley.
Keohane, Robert O. 1982. "The Demand for International Regimes." *Inter-
    national Organization* 36(2): 325–55.
    1984. *After Hegemony: Cooperation and Discord in the World Political
    Economy*. Princeton University Press.
    1986. "Reciprocity in International Relations." *International Organiza-
    tion* 40(1): 1–27.
Kepley, David R. 1988. *The Collapse of the Middle Way: Senate Republicans
    and the Bipartisan Foreign Policy, 1948–1952*. New York: Green-
    wood Press.
Kerry, John. 2004. www.washingtonpost.com/wp-dyn/articles/A25678–
    2004Jul29.html.
Kim, Woosang, and Bruce Bueno de Mesquita. 1995. "How Perceptions
    Influence the Risk of War." *International Studies Quarterly* 39(1):
    51–65.
Kimball, Warren F. 1991. *The Juggler: Franklin Roosevelt as Wartime
    Statesman*. Princeton University Press.
Kinder, Donald R., and Cindy D. Kam. 2009. *Us against Them: Ethno-
    centric Foundations of American Opinion*. University of Chicago
    Press.
Kirk, Russell, and James McClellan. 1967. *The Political Principles of Robert
    A. Taft*. New York: Fleet Press Corp.
Kitschelt, Herbert. 1988a. "Left-Libertarian Parties: Explaining Inno-
    vation in Competitive Party Systems." *World Politics* 40(2):
    194–234.
    1988b. "Organization and Strategy of Belgian and West German Ecol-
    ogy Parties: A New Dynamic of Party Politics in Western Europe?"
    Comparative Politics 20(2): 127–54.
    1994. *The Transformation of European Social Democracy*. Cambridge
    University Press.

Kitschelt, Herbert, and Anthony J. McGann. 1995. *The Radical Right in Western Europe: A Comparative Analysis.* Ann Arbor: University of Michigan Press.

Kluegel, James R. 1990. "Trends in Whites' Explanations of the Black–White Gap in Socioeconomic Status, 1977–1989." *American Sociological Review* 55(4): 512–25.

Kluegel, James R., and Eliot R. Smith. 1986. *Beliefs about Inequality: Americans' Views of What Is and What Ought to Be.* New York: A. de Gruyter.

Knock, Thomas J. 1992. *To End All Wars: Woodrow Wilson and the Quest for a New World Order.* New York: Oxford University Press.

Koremenos, Barbara. 2001. "Loosening the Ties That Bind: A Learning Model of Agreement Flexibility." *International Organization* 55(2): 289–325.

2005. "Contracting around International Uncertainty." *American Political Science Review* 99(4): 549–65.

Koremenos, Barbara, Charles Lipson and Duncan Snidal. 2001. "The Rational Design of International Institutions." *International Organization* 55(4): 761–99.

2004. *The Rational Design of International Institutions.* Cambridge University Press.

Kramer, Roderick M., Marilynn B. Brewer and Benjamin A. Hanna. 1996. "Collective Trust and Collective Action: The Decision to Trust as a Social Decision." In *Trust in Organizations: Frontiers of Theory and Research*, ed. R. M. Kramer and T. R. Tyler, pp. 357–89. Thousand Oaks: Sage.

2004. "Collective Trust and Collective Action: The Decision to Trust as a Social Decision." In *Trust and Distrust in Organizations: Dilemmas and Approaches*, ed. Roderick M. Kramer and Karen S. Cook. New York: Russell Sage Foundation. 357–89.

Krebs, Ronald R., and Jennifer K. Lobasz. 2007. "Fixing the Meaning of 9/11: Hegemony, Coercion and the Road to War in Iraq." *Security Studies* 16(3): 409–51.

Kreps, Sarah. 2008. "When Does the Mission Determine the Coalition?: The Logic of Multilateral Intervention and the Case of Afghanistan." *Security Studies* 17(3): 531–67.

Kruglanski, Arie W., and Donna M. Webster. 1996. "Motivated Closing of the Mind: 'Seizing' and 'Freezing'." *Psychological Review* 103(2): 263–83.

Kuhlman, D. Michael, C. R. Camac and D. A. Cunha. 1986. "Individual Differences in Social Orientation." In *Experimental Social Dilemmas*, ed. H. A. M. Wilke, D. M. Messick and C. G., pp. 151–76. Rutte. Frankfurt am Main: Verlag Peter Lang.

Kuhlman, D. Michael, and Alfred F. Marshello. 1975. "Individual Differences in Game Motivation as Moderators of Preprogrammed Strategy Effects in Prisoner's Dilemma." *Journal of Personality and Social Psychology* 32(5): 922–31.

Kuhlman, D. Michael, and David L. Wimberley. 1976. "Expectations of Choice Behavior Held by Cooperators, Competitors, and Individualists across Four Classes of Experimental Games." *Journal of Personality and Social Psychology* 34(1): 69–81.

Kupchan, Charles A., and Clifford A. Kupchan. 1991. "Concerts, Collective Security, and the Future of Europe." *International Security* 16(1): 114–61.

Kupchan, Charles A., and Peter L. Trubowitz. 2007. "Dead Center: The Demise of Liberal Internationalism in the United States." *International Security* 32(2): 7–44.

Kydd, Andrew H. 2005. *Trust and Mistrust in International Relations.* Princeton University Press.

Lake, David A. 1999. *Entangling Relations: American Foreign Policy in Its Century.* Princeton University Press.

Lake, David A., and Robert Powell. 1999. *Strategic Choice and International Relations.* Princeton University Press.

Landau, Mark J., Sheldon Solomon, Jeff Greenberg, Florette Cohen, Tom Pyszczynski, Jamie Arndt, Claude H. Miller, Daniel M. Ogilvie and Alison Cook. 2004. "Deliver Us from Evil: The Effects of Mortality Salience and Reminders of 9/11 on Support for President George W. Bush." *Personality and Social Psychology Bulletin* 30(9): 1,136–50.

Larson, Deborah Welch. 1997. *Anatomy of Mistrust: US–Soviet Relations during the Cold War.* Ithaca, NY: Cornell University Press.

Leffler, Melvyn P. 1979. *The Elusive Quest: America's Pursuit of European Stability and French Security, 1919–1933.* University of North Carolina Press.

Legro, Jeffrey. 2005. *Rethinking the World: Great Power Strategies and International Order.* Ithaca: Cornell University Press.

Levinson, Daniel J. 1957. "Authoritarian Personality and Foreign Policy." *Conflict Resolution* 1(1): 37–47.

Liebrand, W. B., R. W. T. L. Jansen, V. M. Rijken and C. J. M. Suhre. 1986. "Might over Morality: Social Values and the Perception of Other Players in Experimental Games." *Journal of Experimental Social Psychology* 22: 203–15.

Link, Arthur, ed. 1966. *The Papers of Woodrow Wilson.* Princeton University Press.

Luhmann, Niklas. 1979. *Trust and Power.* New York: J. Wiley.

Maki, Judith E., and Charles G. McClintock. 1983. "The Accuracy of Social Value Prediction: Actor and Observer Influences." *Journal of Personality and Social Psychology* 45(4): 829–38.

Margulies, Herbert F. 1989. *The Mild Reservationists and the League of Nations Controversy in the Senate.* Columbia: University of Missouri Press.

Martin, Lisa L. 1992. "Interests, Power, and Multilateralism." *International Organization* 46(4): 765–92.

Mayer, Arno J. 1969. *Political Origins of the New Diplomacy, 1917–1918.* New York: Howard Fertig.

McCain, John. 2007. "An Enduring Peace Built on Freedom." *Foreign Affairs* 86 (November/December): 19–34.

McCann, Stewart J. H. 1997. "Threatening Times, 'Strong' Presidential Popular Vote Winners, and the Victory Margin, 1824–1964." *Journal of Personality and Social Psychology* 73(1): 160–70.

2008. "Societal Threat, Authoritarianism, Conservatism, and US State Death Penalty Sentencing (1977–2004)." *Journal of Personality and Social Psychology* 94(5): 913–23.

2009. "Political Conservatism, Authoritarianism, and Societal Threat: Voting for Republican Representatives in US Congressional Elections from 1946 to 1992." *Journal of Psychology* 143(4): 341–58.

McCartney, Paul T. 2004. "American Nationalism and U.S. Foreign Policy from September 11 to the Iraq War." *Political Science Quarterly* 119(3): 399–423.

McClintock, Charles G. 1972. "Social Motivation: A Set of Hypotheses." *Behavioral Science* 17(5): 438–54.

McClintock, Charles G., and Wim B. Liebrand. 1988. "Role of Interdependence Structure, Individual Value Orientation, and Another's Strategy in Social Decision Making: A Transformational Analysis." *Journal of Personality and Social Psychology* 55(3): 396–409.

McFarland, Sam. 2005. "On the Eve of War: Authoritarianism, Social Dominance, and American Students' Attitudes Toward Attacking Iraq." *Personality and Social Psychology Bulletin* 31(3): 360–7.

Mearsheimer, John J. 1994. "The False Promise of International Institutions." *International Security* 19(3): 5–49.

Mercer, Jonathan. 1996. *Reputation and International Politics.* Ithaca, NY: Cornell University Press.

2005. "Rationality and Psychology in International Politics." *International Organization* 59(1): 77–106.

Messick, David M., and Marilynn B. Brewer. 1983. "Solving Social Dilemmas: A Review." *Review of Personality and Social Psychology* 4: 11–44.

Messick, David M., and Roderick M. Kramer. 2001. "Trust as a Form of Shallow Morality." In *Trust in Society*, ed. K. S. Cook, pp. 89–118. New York: Russell Sage Foundation.

Messick, David M., and Charles G. McClintock. 1968. "Motivational Bases of Choice in Experimental Games." *Journal of Experimental Social Psychology* 4(1): 1–25.

Miller, David Hunter. 1928. *The Drafting of the Covenant*. Vol. II. New York: G. P. Putnam's Sons.

Miller, Karen A. J. 1999. *Populist Nationalism: Republican Insurgency and American Foreign Policy-Making, 1918–1925*. Westport, Conn.: Greenwood Press.

Miscamble, Wilson D. 1992. *George F. Kennan and the Making of American Foreign Policy, 1947–1950*. Princeton University Press.

Monten, Jonathan. 2005. "The Roots of the Bush Doctrine: Power, Nationalism, and Democracy Promotion in U.S. Strategy." *International Security* 29(4): 112–56.

Moravcsik, Andrew. 1998. *The Choice for Europe: Social Purpose and State Power from Messina to Maastricht*. Ithaca, NY: Cornell University Press.

    2000. "The Origins of Human Rights Regimes: Democratic Delegation in Postwar Europe." *International Organization* 54(2): 217–52.

Murray, Shoon Kathleen, Jonathan A. Cowden and Bruce M. Russett. 1999. "The Convergence of American Elites' Domestic Beliefs with Their Foreign Policy Beliefs." *International Interactions* 25(2): 153–80.

Nail, Paul R., and Ian McGregor. 2009. "Conservative Shift among Liberals and Conservatives Following 9/11/01." *Social Justice Research* 22(2–3): 231–40.

Narizny, Kevin. 2007. *The Political Economy of Grand Strategy*. Ithaca, NY: Cornell University Press.

Notter, Harley A. 1949. *Postwar Foreign Policy Preparation, 1939–1945*. Washington, DC: GPO.

Obama, Barack. 2007a. "Barack Obama's Foreign Policy Speech." www.cfr.org/publication/14356.

    2007b. "Remarks of Senator Barack Obama to the Chicago Council on Global Affairs." www.thechicagocouncil.org/dynamic_page.php?id=64.

    2007c. "Renewing American Leadership." *Foreign Affairs* 86 (July/August): 2–16.

    2008. "The Democratic Presidential Candidate's Foreign Policy Address at the Ronald Reagan Building in Washington, DC." www.guardian.co.uk/world/2008/jul/16/uselections2008.barackobama.

2009. "Obama's Speech to the United Nations General Assembly." www.nytimes.com/2009/09/24/us/politics/24prexy.text.html.

Olson, Mancur. 1971. *The Logic of Collective Action: Public Goods and the Theory of Groups.* New York: Schocken Books.

Orbell, John M., and Robyn M. Dawes. 1993. "Social Welfare, Cooperators' Advantage, and the Option of Not Playing the Game." *American Sociological Review* 58(6): 787–800.

Orbell, John M., Peregrine Schwartz-Shea and Randy T. Simmons. 1984. "Do Cooperators Exit More Readily than Defectors?" *American Political Science Review* 78(1): 147–62.

Osgood, Robert Endicott. 1953. *Ideals and Self-Interest in America's Foreign Relations: The Great Transformation of the Twentieth Century.* University of Chicago Press.

Oskamp, Stuart. 1971. "Effects of Programmed Strategies on Cooperation in the Prisoner's Dilemma and Other Mixed-Motive Games." *Journal of Conflict Resolution* 15(2): 225–59.

Ostrom, Elinor. 2003. "Toward a Behavioral Theory Linking Trust, Reciprocity and Reputation." In *Trust and Reciprocity: Interdisciplinary Lessons from Experimental Research*, eds. E. Ostrom and J. Walker, pp. 19–79. New York: Russell Sage Foundation.

Ostrom, Elinor, and James Walker, eds. 2003. *Trust and Reciprocity: Interdisciplinary Lessons from Experimental Research.* New York: Russell Sage Foundation.

Oye, Kenneth A. 1985. "Explaining Cooperation under Anarchy: Hypotheses and Strategies." *World Politics* 38(1): 1–24.

Parks, Craig D. 1994. "The Predictive Ability of Social Values in Resource Dilemmas and Public Goods Games." *Personality and Social Psychological Bulletin* 20(4): 431–8.

Parks, Craig D., Robert F. Henager and Shawn D. Scamahorn. "Trust and Reactions to Messages of Intent in Social Dilemmas." *Journal of Conflict Resolution* 40(10): 134–51.

Patrick, Stewart. 2009. *The Best Laid Plans: The Origins of American Multilateralism and the Dawn of the Cold War.* Lanham, Md.: Rowman & Littlefield.

Pestritto, Ronald J. 2005. *Woodrow Wilson and the Roots of Modern Liberalism.* Rowman and Littlefield.

Peterson, Bill E., Richard M. Doty and David G. Winter. 1993. "Authoritarianism and Attitudes towards Contemporary Social Issues." *Personality and Social Psychology Bulletin* 19: 174–84.

Pilisuk, Marc, and Paul Skolnick. 1968. "Inducing Trust: A Test of the Osgood Proposal." *Journal of Personality and Social Psychology* 8(2): 121–33.

Pollack, Mark A. 1997. "Delegation, Agency, and Agenda Setting in the European Community." *International Organization* 51(1): 99–134.

Poole, Keith T., and Howard Rosenthal. 1985. "A Spatial Model for Legislative Roll Call Analysis." *American Journal of Political Science* 29(2): 357–84.

1987a. "Analysis of Congressional Coalition Patterns: A Unidimensional Spatial Model." *Legislative Studies Quarterly* 12(1) 55–75.

1987b. "The Regional Realignment of Congress, 1919–1984." In *The Politics of Realignment: Partisan Change in the Mountain West*, eds. P. Galderisi, M. Lyons, R. Simmons and J. Francis. Boulder, Colo.: Westview Press.

1991. "Patterns of Congressional Voting." *American Behavioral Scientist* 35: 228–78.

1993. "Spatial Realignment and the Mapping of Issues in American History: The Evidence from Roll Call Voting." In *Agenda Formation*, ed. W. H. Riker, pp. 13–40. Ann Arbor: University of Michigan Press.

2001. "D-Nominate After 10 Years: An Update to Congress: A Political-Economic History of Roll Call Voting." *Legislative Studies Quarterly* 26(1): 5–29.

2007. *Ideology and Congress*. New Brunswick: Transaction.

Putnam, Robert D. 1993. *Making Democracy Work: Civic Traditions in Modern Italy*. Princeton University Press.

Rathbun, Brian C. 2004. *Partisan Interventions: European Party Politics and Peace Enforcement in the Balkans*. Ithaca, NY. Cornell University Press.

2007a. "Hierarchy and Community at Home and Abroad: Evidence of a Common Structure of Domestic and Foreign Policy Beliefs in American Elites." *Journal of Conflict Resolution* 51(3): 379–407.

2007b. "Uncertain about Uncertainty: Understanding the Multiple Meanings of a Crucial Concept in International Relations Theory." *International Studies Quarterly* 51(3): 533–57.

2008. "Does One Right Make a Realist?: Conservatism, Neoconservatism and Isolationism in the Foreign Policy Ideology of American Elites." *Political Science Quarterly* 123(2): 271–300.

Reynolds, P. A., and E. J. Hughes. 1976. *The Historian as Diplomat: Charles Kingley Webster and the United Nations, 1939–1946*. London: Martin Robertson.

Rieselbach, Leroy N. 1966. *The Roots of Isolationism: Congressional Voting and Presidential Leadership in Foreign Policy*. Indianapolis: Bobbs-Merrill.

Risse-Kappen, Thomas. 1995. *Cooperation among Democracies: The European Influence on U.S. Foreign Policy*. Princeton University Press.

Rokeach, Milton. 1973. *The Nature of Human Values*. New York: Free Press.

Romney, Mitt. 2007. "Rising to a New Generation of Global Challenges." *Foreign Affairs* 86 (July/August): 17–32.

Rosendorff, B. Peter, and Helen V. Milner. 2001. "The Optimal Design of International Trade Institutions: Uncertainty and Escape." *International Organization* 55(4): 829–57.

Rotter, Julian B. 1980. "Interpersonal Trust, Trustworthiness and Gullibility." *American Psychologist* 35(1): 1–7.

Ruggie, John Gerard. 1992. "Multilateralism: the Anatomy of an Institution." *International Organization* 46(3): 561–98.

   1997. "The Past as Prologue?: Interests, Identity, and American Foreign Policy." *International Security* 21(4): 89–125.

Russell, Ruth B. 1958. *A History of the United Nations Charter: The Role of the United States, 1940–1945*. Washington, DC: Brookings Institution.

Sahar, Gail. 2008. "Patriotism, Attributions for the 9/11 Attacks, and Support for War: Then and Now." *Basic and Applied Social Psychology* 30(3): 189–97.

Sales, S. M. 1973. "Threat as a Factor in Authoritarianism: An Analysis of Archival Data." *Journal of Personality and Social Psychology* 28(1): 44–57.

Saucier, Gerard. 2000. "Isms and the Structure of Social Attitudes." *Journal of Personality and Social Psychology* 78(2): 366–85.

Schlenker, Barry R., Bob Helm and James T. Tedeschi. 1973. "The Effects of Personality and Situational Variables on Behavioral Trust." *Journal of Personality and Social Psychology* 25(3): 419–27.

Schlesinger, Arthur M. 1971. *History of American Presidential Elections, 1789–1968*. Vol. II. New York: Chelsea House.

Schlesinger, Stephen C. 2003. *Act of Creation: The Founding of the United Nations: A Story of Superpowers, Secret Agents, Wartime Allies and Enemies, and Their Quest for a Peaceful World*. Boulder, Colo.: Westview Press.

Schmidt, Brian C., and Michael C. Williams. 2008. "The Bush Doctrine and the Iraq War: Neoconservatives versus Realists." *Security Studies* 17(2): 191–220.

Sheldon, Kennon M., and Charles P. Nichols. 2009. "Comparing Democrats and Republicans on Intrinsic and Extrinsic Values." *Journal of Applied Social Psychology* 39(3): 589–623.

Shils, E. A. 1954. "Authoritarianism: 'Right' and 'Left'." In *Studies in the Scope and Method of "The Authoritarian Personality,"* ed. R. Christie and M. Jahoda. Glencoe, Ill.: Free Press.

Shook, Natalie J., and Russell H. Fazio. 2009. "Political Ideology, Exploration of Novel Stimuli, and Attitude Formation." *Journal of Experimental Social Psychology* 45(4): 995–8.

Sinclair, Barbara. 1977. "Party Realignment and the Transformation of the Political Agenda: The House of Representatives, 1925–1938." *American Political Science Review* 71(3): 940–53.

2006. *Party Wars: Polarization and the Politics of National Policy Making*. Norman: University of Oklahoma Press.

Snidal, Duncan. 1985. "The Limits of Hegemonic Stability Theory." *International Organization* 39(4): 579–614.

Sniderman, P. M., and Philip E. Tetlock. 1986. "Interrelationships of Political Ideology and Public Opinion." In *Political Psychology*, ed. M. Hermann, pp. 232–60. San Francisco, Calif.: Jossey-Bass.

Snyder, Glenn H. 1984. "The Security Dilemma in Alliance Politics." *World Politics* 36(4): 461–95.

Snyder, Jack L. 1991. *Myths of Empire: Domestic Politics and International Ambition*. Ithaca, NY: Cornell University Press.

Stein, Arthur A. 1982. "Coordination and Collaboration: Regimes in an Anarchic World." *International Organization* 36(2): 299–324.

Stenner, Karen. 2009a. "'Conservatism,' Context-Dependence, and Cognitive Incapacity." *Psychological Inquiry* 20(2–3): 189–95.

2009b. "Three Kinds of 'Conservatism'." *Psychological Inquiry* 20(2–3): 142–59.

Stettinius, Edward Reilly. 1975. *The Diaries of Edward R. Stettinius, Jr., 1943–1946*, ed. T. M. Campbell and G. C. Herring. New York: New Viewpoints.

Stone, Ralph A. 1970. *The Irreconcilables: The Fight against the League of Nations*. Lexington: University Press of Kentucky.

Stouten, Jeroen, David de Cremer and Eric van Dijk. 2006. "Violating Equality in Social Dilemmas: Emotional and Retributive Reactions as a Function of Trust, Attribution and Honesty." *Personality and Social Psychological Bulletin* 32(7): 894–906.

Sztompka, Piotr. 1999. *Trust: A Sociological Theory*. Cambridge University Press.

Taft, Robert A. 1951. *A Foreign Policy for Americans*. Garden City, NY: Doubleday.

1997. *The Papers of Robert A. Taft*, ed. C. E. Wunderlin. Kent, OH: Kent State University Press.

Tetlock, Philip E. 1983. "Cognitive Style and Political Ideology." *Journal of Personality and Social Psychology* 45(1): 118–26.

1998. "Social Psychology and World Politics." In *Handbook of Social Psychology*, ed. D. T. Gilbert, S. T. Fiske and G. Lindzey, pp. 869–95. New York: McGraw Hill.

Theriault, Sean M. 2008. *Party Polarization in Congress*. Cambridge University Press.

Tomkins, Silvan Solomon, and Carroll E. Izard. 1965. *Affect, Cognition, and Personality: Empirical Studies*. New York: Springer.

Trubowitz, Peter. 1998. *Defining the National Interest: Conflict and Change in American Foreign Policy*. University of Chicago Press.

Tyler, Tom R. 2001. "Why Do People Rely on Others?: Social Identity and Social Aspects of Trust." In *Trust in Society*, ed. K. S. Cook, pp. 285–306. New York: Russell Sage Foundation.

Tyler, Tom R., and Peter Degoey. 1996. "Trust in Organizational Authorities: The Influence of Motive Attributions on Willingness to Accept Decisions." In *Trust in Organizations: Frontiers of Theory and Research*, ed. R. M. Kramer and T. R. Tyler, pp. 331–56. Thousand Oaks: Sage.

Tyszka, Tadeusz, and Janusz L. Grzelak. 1976. "Criteria of Choice in Non-Constant-Sum Games." *Journal of Conflict Resolution* 20(2): 357–76.

US Congress. Various years. *Congressional Record*. Washington, DC: GPO.

US Senate. 1945. "The Charter of the United Nations: Hearings before the Committee on Foreign Relations." Washington, DC: GPO.

1973. *The Vandenberg Resolution and the North Atlantic Treaty*. Hearings, Eightieth Congress, second session on S. Res. 239. Washington: GPO.

Uslaner, Eric M. 2002. *The Moral Foundations of Trust*. Cambridge University Press.

Van Lange, Paul A. M., and D. Michael Kuhlman. 1994. "Social Value Orientations and Impressions of Partner's Honesty and Intelligence: A Test of the Might versus Morality Effect." *Journal of Personality and Social Psychology* 67(1): 126–41.

Van Leeuwen, Florian, and Justin H. Park. 2009. "Perceptions of Social Dangers, Moral Foundations, and Political Orientation." *Personality and Individual Differences* 47(3): 169–73.

Vandenberg, Arthur H. 1952. *The Private Papers of Senator Vandenberg*. Boston: Houghton Mifflin.

Wallace, Henry A. 1948. *Toward World Peace*. New York: Reynal & Hitchcock.

Weber, Katja. 2000. *Hierarchy amidst Anarchy: Transaction Costs and Institutional Choice*. Albany, NY: State University of New York Press.

Weber, Steve. 1992. "Shaping the Postwar Balance of Power: Multilateralism in NATO." *International Organization* 46(3): 633–80.

Webster, Donna M., and Arie W. Kruglanski. 1994. "Individual Differences in Need for Cognitive Closure." *Journal of Personality and Social Psychology* 67(6): 1,049–62.

Weise, David R., Tom Pyszczynski, Cathy R. Cox, Jamie Arndt, Jeff Greenberg, Sheldon Solomon and Spee Kosloff. 2008. "Interpersonal Politics: The Role of Terror Management and Attachment Processes in Shaping Political Preferences." *Psychological Science* 19(5): 448–55.

Wendt, Alexander. 1999. *Social Theory of International Politics.* Cambridge University Press.

Widenor, William C. 1980. *Henry Cabot Lodge and the Search for an American Foreign Policy.* Berkeley: University of California Press.

   1992. "American Planning for the United Nations: Have We Been Asking the Right Questions?" *Diplomatic History* 6(3): 245–66.

Williams, Phil. 1985. *The Senate and US Troops in Europe.* New York: St. Martin's Press.

Wilson, G. D. 1973. "A Dynamic Theory of Conservatism." In *The Psychology of Conservatism,* ed. G. D. Wilson, pp. 257–65. London: Academic Press.

Wilson, Trevor. 1964. "The Coupon and the British General Election of 1918." *Journal of Modern History* 36(1): 28–42.

Wolfers, Arnold. 1940. *Britain and France between Two Wars: Conflicting Strategies of Peace since Versailles.* New York: Harcourt Brace.

Wrightsman, Lawrence S. 1966. "Personality and Attitudinal Correlates of Trusting and Trustworthy Behaviors in Two-Person Games." *Journal of Personality and Social Psychology* 4(3): 328–32.

Wunderlin, Clarence E. 2005. *Robert A. Taft: Ideas, Tradition, and Party in U.S. Foreign Policy.* Lanham, Md.: SR Books.

Yamagishi, Toshio. 2001. "Trust as a Form of Social Intelligence." In *Trust in Society,* ed. K. S. Cook, pp. 121–47. New York: Russell Sage Foundation.

Yamagishi, Toshio, and Karen S. Cook. 1993. "Generalized Exchange and Social Dilemmas." *Social Psychology Quarterly* 56(4): 235–48.

Yamagishi, Toshio, Karen S. Cook and Motoki Watabe. 1998. "Uncertainty, Trust, and Commitment Formation in the United States and Japan." *American Journal of Sociology* 104(1): 165–94.

Yamagishi, Toshio, and Midori Yamagishi. 1994. "Trust and Commitment in the United States and Japan." *Motivation and Emotion* 18(2): 129–66.

Index

abandonment, 8, 21, 22, 23, 30, 43, 45, 57, 63, 65, 73, 89, 125, 141, 191, 193, 195, 207

absolute veto, 112, 113, 115, 134–46, 147, 148, 150

Acheson, Dean, 118, 122, 181, 189, 190, 191, 198, 199, 203, 204

Achilles, Theodore, 171, 178, 180

Article 51, 150–3

assurance, 6, 23, 28, 34, 38, 41, 53, 64, 102, 132, 145, 153, 154, 169, 170, 175, 177, 179, 180, 190, 200

assurance game, xiii, 5–6, 10, 17, 25, 34, 36, 37, 46, 58, 172, 175

Bevin, Ernest, 168, 169, 202

bipartisanship, 4, 135, 187, 188
    in creation of United Nations, 130, 134
    in drafting of North Atlantic Treaty, 176–81, 189
    myth of, 2, 8–9, 176

Borah, William, 81–6, 98, 100, 103, 123, 194

British Conservative Party
    and League of Nations, 86–90, 161
    and United Nations, 138–42

British Dominions
    and United Nations, 144–6

Cecil, Lord Robert, 87, 88, 89, 90, 91, 92–4, 95, 101, 119

Churchill, Winston, 92, 138, 139, 140, 141

collective security, 39, 49, 55, 57, 58, 61, 62, 102
    in United Nations, 119, 133

Woodrow Wilson's conception of, 62

community circle, 3, 12, 14, 17, 22, 26, 29, 58, 93, 152, 175, 177, 191, 196, 223, 227

competitive social orientation, 5–6, 8, 59, 72–7, 110, 139, 142, 172–6, 190
    and generalized trust, 5–6, 8, 32–4
    and institutional design, 38

concert
    British conservatives' preference for, 86, 93, 138–42
    in United Nations, 133, 138
    Republican preference for, 78, 123
    Roosevelt's preference for, 117

conflict resolution, 4, 20, 22, 37, 41, 42, 62, 63, 64
    and social orientation, 36–7
    exploitation in, 21–2
    hypotheses on, 40–2
    in United Nations, 121

Connally resolution, 129

Connally, Tom, 128, 159, 184, 189, 190, 191, 192, 197, 206

conservative internationalists, 59, 60, 72, 73, 76, 77, 78, 79, 80, 81, 82, 97. *See also* Republican Party
    and League of Nations, 72–7
    and North Atlantic Treaty, 172–6
    and United Nations, 126

constructivism, 39–40
    and North Atlantic Treaty, 201–5

cooperation, 2
    and generalized trust, 31–7
    and trust, 2–3, 4–5
    in rationalist accounts, 12–15
    initiation of, 17–18, 34, 39–40

Cambridge Studies in International Relations